120:2 · April 2021

Crip Temporalities
Ellen Samuels and Elizabeth Freeman, Special Issue Editors

AGAINST the DAY

Protests in Lebanon
Karim Makdisi, Editor

Ellen Samuels and Elizabeth Freeman

Introduction: Crip Temporalities

When we proposed this special issue to the editor of the *South Atlantic Quarterly* nearly two years ago, we knew that crip temporality was an important and pressing matter, not just for disabled and chronically ill people but for all subjects living under the conditions of late capitalism, global technocracy, and medicolegal regimes. As academics, we knew that our lives were structured by time as a vector of power, from minutiae, such as class schedules, through annual reviews and milestones, such as merit steps and promotions, through the larger temporal systems that govern invisibly, which Michel Foucault ([1975] 1995) understood as the heart of discipline and which one of us calls "chrononormativity" (Freeman 2010). As scholars of temporality, we understood that the legal category of disability has been constructed through an elaborate artifice of permanence, of bodies and minds that cannot move through time along the smooth rails of normative life stages but are always being asked, "Will you ever work again? Will you ever walk again? Will you ever get better?" As disabled people, we knew that medicine, too, conceives disability and illness in linear temporal terms, such as *prognosis, remission, recurrence, chronic,* and/or *terminal* (see Jain 2007; Kafer 2013; Samuels 2017;

The South Atlantic Quarterly 120:2, April 2021
DOI 10.1215/00382876-8915937   © 2021 Duke University Press

Clare 2017).[1] And as denizens of the twenty-first century, we knew that the world had been accelerating out of control through hypercapitalization, the high-speed growth of private enterprise, and the digital transformation and that, at the same time, it was being consumed by the slow violence of climate change (Nixon 2011) and the forced stagnation of the public sector, with both temporal regimes literally disabling more bodies and minds.

What we could not have anticipated, though, is how the advent of the COVID-19 pandemic in early 2020 would transform the social and temporal landscape in ways that are still ongoing and impossible to fully predict. As we write this, we don't yet know exactly when the pandemic began or when it will end, or what the world "after" COVID-19 will look like. Those of us residing in the United States are subject to constant, destabilizing change and unpredictability in governmental and institutional responses to the pandemic, while here, as well as in other parts of the world, its impact exacerbates existing states of debility and violence. In this new and evolving situation, crip temporality feels even more urgent than before. And more than ever before, it can be said that all of us now are living in crip time (see Shew 2020).

Let us give a concrete example of this universalization of crip time, from US academe. As pandemic time arrived, professors had to move their classes online, often very quickly and with little or no training in how to teach online or to use the various technologies involved. Think pieces quickly proliferated about how to navigate this change: how to teach effectively or, ironically, how to do a terrible job teaching.[2] What all parties could agree on, however, was that this shift was difficult, imperfect, physically and mentally draining, and profoundly time-consuming. Instructors had not only to do all the usual work of teaching—writing and delivering lectures, creating Power-Points, leading discussions, responding to students' questions, crafting assignments, and grading assigned work—but also to master a variety of technologies for doing so: learning how to record lectures and upload them to course management systems, to create and host Zoom classrooms, to give assignments that students could complete from home, perhaps with limited computer or internet access, and to do all of this under the pressure and duress of both a frightening physical contagion and the normative timeline of the usual semester or quarter.

This move to pandemic pedagogy mirrors in many ways the prior experiences of disabled instructors and students. Those of us fortunate or persistent enough to receive reasonable accommodations must generally put in massive effort and time in order to use them, even as we are expected to adhere to the same timelines of study and instruction as nondisabled peers. Most nondisabled people (or even disabled people who don't use a particular technology) are unaware of how very imperfect and time-consuming many alternative technologies are. Screen reading and voice recognition software programs, for example, are not seamless tools but vary widely according to which hardware and software platforms they must interface with, what tasks must be performed, and how conscientious designers have been in making various platforms accessible. Every time new course software is adopted or an email system is updated, many disabled users must spend additional tedious hours figuring out how to use it with their adaptive tech, if the new platforms are even usable (often they are not, despite legal requirements in the United States). Even as simple an adaptation as changing from a sitting to a standing or reclining workstation involves expense, trial and error, a certain amount of bodily and mental achiness, and a certain number of well-placed curses.

What is nearly always true, however, is that using a different form of technology for access reasons means that everything takes longer. And this is true not just for users of complex technologies like screen readers: differences such as having only limited fingers available for typing, or using one's mouth to hold a pen, or being able to look at screens for only an hour per day, or processing written information better than aural or the other way around—all of these differences from the presumed norm mean that disabled academics have always done the same work as our peers in profoundly different temporalities.

With the advent of the COVID-19 pandemic, suddenly US academics and other white-collar workers who had previously resided in the sheltered space of the norm were thrust into the time-consuming, often frustrating space of crip time. They found themselves grappling with Zoom and other video chat technologies, struggling to balance exigencies of groceries and childcare with expectations of professional performance, running out of hours in the day and energy in their bodyminds to keep up. They remarked on social media that it was taking much longer to get anything accomplished, that they could not focus, that unstructured days indoors were strangely tiring, that instructional technologies themselves produced strange effects on their energy and motivation.[3] In the time of COVID-19, those who had lived previously with the privilege of normative ability began to learn what sick and disabled people have known forever: that crip time isn't easy, it isn't fair, it cannot be reasoned with.

But at the same time that disabled people see nondisabled people now contending with a cripped workplace, we also see approaches to work and study long denied to us as "unreasonable" accommodations—too expensive, too burdensome, not the way it's done—suddenly implemented quickly, universally, and with total social acceptance.[4] Not only did universities and colleges suddenly supply to some or all of their faculty en masse the technologies, flexibility with deadlines, and professional clock extensions often denied to disabled people, but also, at the time of this writing, all public universities and colleges in the United States, as well as private ones with fewer than five hundred employees, are required to comply with the federal Families First Coronavirus Response Act that expands paid leave time.[5] These are technological, medical, and financial accommodations that many colleges and universities have not previously extended to their disabled and/or chronically ill faculty with any consistency. Furthermore, in the time of COVID-19, many academic institutions have advised or mandated accommodations for students, such as pass/fail grading and flexibility with due dates and attendance policies, that are ordinarily extended only to students with learning disabilities or other cognitive diagnoses and unevenly adhered to by nondisabled faculty (Burke 2020). Finally, there has been widespread acknowledgment and destigmatization of (though not necessarily help for) the emotional distress of faculty and students, whereas mentally disabled members of academe have generally stayed closeted about their condition or have been forced to leave their campus if it becomes unmanageable (Price 2011; see also Cepeda, this issue).

Many of these newly extended accommodations for the nondisabled or for the suddenly disabled—slowdowns, flexibility, time to care for others, the right to paid time away from work to heal, acknowledgment of grief and trauma—implicitly acknowledge that most workers and students are now living crip temporality. The contributions to this issue, on the other hand, come from people for whom crip temporality is nothing new. In conceiving this special issue, we felt it was vitally important to put the existing and crucial work on crip temporality by disability scholars and artists into conversation with writing from new or underrepresented perspectives in order to challenge and expand the range of "crip temporalities" in scholarly thought and creative practice. In particular, we wanted to explore the affects of living in crip time and with crip temporalities, affects including but not limited to alienation, grief, anger, and exhaustion. The notion of crip time as flex time—as what Alison Kafer (2013: 27) has eloquently called "flex time not just expanded but exploded"—has been vitally important for disabled people finding ways to survive, to wedge our nonnormative bodyminds into the apparatus of capitalist production far enough to keep a roof over our heads.

But the danger of equating crip time with flex time, as Margaret Price notes in her contribution to this issue, is that it suggests a kind of freedom, an ease, a metaphoric stretching of the limbs. Rather than only calling for this kind of relief from capitalist temporality, we also wanted to explore the freedoms offered by the positive experiences of crip life and crip temporality, such as exultance, solidarity, grace, the simple rhythm of the breath. The stories of disabled people, as Price and others in this issue show, reveal crip time as paradoxically both liberating and confining, because it breaks open rigid socioeconomic structures of time and affords others, and because that breaking is not a choice but a necessity, an enforcement issued by the physical and mental strictures of the crip bodymind.

Many of the contributions in this issue, in some way or another, discuss crip temporality in terms of confinement. For example, Price's article extends her earlier work, which centered on mental and cognitive disability in her analysis of temporality in the academy, to foreground slowness as a key feature of academic crip time. In her article, María Elena Cepeda draws on Price's work as she offers *testimonio* of her experience as a mentally disabled Latina academic negotiating dynamics of power and passing in both academic and psychiatric institutions. Similarly, Mimi Khúc describes the process of creating *Open in Emergency*, a multimedia project centered on Asian American mental health, as enacting a temporality of unwellness that at once exposes and seeks to repair deep fissures of distress in her communities. And Jasbir K. Puar's article on "slow life" discusses how, in addition to maiming rather than killing Palestinians, the Israeli military has "create[d] an entire population with mobility impairments," holding Palestinians' time hostage through checkpoints, roadblocks, walls, and segregated highways that reinforce the suspended state of fearful waiting for death and destruction in which this population lives. These articles, like all contributions in this collection, proceed from a deeply intersectional understanding of crip temporality in which race, colonialism, gender, and sexuality entwine with disability to produce compelling particular temporal landscapes.

But crip time is also a time of survival and even of world making, and several of the articles in this issue offer both strategies for surviving the normative violences of capitalist time and, in the key of liberation, strategies for inventing new models of work, sociability, and being. Moya Bailey, for example, offers the "ethics of pace" as a strategy for multiply marginalized subjects, particularly sick and disabled women of color, to navigate the academy without succumbing to the death drive of productivity that has too often claimed their health and even their lives. Jake Pyne's article articulates a model of trans autistic temporality in which neurodivergence and gender nonconformity intertwine to shape new ways of being and responding to the world. In their coauthored article, Jina B. Kim and Sami Schalk discuss self-care as a temporal practice for people of color, reconceiving crip time through a crip-of-color critique that follows the foundational work of Audre Lorde to center care as a "taking of time" for community and personal survival while rejecting neoliberal notions of "self-care" in service of maintaining or restoring productivity. Alison Kafer explores the possibility that crip time, rather than just being an extension of normative time ("more"), might unfold into new solidarities and forms of relationality, obviating the "before" and "after" time of disability.

Even as crip time is a space of frustration and often of loss, then, it is also a space that offers new kinds of connections and presence that are fundamental to imagining a new world into being. The artwork and poetry that we include in this issue profoundly engage with that project. In his powerful invocational poem "May Day, 2020," Eli Clare weaves together the voices of many disabled and precarious lives affected by the COVID-19 pandemic, insisting on both survival and imagination—indeed, on imagination as key to survival. This is a powerful and necessary reminder in these times of bare-bones utilitarian thinking, as is the poem's resistance to the destructive logics of capital. Similarly, Leah Lakshmi Piepzna-Samarasinha's text for the tarot card *The Crip* calls and challenges us to "dream disabled dreams," to "consider how you are finding and claiming your power," while Matt Huynh's visuals work a constant tension between power and vulnerability, envisioning kneeling as both a position of rest and of launching to action, swords as both destructive and constructive tools. Finn Enke's four drawings also work a tension, in this case more abstractly, between bodies, gender, vulnerability, and empowerment, circling around the concept of dysphoria as their blockish figures negotiate comic frames that both open and foreclose possible bodily arrangements—visually performing the "square peg in the round hole" misfitting of gender and disability also echoed in the narratives of trans autistic authors discussed by Pyne. In their cover art for this issue, *Man in the Mirror,* Enke explores through watercolor another version of this tension, in this case between the body and the natural world, acknowledging that those boundaries are far more porous than either capitalism or materialist politics often acknowledges.

Moving further into this phenomenological realm, Christine Sun Kim's series *Six Types of Waiting in Berlin* synesthetically merges the visual, textual, and musical in its minimalistic display of the tedium of waiting that is central to the crip experience of chronic illness, located in Berlin to foreground how cultural differences in temporality shape subjective experience. Like Sun Kim's visual art, Michael Snediker's four poems make use of both text and the white space left in between to enact embodiment as a kind of music or dance, with the spacing of words, line breaks, and enjambment evoking the sense of a body quivering at the edge of a cliff, "the body's / pendulum" marking time, not with the contained pulse of a metronome but like a ballerina or circus acrobat ecstatic in motion.

So, if pandemic time is crip time for all—even as features such as seemingly interminable waiting, long days indoors, fear of foreshortened mortality, an increase in or sudden loss of hours spent working, and time lost to managing technology are still unevenly distributed—what forms of justice, human connectivity, and pleasure might emerge from it? In her set of meditations on crip temporalities, Alison Kafer suggests that we think less about what crip time *is* and more about what it *does*. Here are some of those "doings" at the time of this writing. Among disabled and nondisabled people alike, pandemic time has brought the systems of mutual aid detailed by scholar-activists such as Leah Lakshmi Piepzna-Samarasinha (2018), Dean Spade (2015), and Hi'ilei Julia Kawehipuaakahaopulani Hobart and Tamara Kneese (2020).[6] And sheltering in place, though it has led to a spike in reported mental health difficulties, has also given rise to such virtual-communal forms of generosity and enjoyment as Zoom game nights, 7:00 p.m. neighborhood noisemaking to thank health care workers, social media posts of individuals and households re-creating famous paintings, socially mediated mask-making bees, city sourdough starter giveaways, and online performances by choirs, orchestras, and theater and dance troupes whose members record their parts individually and whose directors combine them into a beautiful whole. Crip temporalities seem to have given broader access, at least for some of us, to the kinds of compassion, empathy, and relationality that have regularly structured disabled communities.[7] These values and the activities they engender, or these activities and the values they engender, depart from what Kafer calls the temporalities of late capitalism, which include "productivity, capacity, self-sufficiency, independence, [and] achievement." They are about neither speed nor slowness, precisely, but about new rhythms, new practices of time, new sociotemporal imaginaries.

These new practices of pandemic time raise intriguing and important questions for the new world we are making. What if we all simply took as much of our time as possible back from late capitalism? What if we developed new forms of punctuality centering on presence, simultaneity, and concurrence: new ways of being together in time—perhaps even ones that valued stasis and the present rather than motion and the future (see Freeman

2019; Baraitser 2017)? What if temporal rhythms and their attached notions of normalcy, productivity, and community were forever cripped, detached from chrononormative capitalist structures and predicated instead on the myriad realities of bodyminds along a spectrum of abilities? These possibilities, these revolutions, are explored in multiple and compelling ways by the contributions in this issue, and so we offer them to all readers, regardless of disability status, as invocations of crip timescapes we all may create and share together.

Notes

We both offer profuse thanks to Bethany Qualls, who helped us through the final push getting the issue ready, and to our authors, artists, and curators who wrote and revised throughout the pandemic and saw this project through. And we are deeply grateful to each other. Elizabeth Freeman also wishes to thank Candace Moore, whose love has meant everything, along with the many activists, scholars, friends, and other kinds of kin whose crip solidarity makes and remakes the world. Ellen Samuels would also like to thank Alison Kafer, Margaret Price, and Eli Clare for their friendship and wisdom; her graduate students in feminist disability studies at the University of Wisconsin–Madison for pushing her thinking on crip worlds further; and Jonathan Zarov for everything else.

1   A note regarding positionality: one of us (Samuels) identifies as a disabled person; one of us (Freeman) has, as we worked on this project, found herself in an ongoing medical crisis that has necessitated what Sami Schalk (2013) calls "coming to claim crip." In writing this joint introduction, we are using the first-person *we* to refer to disabled people and communities, not only to reflect our own status as disabled people but also to signal our solidarity with disability activism and scholarship. For further discussion of strategic identifications as disabled and crip, see Schalk 2013 and McRuer 2006.

2   Here are a very few examples from the vast online archive of resources for teaching effectively online, from academic professional journals and our own institutions: Darby 2019; Moore and Hodges 2020; Barrett-Fox 2020; and University of California, Davis, n.d.

3   On instructional technologies and fatigue, see, e.g., Sklar 2020. On general pandemic fatigue, see, e.g., Zerbe 2020. On how this fatigue is temporal, see, e.g., Breen 2020.

4   Consider, for example, the University of California's systemwide licensing agreement with Zoom (Trappler 2016). See also articles on adjusting tenure expectations and clocks, such as Connolly 2020. For reflection on these dynamics, see Doyle 2020.

5   The Families First Coronavirus Response Act mandates two weeks of paid sick leave for illness or quarantine; two weeks at two-thirds pay for caretakers of the quarantined or ill and for workers with childcare responsibilities due to the closure of schools and daycare; and an additional ten weeks of paid expanded family and medical leave at two-thirds pay for COVID-19-related reasons. See US Department of Labor, n.d. See also CUPA-HR Knowledge Center 2020.

6   See also *New Inquiry* and Agbebyiyi 2020 on the Disability Justice Mutual Aid Fund.

7   For a beautiful example of these values in action, and their interconnection with social justice, see the film *Crip Camp* (Newnham and LeBrecht 2020).

References

Baraitser, Lisa. 2017. *Enduring Time*. London: Bloomsbury Academic.

Barrett-Fox, Rebecca. 2020. "Please Do a Bad Job of Putting Your Courses Online." *Any Good Thing* (blog), March 12. anygoodthing.com/2020/03/12/please-do-a-bad-job-of-putting-your-courses-online/.

Breen, Kerry. 2020. "Why Am I Tired All the Time? Experts Share How to Feel More Rested during Pandemic." *Today*, May 20. www.today.com/health/why-am-i-so-tired-how-deal-exhaustion-during-pandemic-t182125.

Burke, Lilah. 2020. "#PassFailNation." *Inside Higher Ed*, March 19. www.insidehighered.com/news/2020/03/19/colleges-go-passfail-address-coronavirus.

Clare, Eli. 2017. *Brilliant Imperfection: Grappling with Cure*. Durham, NC: Duke University Press.

CUPA-HR (College and University Professional Association for Human Resources) Knowledge Center. 2020. "COVID-19 Emergency Leave Q&A for Higher Education HR." April 5. cupahr.org/knowledge-center/covid-19-resources/faq-leave-provisions-ffcra/.

Connolly, Joyce. 2020. "We Need to Think about What Counts for Tenure Now." *Inside Higher Ed*, April 9. www.insidehighered.com/advice/2020/04/09/covid-19-demands-reconsideration-tenure-requirements-going-forward-opinion.

Darby, Flower. 2019. "How to Be a Better Online Teacher: Advice Guide." *Chronicle of Higher Education*, April 17. www.chronicle.com/interactives/advice-online-teaching.

Doyle, Nancy. 2020. "We Have Been Disabled: How the Pandemic Has Proven the Social Model of Disability." *Forbes*, April 29. www.forbes.com/sites/drnancydoyle/2020/04/29/we-have-been-disabled-how-the-pandemic-has-proven-the-social-model-of-disability/.

Foucault, Michel. (1975) 1995. *Discipline and Punish: The Birth of the Prison*, translated by Alan Sheridan. New York: Vintage.

Freeman, Elizabeth. 2010. *Time Binds: Queer Temporalities, Queer Histories*. Durham, NC: Duke University Press.

Freeman, Elizabeth. 2019. *Beside You in Time: Sense Methods and Queer Sociabilities in the American Nineteenth Century*. Durham, NC: Duke University Press.

Hobart, Hi'ilei Julia Kawehipuaakahaopulani, and Tamara Kneese. 2020. "Radical Care: Survival Strategies for Uncertain Times." In "Radical Care," edited by Hi'ilei Julia Kawehipuaakahaopulani Hobart and Tamara Kneese. Special issue, *Social Text* 38, no. 1 (142): 1–16. doi.org/10.1215/01642472-7971067.

Jain, S. Lochlann. 2007. "Living in Prognosis: Toward an Elegaic Politics." *Representations* 98, no. 1: 77–92.

Kafer, Alison. 2013. *Feminist Queer Crip*. Bloomington: Indiana University Press.

McRuer, Robert. 2006. *Crip Theory: Cultural Locations of Disability and Queerness*. New York: New York University Press.

Moore, Stephanie, and Charles B. Hodges. 2020. "So You Want to Teach Temporarily Online." *Inside Higher Ed*, March 11. www.insidehighered.com/advice/2020/03/11/practical-advice-instructors-faced-abrupt-move-online-teaching-opinion.

Newnham, Nicole, and Jim LeBrecht, dirs. 2020. *Crip Camp: A Disability Revolution*. Produced by Higher Ground Productions, distributed by Netflix, Los Gatos, CA. netflix.com/title/81001496?s=i&trkid=13747225&t=amsg.

New Inquiry and K. Agbebyiyi. 2020. "Redistribution and World Building: A Conversation with K Agbebiyi, Creator of the Disability Justice Mutual Aid Fund." *New Inquiry*, June 10. thenewinquiry.com/redistribution-and-world-building/.

Nixon, Rob. 2011. *Slow Violence and the Environmentalism of the Poor.* Cambridge, MA: Harvard University Press.

Piepzna-Samarasinha, Leah Lakshmi. 2018. *Care Work: Dreaming Disability Justice.* Vancouver: Arsenal Pulp Press.

Price, Margaret. 2011. *Mad at School: Rhetorics of Mental Disability and Academic Life.* Ann Arbor: University of Michigan Press.

Samuels, Ellen. 2017. "Six Ways of Looking at Crip Time." *Disability Studies Quarterly* 37, no. 3. doi.org/10.18061/dsq.v37i3.5824.

Schalk, Sami. 2013. "Coming to Claim Crip: Disidentification with/in Disability Studies." *Disability Studies Quarterly* 33, no. 2. doi.org/10.18061/dsq.v33i2.3705.

Shew, Ashley. 2020. "Let COVID-19 Expand Awareness of Disability Tech." *Nature*, May 5. www.nature.com/articles/d41586-020-01312-w

Sklar, Julia. 2020. "'Zoom Fatigue' Is Taxing the Brain: Here's Why That Happens." *National Geographic*, April 24. www.msn.com/en-us/health/wellness/zoom-fatigue-is-taxing-the-brain-heres-why-that-happens/ar-BB138Eym.

Spade, Dean. 2015. *Normal Life: Administrative Violence, Critical Trans Politics, and the Limits of Law.* Durham, NC: Duke University Press.

Trappler, Thomas. 2016. "New UC Zoom Agreement for Video, Web, and Audio Conferencing." *University of California UC IT Blog*, July 28. cio.ucop.edu/new-uc-zoom-agreement-for-video-web-and-audio-conferencing/.

University of California, Davis. n.d. "Keep Teaching." keepteaching.ucdavis.edu/teach (accessed June 11, 2020).

US Department of Labor. n.d. "Families First Coronavirus Response Act: Employer Paid Leave Responsibilities." www.dol.gov/agencies/whd/pandemic/ffcra-employer-paid-leave (accessed June 11, 2020).

Zerbe, Kathryn. 2020. "'Pandemic Fatigue' Takes a Toll on Relationships." *Psychology Today*, May 4.

Eli Clare

May Day, 2020

Yesterday your words came in a burst:
i cannot imagine a world without capitalism

and my heart shivered. I wanted to argue,
quote Karl Marx, curl into a hollowed out

redwood stump. In this time
of epidemic, our doors closed, windows

open, as we ward off virus
and worry about death, let us

turn off the news—funerals doubling
every three days. We who sing

from balconies and play klezmer music
on front stoops. We who check in

every day over text, phone, Zoom, Skype,
Facebook, FaceTime: *how are your lungs,*

can you make rent this month, did you lose your job today,
are you hungry right now, do you have enough

insulin, estrogen, Prozac, Klonopin, blood pressure meds?
We who drive across town to deliver saltines,

fresh kale, chicken soup, half bottles
of Tylenol, the last box of face masks

to ex-lovers and best friends. We who have always
shared everything we had. We who keep

The South Atlantic Quarterly 120:2, April 2021
DOI 10.1215/00382876-8915952   © 2021 Duke University Press

each other alive. We who will be turned away
from emergency rooms and denied

ventilators. We who will never
go to the hospital. We who will die

and we who will live. Wall Street is crashing,
cruise ships docked, World Bank

panicked, renters and Amazon workers
on strike. It is time. It is time. It is time

to listen to our grief and soothe our jangled nerves—
we cannot afford to forfeit imagination.

Margaret Price

Time Harms: Disabled Faculty Navigating the Accommodations Loop

I needed time, but time doesn't help that much.
—Camille, interviewee in the Disabled Faculty Study

We are accustomed to saying that "time heals."
But time also harms, and that less-well-acknowl-
edged fact is a central tenet of crip spacetime. The
theory of crip spacetime builds on crip time and
critical disability studies to explain what it means
to be disabled in specific spaces. I developed this
theory while working on an eight-year project, the
Disabled Faculty Study, that focuses on everyday
academic life as experienced by disabled faculty.[1] It
draws on a survey (Price et al. 2017; Kerschbaum
et al. 2017), in-depth interviews conducted with
thirty-six disabled faculty members, and published accounts by or about disabled faculty. One
of the most important findings from the study is
that access, as envisioned and practiced in the contemporary university, actually worsens inequity
rather than mitigating it. In other words, even
when policy makers, scholars, and everyone else
involved in the academic enterprise make sincere
efforts to "include" disabled people, the disparities
between disabled and nondisabled life only
become more pronounced.

The South Atlantic Quarterly 120:2, April 2021
DOI 10.1215/00382876-8915966   © 2021 Duke University Press

Crip spacetime helps explain why that happens. This theory turns attention away from individual disabled bodies and the obsession with "accommodating" those individual bodies, focusing instead on relations, systems, objects, and discourses. Essentially, crip spacetime shows that thinking about disability and access in terms of individual bodies not only does an inadequate job of explaining both disability and access but also tends to exacerbate inequity and block efforts at inclusivity.[2] In this article, I explore one specific theme—slowness—to demonstrate how crip spacetime works. My aim is not only to provide empirical evidence that disabled faculty are appallingly underserved by their academic employers but also to slow down with time itself—to analyze, carefully and bit by bit, the textures and shapes of time in higher education, so that we can better understand how it is mobilized to divide workers against one another and against themselves. Understanding this dynamic positions us to take collective action, to "imagine possible futures, a place where life could be lived differently" (hooks 1994: 61).

Some of my insights draw on previous scholarship in critical temporality studies, including Lauren Berlant's (2007) slow death, Mel Y. Chen's (2016) slow constitution, Elizabeth Freeman's (2010) chrononormativity, and Alison Kafer's (2013) and Ellen Samuels's (2017) versions of crip time. Some may be new, for example, my argument that recovery, loops, and conditionality are important aspects of critical temporality studies. Overall, I argue that time is part of a material-discursive field through which body-minds[3] are sorted. Further, as my analysis of interviews shows, time is not separable from cost (see Patsavas 2018). Perhaps we already knew this—we "spend time," after all, and "time is money," and, I guess inevitably, we now have "time poverty" (Williams, Masuda, and Tallis 2016; Zilanawala 2016). But I think we need to notice, again, how those costs are rung up in specific moments, for specific subjects.

Deceleration: A Love Affair

The slow movement, usually reported to have begun in 1986 with a "slow food" protest against McDonald's, has proliferated through slow fashion, slow cinema, slow parenting, and slow travel. Some of the movement's versions within academe include slow agency (Micciche 2011), slow counseling (Astramovich and Hoskins 2012), and slow medicine (Sweet 2017). The concept of slow professoring (Berg and Seeber 2016) has been rightly criticized for its failure to address the privileges necessary to take up its recommendations, and yet its tenets are echoed with increasing frequency within aca-demic spaces: *Take time off. No email after work hours. Say no.* Except in rare cases, such as the insightful coauthored article "For Slow Scholarship" by Alison Mountz et al. (2015),[4] the complex costs of such slowness are ignored. Not everyone can work slowly and be rewarded for it (or even survive doing it). I note, but do not dwell on, the inevitably neoliberal tilt of arguments for slowing down in the service of greater overall productivity, with happiness marshaled as part of one's performance.

Temporality has been a focus of queer studies for at least fifteen years (Freeman 2010; Halberstam 2005; Love 2007) and is now being mentioned more frequently as materialist scholars explore various implications of becoming as theorized by Gilles Deleuze and Félix Guattari (1987, 1994). Much of the materialist scholarship (both new and structural) calls attention to the use of time as a metric of production in late capitalism. As Rosi Braidotti (2019: 41) argues, acceleration leads to "the negative, entropic frenzy of capi-talist axiomatic," while "the political starts with de-acceleration." Braidotti is joined by many other scholars in exploring the relationships between time and materiality. For example, Rachel Loewen Walker (2014: 54) argues for the value of a "living present" as a resistant feminist imaginary. She elaborates:

> Just as we cannot expect to jump up and run away the minute after we twist an ankle, we cannot erase a history of exclusion with the great big stroke of "legalizing same-sex marriage in Canada." . . . The living present is heavy with lineages that mimic, critique and undo our assumed histories, and, rather than wiping away the past or seeking absolution for our actions, we can embrace this thick temporality, recognizing its ability to deepen our accountabilities to those pasts and their possible futures. (56)

In other words, Walker suggests, the living present forms a thick temporality (which echoes, without directly citing, Clifford Geertz). This means that past and future matter through what we imagine to be the present.

Further, Walker's theory includes the key construct of accountability, which I argue is the ethical component missing from many new materialist theories calling for "alternative modes of becoming" and "new alliances" (Braidotti 2019: 49–50) between subjects and also between fields of study. And yet, the matter of disability is both foregrounded and strangely unac-counted for in most new materialist theories. Taking Walker's article as an example, we might ask: Is the twisted ankle in this example meant to be a minor inconvenience experienced by a generally nondisabled person? Will the ankle turner be able to run and jump, not the minute after their accident but maybe five minutes later? Or is the metaphor meant to indicate the kind of slow, painful change and healing that might follow sweeping progressive legislation on a national scale? This is not a problem with Walker's theory of a living present but, rather, an indication that it could extend further. What *about* the matter of disability—especially since disability studies has a long history of theorizing time?

Crip time in many ways parallels Walker's theory of a "living present" but moves beyond it as well. For example, Ellen Samuels's (2017) "Six Ways of Looking at Crip Time" presents crip time as layered and marked by loss—not the temporary loss of a twisted ankle but scarring, life-changing loss. She writes:

> I look 25, feel 85, and just want to live like the other 40-somethings I know. I want to be aligned, synchronous, part of the regular order of the world.
>
> Like the leaves just now turning as the year spins toward its end, I want sometimes to be part of nature, to live within its time. But I don't. My life has turned another way. (n.p.)

Samuels's essay deliberately emphasizes the painful and difficult aspects of crip time, those "that are harder to see as liberatory, more challenging to find a way to celebrate." Samuels thus presents an important counterpoint to the optimistic and desire-oriented approach to disability that characterized much disability studies theory in the 1990s and early 2000s. As necessary as optimism and desire are, disability studies must also incorporate the painful and sometimes unbearable aspects of being disabled, or the discipline itself will include only some of its purported demographic (see Price 2015).

Alison Kafer's *Feminist, Queer, Crip* (2013) similarly grapples with the paradox of disability as the simultaneous site of hopeful futures and painful loss. References to *Feminist, Queer, Crip* often quote one of its most uplifting statements about crip time: "Rather than bend disabled bodies and minds to meet the clock, crip time bends the clock to meet disabled bodies and minds" (27). However, if we explore Kafer's discussion of crip/queer time throughout her book, we find a more complicated mix of takes, especially the potential of theories of futurity to reinscribe harm, abuse, colonization, and slavery, all while claiming to leave them behind. In her chapter on the cyborg, for example, Kafer argues that, while the future-pointing potential of the cyborg is invigorating, it also demands "a reckoning, an acknowledgement, of the cyborg's history in institutionalization and abuse" (128). A key part of Kafer's approach to crip time[5] is its acknowledgment that no history can really be moved past; no future, no matter how liberatory, really leaves anything behind.

As we reconsider time vis-à-vis these scholars, an important divide is apparent between those whose theories center questions of accountability and harm as a constitutive element of development, and those whose do not. The common theme of accountability causes me to add Nirmala Erevelles as a theorist whose ideas shape crip understandings of time, although her book *Disability and Difference in Global Contexts* (2011) does not name crip time directly. In *Disability and Difference,* Erevelles presents time as a necessary part of the intertwining of race and disability through the process of becoming. Drawing on Hortense J. Spillers's "Mama's Baby, Papa's Maybe" (1987), Erevelles (2011: 26) argues that race and disability must be understood in terms of each other, because "it is the materiality of racialized violence that becomes the originary space of difference." The contemporary understanding of disability that underlies such logics as fitness and stamina has formed, Erevelles argues, not after the Middle Passage or as a consequence of the Middle Passage but through the Middle Passage. This makes Erevelles's reading of becoming quite different from, for example, Margaret Shildrick's (2009) (also examined by Erevelles), and more like M. Jacqui Alexander's (2006: 190) use of "palimpsestic time," which measures change through experience, including the experience of trauma—and which emphasizes the constant layering and relayering of history on the present.

Drawing on Erevelles, Kafer, and Samuels, I argue that time and accountability are inseparable. In their different ways, these three authors argue not simply that we could recognize harm as a constituent aspect of time but that we must recognize it as such. That recognition informs my understanding of academic time: it is composed not only of a fast-moving, bell-ringing present but also of histories of inequality and abuse, as well as uncertain futures that could point toward either transformation or further eugenic projects.

Academe as a workplace has rhythms unlike most others. For example, most faculty and students are not expected to follow any particular timetable outside of classes and meetings, while staff are usually expected to follow a more conventional nine-to-five schedule. At least twice a year its inhabitants experience a temporal break (not necessarily time off), followed by a fresh, sometimes jarring restart. These temporal breaks are rigorously scheduled, often years in advance. Time is constantly referenced: "time to degree," "extended time on tests," "stop the clock." Yet, because academic time blends premodern and postmodern ways of working (Walker 2009), most faculty do not use billable hours, nor do many of us even keep track of our hours, despite the percentages that are supposed to structure our labor.

Highly privileged academic employees (the 1 percent, you might say) are allowed to take part in premodern customs such as tenure and the sabbatical, both of which assume time is required to develop knowledge and creativity. However, even tenured faculty are constantly exhorted to "do more with less" and, in general, as Judith Walker (2009: 500) shows, are forced to participate in an "ever-increasing exigency to justify time and to take individual responsibility for doing so." Further, the scarcity of time for academic workers takes place in a context of decadent abundance for certain pursuits, including marketing, building, and athletics (Meyerhoff, Johnson, and Braun 2011).

The COVID-19 pandemic has altered some of these rhythms. People accustomed to moving easily through the spacetime of their universities have found themselves dropped into another world: housebound, unable to predict what might happen next week, trying to plan in advance for future debilitation, anxious, frightened, and suddenly dependent on strangers for their own health and safety. Disabled academics have written many pieces, on social media and elsewhere, pointing out that this so-called new normal is in fact the old normal for many (Wilde 2020). And yet, despite the monumental changes brought by COVID-19, many temporal patterns remain intact. The compression of more work into increasingly limited time frames is, if anything, amplified. Budgets have been slashed and jobs cut, while those still employed are expected to do (even) more with (even) less. For example, as I write during the summer of 2020, faculty are expected to prepare multiple versions of syllabi to meet a number of different possible scenarios for our autumn courses: in person, online, hybrid, or, in a puzzling new term, "HyFlex." Women and minoritized faculty are bearing most of the burden. According to both the UK *Guardian* and the US *Inside Higher Education*, women's submissions of research have dropped sharply (Fazackerley 2020; Flaherty 2020). Meanwhile, Black people and other people of color are not only bearing professional burdens but also dying from COVID-19 at much higher rates. The pandemic, while sometimes extolled as a chance to slow down, offers that pleasant kind of slowness only to the most privileged.

Given this context, academic time has a particular ability to intensify and sustain structural inequities. It draws on both postmodern (for the masses) and premodern (for the elite) systems of timekeeping and practices a special regime of nontransparency with regard to how time is spent, while at the same time increasing technologies of surveillance and encouraging self-surveillance. Walker (2009) speculates, in her article's conclusion, that future studies of academic time will show "differential effects" based on subject position (race, class, gender, age, discipline). This has turned out to be true in the case of the Disabled Faculty Study. Although time was not a main focus of the initial research questions, it turned out to be an important topic for nearly every interviewee. Further investigation led to my realization that not all of us, in academia, are inhabiting the same spacetime.

Exploring the Textures and Shapes of Time: The Disabled Faculty Study

The Disabled Faculty Study was launched in 2012 as a collaborative effort among Stephanie Kerschbaum (rhetoric/composition, University of Delaware), Amber O'Shea (psychology, Temple University), Mark Salzer (rehabilitation psychology, Temple University), and me (English, Spelman College and Ohio State University). Over one hundred people volunteered for interviews, and thirty-six interviews were eventually completed. Following interviewees' preferences, interviews took place in a variety of modes, including face-to-face, videoconference, telephone, instant-message chat, and email. Some interviews were oral, some signed, and some were a mix; we also worked with interpreters, captionists, and/or vocal assistants at various times, both remotely and in person.[6]

I analyzed the interviews using an approach to coding described by Cheryl Geisler (2018) and Geisler and Jason Swarts (2019). My early categories, including ambient uncertainty, gaslighting, and bodymind event (see Price 2017, 2018), showed me that disabled faculty members often seem to inhabit a different reality than their nondisabled colleagues. Or, to put it less dramatically, a disabled faculty member's everyday life and choices may be extraordinarily hard to understand from a nondisabled point of view. Interviewees described grappling with such commonsense questions as "Why don't you just explain the problem to your chair?" or "Why not just use the elevator, then?" and struggling to elucidate, even to themselves, the nature of the barriers they faced. Working from those early codes, I identified a set of more robust categories (including space, time, cost, and accountability) that formed the basis for a more targeted round of analysis. This article focuses mainly on subcodes within the broader code of time, such as stamina, conditional (if/then) time, and time needed to get accommodations in place. The purpose of identifying codes is to learn more about how they work together—in a sense, what story they are telling. The following section tells one of the stories that became apparent when I studied the various time subcodes together. I call this story the accommodations loop (Figure 1).

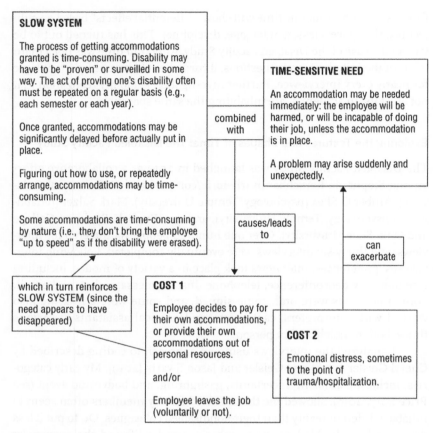

Figure 1

Mapping Crip Spacetime: The Accommodations Loop

Think pieces about slow professoring or slow medicine tend to focus on the speed of individual work, and indeed, individual work did receive significant attention from interviewees. However, interviewees also spoke at length about the speed at which systems and processes move. Analysis of the time subcodes revealed that, when processes move slowly, academic workers experience material costs—harms—for which they then must figure out some way to compensate. Often those compensations come at painful cost, such as paying for one's own accommodations, giving up research and creative opportunities, or even having to leave one's job.

Interviewees described two ways in which the system moves slowly: first, accommodations may take a long time to put in place; and second, once put in place, accommodations may be time-consuming to use. Both phenomena require detailed unpacking, because the dominant narrative about academic accommodation is that it proceeds smoothly, linearly, and promptly. For example, even a pro-faculty and disability-studies-informed publication like *Accommodating Faculty Members Who Have Disabilities* by the American Association of University Professors (Franke et al. 2012: 32) contributes to that narrative by announcing, "Once a faculty member indicates, whether orally or in writing, that he or she has a disability, a structured process involving several steps begins." Such statements imply that the process leading to adequate accommodation is clearly laid out, but the experiences of disabled employees tell a different story.

Roger[7] is a white gay man who has tenure at a liberal arts college. During his interview, he talked about trying to reach his office, located on the fourth floor of his department's building. Like many disabled faculty, Roger had arranged accommodations with his department chair rather than register with the human resources department (HR). He ran into difficulty, however, when he discovered that the elevator in his building was shut off on weekends.

> There's a very bad, fairly unsafe elevator that I am sure was put in years ago, strictly to meet some certain kinds of standards, but they barely do. But worse is that on weekends the janitors would shut the elevator down. . . . I made a point of, yeah, of talking to people in, say, in the administrative and the dean's office about it. And the administrative assistant rather curtly told me that, you know, if I wanted anything done about it that I'd have to go to Human Resources and register as a person with a disability.

Registering with HR not only would require that Roger go on record as a disabled employee but also would take the time required to make the appointment, get whatever tests or certifications might be required (and pay for them), and then convince HR to change building policy. As it turned out, there was a much simpler (and quicker) approach available: Roger brought his question to his school's affirmative action officer, who cut through the red tape by contacting the building manager directly. The building manager ensured that the elevator would not be shut down on weekends.

Roger's accommodation story is one of the simpler ones. Jacky, a blind woman of color, described starting a tenure-track job at a large, public state university.[8] Her institution was slow to provide the accommodations she needed: a reader (i.e., a sighted person to read inaccessible material aloud), JAWS screen-reading software, and a scanner. Although her university was "working on" her accommodations, weeks and months passed. She described the situation:

> First year was really, like, in that sense shaky, like, I did not have a reader when I came, I did not have assistive technology. I just came and straightaway I had to start teaching. . . . I had to look for the reader. I had to put the ads for it, interview people, and for one or two months I did not have a reader, either JAWS or this. . . . Thankfully I taught one course, but that meant like I bought so many of my courses just to accommodate myself.

What does "I bought . . . my courses" mean? All tenure-track faculty at Jacky's institution received eight course releases ("buyouts") in the first five years (against an annual 3/3 load: three classes in Fall semester, three in Spring semester), intended to support research activity. The first reader she hired, who was "wonderful" and "[made] sure everything was accessible," left the institution after a brief time, at which point, Jacky reported, "everything was stalled." (As other interviewees pointed out, the academic custom of hiring students as assistants means that, if a worker must be replaced midsemester, few applicants are available, since most students have made their arrangements already.) Left with no in-person reader and no screen reader software, Jacky used up half her course buyouts in her first three semesters.

At that point, Jacky said, she realized that she couldn't go on as she was and appealed to her department chair for help. She asked for extra course releases to make up the ones she had used while self-accommodating, and at first she received apologies: "[My chair] knew, everybody knew that [accommodations] got delayed and all that, and they kept apologizing: 'Oh we're so sorry about it, we're so sorry about it.' I said, 'Wait, like, sorry does not solve anything. I am literally, you know, halfway through with my course releases and it's my second year.' . . . Then the whole bargaining started (chuckling)." The apology is a common theme in the accommodations loop: apologies are routinely offered along with harmful delays. Jacky's succinct response— "sorry does not solve anything"—points out that apologies do not redress the actual harms occurring.

Jacky's story shifts at this point to a series of exhausting, and sometimes insulting, discussions about what accommodations would be adequate. In this part of the accommodations loop, disabled employees are often asked to prove that they are disabled and/or how badly they actually need the requested accommodation. This is a question of time in a different way: how much is loss of time actually affecting the employee? And by *affecting*, the counterbargainer does not mean "How much pain is it costing you?" but, rather, "How much is it affecting your productivity?"

Jacky recounted extensive conversations during her second year between multiple administrators and staff at her institution:

> Jacky: So back and forth between the dean and the provost and dean and pro—and they were like—the second year was full of all this drama, [and] I was not in any of those meetings. . . . [But] I got to hear a lot of nasty things from the provost and, like, from the administration. Like, first of all, they said, like, I'm being too needy and demanding.
>
> Margaret: Really.
>
> Jacky: Yeah, too demanding. They were, like, her needs never get over, like she wanted a scanner, $1,700 scanner, we got it. She wanted the second reader, she wanted, she got it. Now she wants course releases, she doesn't want to teach.

Jacky was not called needy or demanding to her face.[9] Rather, an ally in the Office of Diversity reported this back to her, not in an effort to hurt her but to note that the administration was being "nasty" and that they would have to advocate more forcefully. As Jacky said, this process not only delayed her work even further but also carried significant emotional cost: "I was in tears, I was in tears." During her interview, Jacky cried again, recalling the pain of these events.

At this point, the administration began to discuss granting the course releases but insisted that they be awarded on the basis of low productivity rather than calling them an accommodation. This introduced a temporal paradox into the loop. Jacky was asked to sign a form stating that she would be granted the course releases because she had not been productive enough, despite the fact that she had already obtained three grants in her first two years: "I said, that doesn't make sense." Jacky refused to sign and consulted with her chair: "I was, like, okay, what should I do? I don't want to sign. She's, like, just forget about it, don't sign it. Just fizzle it—let it fizzle away. . . . I had asked for five course releases. They gave me two, and then they said, we will review the request for the other two courses releases next year, depending if you do these [things]." Numerous other faculty members told stories about being taken through similar bends and twists while attempting to gain accommodations. Jacky had an outstanding work record ("I said, just look at my CV") but was met with a double-bind response: if you need accommodations, you must be able to show that you are performing poorly; but then, poor performance means you are not a competent faculty member, and thus you should not receive benefits like course releases. This paradoxical logic often has a clear purpose: in Jacky's case, as she noted herself, the institution wanted to avoid admitting that "they had not complied" with their obligation to accommodate her adequately. Numerous other interviewees in the Disabled Faculty Study reported being caught in a similar paradox. As Iris put it, "It's like, [I have to] explain what's happening that's difficult, and then explain how great I'm doing anyway, and I kind of rhetorically move back and forth."[10]

Jacky was not asked to prove she was blind or to take a vision test. However, many interviewees reported being asked to do just that: demonstrate or certify their disabilities in specific ways, vetted by specific authorities, a process that Samuels (2014) theorizes as biocertification. Some interviewees were forced to obtain letters from their doctors or undergo expensive tests, while others proactively sought documentation in an effort to avoid at least part of the accommodations loop. One deaf faculty member, already tenured, arranged a new audiology test when moving to a different (also tenured) job and requested that the results be placed in her personnel file. Unfortunately, depending on specific circumstances, an employee's disability may be disbelieved—either its specific effects or even the fact that it exists in the first place.[11] These narratives are familiar parts of the accommodations loop for many disabled employees: first, negotiate the question of whether one is faking one's disability or faking one's need (engage in biocertification), and next, undergo some process of surveillance designed to test whether one's biocertification is valid.

These parts of the accommodations loop were a central part of Miyoko's story.[12] Miyoko is an Asian American woman who left a tenured position at a midsize private university due to the stress of trying to navigate accommodations. Her disabilities include chronic pain in her legs, arms, back, and neck, as well as chronic fatigue. During the first several years at her job, she self-accommodated in many ways, for example, remaining seated while teaching and avoiding use of classroom blackboards. However, work that required extensive use of computer keyboard and mouse (such as using her school's course management system) was especially problematic. Eventually, and after undergoing two medical leaves, Miyoko formally requested disability accommodation from her university's HR department.

An aspect of bureaucracy that is not often recognized but that is a key part of the accommodations loop is its tendency to slow down processes through seeming failure to understand the problem.[13] For Miyoko, failures to understand her accommodation requests stalled her case repeatedly. She sent her initial request letter at the beginning of a summer, several months before she hoped accommodations would be implemented. The first stall was caused by the fact that she requested a different computer. She had originally been issued a Mac but then learned (after her conditions became debilitating) that Dragon Dictate software worked much better on Windows. Her request was misinterpreted to mean that Dragon could not work on a Mac, yet instead of contacting Miyoko for clarification or even rejecting the request, HR simply did not respond. A second misunderstanding centered upon her request to reallocate her teaching load. Miyoko's usual load was 3/3 (three fall, three spring), which she asked to have reallocated to 2/2/1/1 (two fall, two spring, two summer). She explained:

> Basically this first HR [employee] persisted over the summer in being very slow to respond . . . and at some point I figured out that . . . her main objection was that she thought that I was asking for a course reduction. (Laughs) So then I couldn't believe it, but I wrote a letter saying, you know, that 3 plus 3 is the same as 2 plus 2 plus 1 plus 1, and I actually made a little table to, you know, [show that].

Both of these stalls were exacerbated by the fact that responses (when given) took more than a month and were sent by certified mail, despite repeated requests from Miyoko to use email or the telephone or to meet in person. When she received her first certified letter, Miyoko reported, "I realized that it had become this very legal thing."

Like Jacky, Miyoko was not usually permitted to advocate on her own behalf. She in fact never learned from HR directly that they had misunderstood that 2/2/1/1 was not a course reduction. Her dean revealed that error while admonishing her for asking for "less teaching," at which point Miyoko wrote the corrective letter. This accommodation was then granted, but only for one year—"subject to renewal." She was also required to obtain medical documentation—again, the biocertification stage of the accommodations loop.

After she sent documentation from her doctor, Miyoko entered a new and alarming part of the accommodations loop: being surveilled. "Then I got a letter back from them saying that they had Googled me online and they had seen certain YouTube videos in which I appeared to be raising my arms above my head and doing things inconsistent with my claims that I had made in the letter [from my doctor]. . . . I was really shocked." As Miyoko discussed her reaction to this new twist, she pointed out a problem with the university's way of measuring time that was echoed by other interviewees: requests for accommodation often turn on precise measurements of chronological time, but most disabilities don't run on chronological time—they run on crip time. Pain might change a five-minute walk to one's classroom on one day to a twenty-minute walk the next. "Inability" to use the phone might mean "inability to use the phone for calls longer than two or three minutes" rather than "total inability to use the phone at any point, for any reason." Interviewee after interviewee described the complex, subtle calculations they made when trying to manage and predict their stamina.[14] One interviewee, Nicola, said that she routinely turned down invitations to attend social events after teaching because she knew "if I do this I won't be able to teach tomorrow."[15] Yet another, Trudy, described a long series of such calculations, affecting every aspect of her work and personal life: "I have to be super organized about the semester, assuming that at some point in there I'm not going to be doing well. . . . I probably look at my Google calendar more than anybody else I know because I have to anticipate what kind of energy this day is going to take, where I'm going to find time to rest."[16]

As these stories indicate, attempting to fill out an accommodation request truthfully can feel like writing one's own book-length autobiography. Yet fitting one's story into the yes/no, possible/impossible, reasonable/unreasonable discourse of the Americans with Disabilities Act makes it extremely difficult to express one's access needs accurately. At a particular moment in Miyoko's story, some authority at her university saw her (in a video) raise her arms above her head once and assumed that was an ability she could flex any time, all the time. And yet she would be required to re-biocertify her impairment, by means of doctor's letters and certified mail, every year. In summary, institutional discourses required Miyoko's disability to be constant and certain, yet the accommodations themselves were temporary.

In a desperate effort to keep her job, Miyoko paid out of pocket for many kinds of software, keyboards, and computer mice, as well as a personal assistant to help her manage the dozens of hours of computer work required of her each week. One of the last events that occurred before she quit her tenured job was learning that her assistant would be barred from campus:

> I hired my own assistant because I realized that the university was not moving quickly enough and I needed somebody to help me prep for class. . . . So I did that and then I got a letter [from HR] saying you must not allow this person—this person will not be allowed onto campus because she was not hired through the payroll system. Any person that you have as an assistant has to be hired by [this university].

Miyoko received that letter just before the autumn semester began, and in accordance with its directive, she began working at home more, continuing to pay the assistant out of pocket. Matters did not improve, though, and although she had been tenured only the year before, she ended up quitting in December. As she spoke about the decision, Miyoko emphasized how carefully it was made. She wrote a goodbye email to her colleagues, hoping her actions would not be misconstrued: "[I wouldn't] quit my job to make a point, you know, I'm not that kind of person. I know some activist people might resign out of protest but I was, like, no, I threw away a tenured position knowing exactly what I was doing. And I would have kept it if I could, but I just didn't have the energy." Miyoko's decision to resign came after years of self-accommodation and "about seven months of trying to work within the system." She added that if she ever had another academic job, "I would give myself like two years to get (chuckling) accommodations." However, asked if she would work as a professor again, Miyoko responded that she probably would not. "It takes a long time for academia to change," she reflected, "and so in the meantime I will be doing other things."

Many academics know that accommodations can be difficult to put in place. But the extreme delays, and the actual cruelty, that are routine parts of the accommodations loop might not be as familiar. Also unfamiliar might be that, even when accommodations are granted fairly readily, they often cannot be used without investing huge chunks of time. For example, in "Time, Speedviewing, and Deaf Academics," Teresa Blankmeyer Burke (2016: n.p.), a Deaf professor of philosophy, describes the time and effort she dedicated to locating American Sign Language interpreters when she was invited to give two talks at two different schools within the same time frame:

> What I cannot predict is how much time to spend on dealing with the universities or other academic organizations. In the case of the two universities mentioned above, one took 3 emails to resolve (my detailed request, university response and confirmation, then my response) and the other took close to 200 emails. Contrary to what you might think, the wealthy [Ivy League] university was obstructionist; the impoverished state university, expedient.

Even if both her hosts had been quickly accommodating, Burke notes, arranging interpreters is still a time-consuming task and cannot usually be handed off to a proxy (such as a departmental assistant), because "even highly skilled ASL-English interpreters are not fungible." That is, for a philosophy professor like Burke, interpreters must be well versed not just in general "academic" interpreting but in interpreting within the discipline of philosophy. Added to that are many more complications of language, location, and familiarity, which Burke elaborates further in this and other articles (e.g., Burke 2017).

Thus, although accommodations are often referred to as measures that "level the playing field," this metaphor represents a dangerous misrepresentation. Close study of the accommodations loop shows why. The loop is arduous to traverse, must be traversed over and over again, and exacts costs not only of time and money but also of emotion. The loop must be traversed by anyone seeking accommodations, whether they are quickly granted or fiercely contested. And, perhaps most important, the loop is almost always invisible to those not traversing it. Its travelers either continue funding their own accommodations or find a way to manage the constant labor of justification and biocertification, or they disappear from the system (dropping out, not having contracts renewed, not getting tenure). When a disabled person leaves the university system, the loop closes, for their disappearance removes both the need for accommodation and any trace of its history.

Mapping Otherwise

Institutional discourses suggest that waiting for an accommodation is a value-neutral event. It might be inconvenient or frustrating, but if the accommodation is eventually forthcoming (and if everyone has good intentions), no real harm is done. I argue that we must counter that assumption by recognizing a basic law of crip spacetime: time can cause harm. The need to assert and reassert access needs becomes a kind of repetitive stress injury, called "access fatigue" by Annika Konrad (2016).[17] Repetition has received considerable attention in the philosophy of time: Sara Ahmed (2006: 57) points out that "the work of repetition is not neutral work; *it orients the body in some ways rather than others.*" Thus, when interviewees referred to the need to negotiate vis-à-vis their disabilities "all the time," they were not describing a mere nuisance; they were describing a drain on their emotional and physical resources that often led to a drain of professional and financial resources as well.

The landmarks of crip spacetime are well known to most disabled faculty members, and in fact to all minoritized faculty members: surveillance, disbelief, minimizing, apparent inability to understand straightforward requests, gaslighting, microaggressions, open cruelty. Yet those same landmarks remain mysterious to those who continue to wonder, Why don't you just ask? Why would you leave a tenured position with no secure alternative? Why are you always bringing it up? Why aren't you ever satisfied?

As I write this conclusion, injustices of appalling scale are sweeping the United States and the world, dragged to light and inflamed—but not created—by the COVID-19 pandemic. Millions of people are taking action in response to the murders of Black people by police, with a new surge of energy around the years-long Movement for Black Lives. In this context, I am moved to reflect that, in its eight years thus far, the Disabled Faculty Study has yielded one finding more urgent than any other: not just collective action but collective accountability is the only way forward. Individual accommodations—and, by extension, individual efforts—no matter how well executed or how enthusiastically put in place, will only lead us further from equity and justice. Collective accountability is not just desirable but necessary if we want academic life to change for the better.

This work will take a long time. It will be an ongoing practice, not an event, and I can't predict how it will unfold. But I'll leave you with this one suggestion for breaking out of the accommodations loop, one step toward collective accountability in crip time: the next time someone tells you they need something—anything, any accommodation for any reason—*believe them.*

Notes

1   Due to limitations on funding and my research capacity, I did not include academics other than faculty in the interview sample. However, I hope to continue broadening this study, and my coresearchers and I encourage other researchers to make use of our instruments (a survey and an interview protocol) if they wish. For details see margaretprice .wordpress.com/disabled-faculty-study/.

2   For more on this theory, see Price 2017, 2018.

3   For a fuller explanation of why I use *bodymind* rather than *body and mind*, see Price 2015.

4   This open-source article, written by a collective of feminist geographers, directly engages structural inequity rather than offering glib advice about individual fixes. It does provide a list of recommended actions, but these are deliberately framed as both collective and complicated in nature. For example, "Organize" is number 3 on the list (Mountz et al. 2015: 16); "write fewer emails" is accompanied by a discussion of the political implications of refusing to respond (17); and "Say No" is paired with "Say Yes," to encourage discussion of the ways that more secure academics can make a material difference to, and/or share resources with, less secure academics (18).

5   This theme continues in Kafer 2016 on trauma and in Kafer's contribution to this issue of *South Atlantic Quarterly*.

6   We recruited participants from a range of backgrounds, types of institutions, areas of study, academic ranks (including non-tenure-track and clinical roles), and types of self-identified disabilities. This method, maximum variation sampling, aims to learn from varied experiences rather than achieve a "representative" sample. For more details on the study's methodology, see Kerschbaum and Price 2017 and Price and Kerschbaum 2016. Some details of interviewees' positions or backgrounds are omitted to maintain confidentiality. Interviewees were offered the chance to shape their own

descriptions. For example, the interviewee Jacky chose to be described as a "woman of color."

7   Telephone interview, conducted orally by Stephanie Kerschbaum, working with captioning service (CapTel). All interviewee names given are pseudonyms.

8   In-person interview, conducted orally by Margaret Price.

9   Maximum variation sampling does not permit comparisons across demographics, for example, how often an event was experienced by disabled women of color or disabled queer people compared to disabled white straight men. However, the many belittling remarks and frankly horrible treatment faced by multiply minoritized disabled faculty members indicate that this is an important area for future study.

10   In-person interview, conducted orally by Margaret Price.

11   For more on the "disability con" and its frequent appearance in stereotypes of dishonest or scheming disabled people, see Samuels 2014; Brune and Wilson 2013; Dolmage 2014, 2017; and Dorfman 2019.

12   Videoconference interview, conducted orally by Margaret Price.

13   For a thoughtful discussion of bureaucracy and its role in shaping the experience of disability in higher education, see Titchkosky 2011: 39, 94–96.

14   For further empirical evidence of these constant calculations, see Bê 2019: 1344.

15   In-person interview, conducted orally by Margaret Price.

16   In-person interview, conducted orally by Stephanie Kerschbaum.

17   Intertwined with access fatigue are phenomena specific to different but interlocking systems of oppression, for example, "racial battle fatigue," identified and studied by William A. Smith (Smith, Allen, and Danley 2007; Smith, Hung, and Franklin 2011).

References

Ahmed, Sara. 2006. *Queer Phenomenology: Orientations, Objects, Others.* Durham, NC: Duke University Press.

Alexander, M. Jacqui. 2005. *Pedagogies of Crossing: Meditations on Feminism, Sexual Politics, Memory, and the Sacred.* Durham, NC: Duke University Press.

Astramovich, Randall, and Wendy Hoskins. 2012. "Slow Counseling: Promoting Wellness in a Fast World." *Journal for International Counselor Education* 4, no. 1. digitalscholarship .unlv.edu/jice/vol4/iss1/4.

Bê, Ana. 2019. "Disabled People and Subjugated Knowledges: New Understandings and Strategies Developed by People Living with Chronic Conditions." *Disability and Society* 34, no. 9–10: 1334–52. doi.org/10.1080/09687599.2019.1596785.

Berg, Maggie, and Barbara Karolina Seeber. 2016. *The Slow Professor: Challenging the Culture of Speed in the Academy.* Toronto: University of Toronto Press.

Berlant, Lauren. 2007. "Slow Death (Sovereignty, Obesity, Lateral Agency)." *Critical Inquiry* 33, no. 4: 754–80. doi.org/10.1086/521568.

Braidotti, Rosi. 2019. "A Theoretical Framework for the Critical Posthumanities." *Theory, Culture, and Society* 36, no. 6: 31–61. doi.org/10.1177/0263276418771486.

Brune, Jeffrey A., and Daniel J. Wilson, eds. 2013. *Disability and Passing: Blurring the Lines of Identity.* Philadelphia: Temple University Press.

Burke, Teresa Blankmeyer. 2016. "Time, Speedviewing, and Deaf Academics." *Possibilities and Finger Snaps,* March 20. possibilitiesandfingersnaps.wordpress.com/2016/03/20/time -speedviewing-and-deaf-academics/.

Burke, Teresa Blankmeyer. 2017. "Choosing Accommodations: Signed Language Interpreting and the Absence of Choice." *Kennedy Institute of Ethics Journal* 27, no. 2: 267–99. doi.org /10.1353/ken.2017.0018.

Chen, Mel Y. 2016. "'The Stuff of Slow Constitution': Reading Down Syndrome for Race, Disability, and the Timing That Makes Them So." *Somatechnics* 6, no. 2: 235–48. doi.org /10.3366/soma.2016.0193.

Deleuze, Gilles, and Félix Guattari. 1987. *A Thousand Plateaus: Capitalism and Schizophrenia.* Minneapolis: University of Minnesota Press.

Dolmage, Jay. 2014. *Disability Rhetoric.* Syracuse, NY: Syracuse University Press.

Dolmage, Jay. 2017. *Academic Ableism: Disability and Higher Education.* Ann Arbor: University of Michigan Press.

Dorfman, Doron. 2019. "Fear of the Disability Con: Perceptions of Fraud and Special Rights Discourse." *Law and Society Review* 53, no. 4: 1051–91. doi.org/10.1111/lasr.12437.

Erevelles, Nirmala. 2011. *Disability and Difference in Global Contexts: Enabling a Transformative Body Politic.* New York: Palgrave Macmillan.

Fazackerley, Anna. 2020. "Women's Research Plummets during Lockdown: But Articles from Men Increase." *Guardian*, May 12. theguardian.com/education/2020/may/12/womens- research-plummets-during-lockdown-but-articles-from-men-increase.

Flaherty, Colleen. 2020. "No Room of One's Own: Early Journal Submission Data Suggest COVID-19 Is Tanking Women's Research Productivity." *Inside Higher Ed*, April 21. insidehighered.com/news/2020/04/21/early-journal-submission-data-suggest-covid -19-tanking-womens-research-productivity.

Franke, Ann H., Michael F. Bérubé, and Robert M. O'Neil. 2012. *Accommodating Faculty Members Who Have Disabilities.* American Association of University Professors. www .aaup.org/sites/default/files/disabilities.pdf.

Freeman, Elizabeth. 2010. *Time Binds: Queer Temporalities, Queer Histories.* Durham, NC: Duke University Press.

Geisler, Cheryl. 2018. "Coding for Language Complexity: The Interplay among Methodological Commitments, Tools, and Workflow in Writing Research." *Written Communication* 35, no. 2: 215–49. doi.org/10.1177/0741088317748590.

Geisler, Cheryl, and Jason Swarts. 2019. *Coding Streams of Language: Techniques for the Systematic Coding of Text, Talk, and Other Verbal Data.* Ft. Collins, CO: WAC Clearinghouse.

Halberstam, Jack. 2005. *In a Queer Time and Place: Transgender Bodies, Subcultural Lives.* New York: NYU Press.

hooks, bell. 1994. *Teaching to Transgress: Education as the Practice of Freedom.* New York: Routledge.

Kafer, Alison. 2013. *Feminist, Queer, Crip.* Bloomington: Indiana University Press.

Kafer, Alison. 2016. "Un/Safe Disclosures: Scenes of Disability and Trauma." *Journal of Literary and Cultural Disability Studies* 10, no. 1: 1–20.

Kerschbaum, Stephanie L., Amber M. O'Shea, Margaret Price, and Mark S. Salzer. 2017. "Accommodations and Disclosure for Faculty Members with Mental Disability." In *Negotiating Disability: Disclosure and Higher Education*, edited by Stephanie L. Kerschbaum, Laura T. Eisenman, and James M. Jones, 311–26. Ann Arbor: University of Michigan Press.

Kerschbaum, Stephanie L., and Margaret Price. 2017. "Centering Disability in Qualitative Interviewing." *Research in the Teaching of English* 52, no. 1: 98–107.

Konrad, Annika. 2016. "Access as a Lens for Peer Tutoring." *Another Word* (blog), February 22. dept.writing.wisc.edu/blog/access-as-a-lens-for-peer-tutoring/.

Love, Heather. 2007. *Feeling Backward: Loss and the Politics of Queer History.* Cambridge, MA: Harvard University Press.

Meyerhoff, Eli, Elizabeth Johnson, and Bruce Braun. 2011. "Time and the University." *ACME: An International E-Journal for Critical Geographies* 10, no. 3: 483–507.

Micciche, Laura R. 2011. "For Slow Agency." *Writing Program Administration* 35, no. 1: 73–90. Gale Academic OneFile.

Mountz, Alison, et al. 2015. "For Slow Scholarship: A Feminist Politics of Resistance through Collective Action in the Neoliberal University." *ACME: An International Journal for Critical Geographies* 14, no. 4: 1235–59.

Patsavas, Alyson. 2018. "Time, Accounting, and the Pained Bodymind." Paper presented at the Conference on College Composition and Communication, Kansas City, Missouri, March 17.

Price, Margaret. 2015. "The Bodymind Problem and the Possibilities of Pain." *Hypatia* 30, no. 1: 268–84. doi.org/10.1111/hypa.12127.

Price, Margaret. 2017. "Un/Shared Space: The Dilemma of Inclusive Architecture." In *Disability Space Architecture: A Reader*, edited by Jos Boys, 155–72. London: Routledge.

Price, Margaret. 2018. "The Precarity of Disability/Studies in Academe." In *Precarious Rhetorics*, edited by Wendy S. Hesford, Adela C. Licona, and Christa Teston, 191–211. Columbus: Ohio State University Press.

Price, Margaret, and Stephanie L. Kerschbaum. 2016. "Stories of Methodology: Interviewing Sideways, Crooked, and Crip." *Canadian Journal of Disability Studies* 5, no. 3: 18–56.

Price, Margaret, Mark S. Salzer, Amber M. O'Shea, and Stephanie L. Kerschbaum. 2017. "Disclosure of Mental Disability by College and University Faculty: The Negotiation of Accommodations, Supports, and Barriers." *Disability Studies Quarterly* 37, no. 2. doi.org/10.18061/dsq.v37i2.5487.

Samuels, Ellen. 2014. *Fantasies of Identification: Disability, Gender, Race.* New York: NYU Press.

Samuels, Ellen. 2017. "Six Ways of Looking at Crip Time." *Disability Studies Quarterly* 37, no. 3. doi.org/10.18061/dsq.v37i3.5824.

Shildrick, Margaret. 2009. *Dangerous Discourses of Disability, Subjectivity and Sexuality.* New York: Palgrave Macmillan.

Smith, William A., Walter R. Allen, and Lynette L. Danley. 2007. "'Assume the Position . . . You Fit the Description': Psychosocial Experiences and Racial Battle Fatigue among African American Male College Students." *American Behavioral Scientist* 51, no. 4: 551–78. doi.org/10.1177/0002764207307742.

Smith, William A., Man Hung, and Jeremy D. Franklin. 2011. "Racial Battle Fatigue and the Miseducation of Black Men: Racial Microaggressions, Societal Problems, and Environmental Stress." *Journal of Negro Education* 80, no. 1: 63–82.

Sweet, Victoria. 2017. *Slow Medicine: The Way to Healing.* New York: Riverhead Books.

Titchkosky, Tanya. 2011. *The Question of Access: Disability, Space, Meaning.* Toronto: University of Toronto Press.

Walker, Judith. 2009. "Time as the Fourth Dimension in the Globalization of Higher Education." *Journal of Higher Education* 80, no. 5: 483–509. doi.org/10.1353/jhe.0.0061.

Walker, Rachel Loewen. 2014. "The Living Present as a Materialist Feminist Temporality." *Women: A Cultural Review* 25, no. 1: 46–61. doi.org/10.1080/09574042.2014.901107.

Wilde, Alison. 2020. "COVID-19 and the Academy." With Sara Ryan and Sarah Woodin. *Everyday Society*, May 21. es.britsoc.co.uk/covid-19-and-the-academy/.

Williams, Jason R., Yuta J. Masuda, and Heather Tallis. 2016. "A Measure Whose Time Has Come: Formalizing Time Poverty." *Social Indicators Research* 128, no. 1: 265–83. doi.org /10.1007/s11205-015-1029-z.

Zilanawala, Afshin. 2016. "Women's Time Poverty and Family Structure: Differences by Parenthood and Employment." *Journal of Family Issues* 37, no. 3: 369–92. doi.org/10.1177 /0192513X14542432.

Christine Sun Kim, curated by Amanda Cachia

Six Types of Waiting in Berlin, 2017
Charcoal on Paper
50 x 65 cm or 19.68 x 25.6"

Artist Statement: Christine Sun Kim

Every culture's sense of pacing is different. After moving to Berlin from New York City a few years ago, I've noticed that I run errands much slower and that I receive undivided attention only if I've waited my turn. Once your turn comes, you can ask as many questions as you like. In New York City, on the other hand, you can easily get your quick questions answered very quickly, unless they're questions with longer answers. I have transitioned between musical notes and dynamics, which indicates being either aware of time or losing track of time.

Reference

Kim, Christine Sun. 2017. Artist statement from website. Accessed June 17, 2019. christinesunkim.com/work /six-types-of-waiting-in-berlin/.

Curator Statement: Amanda Cachia

In *Six Types of Waiting in Berlin*, Christine Sun Kim's drawings provide a fascinating constellation of cultural and sensorial experiences with time. Originally from the United States, the artist

The South Atlantic Quarterly 120:2, April 2021
DOI 10.1215/00382876-8915980   © 2021 Duke University Press

shares her account of how time (and waiting) is measured differently according to the cities in which she has lived, with each place having its own advantages and drawbacks. While each environment in which one must tediously wait—an immigration office, the health insurance office, the doctor's office, the bank, an art supplies shop, and the grocery store—is familiar, the subtext of the drawings is how the artist's relationship with time is also measured by her style of communication. Kim uses American Sign Language and asks questions in a written form using an iPhone on a daily basis as she goes about her chores. "Crip time" is thus also punctuated by the pauses in writing/scrawling questions, in reading, and the creativity involved in ad-lib responding between deaf and non-deaf sensorial modalities.

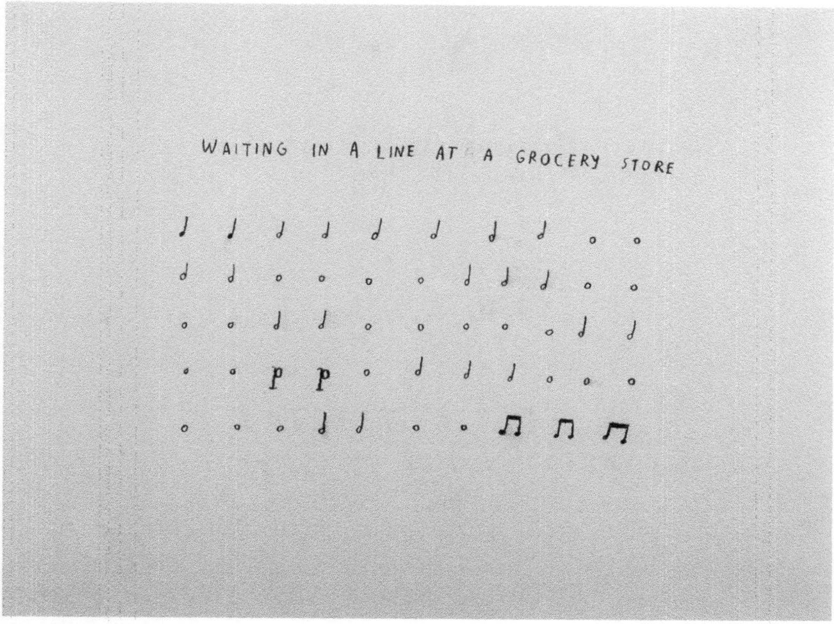
WAITING IN A LINE AT A GROCERY STORE

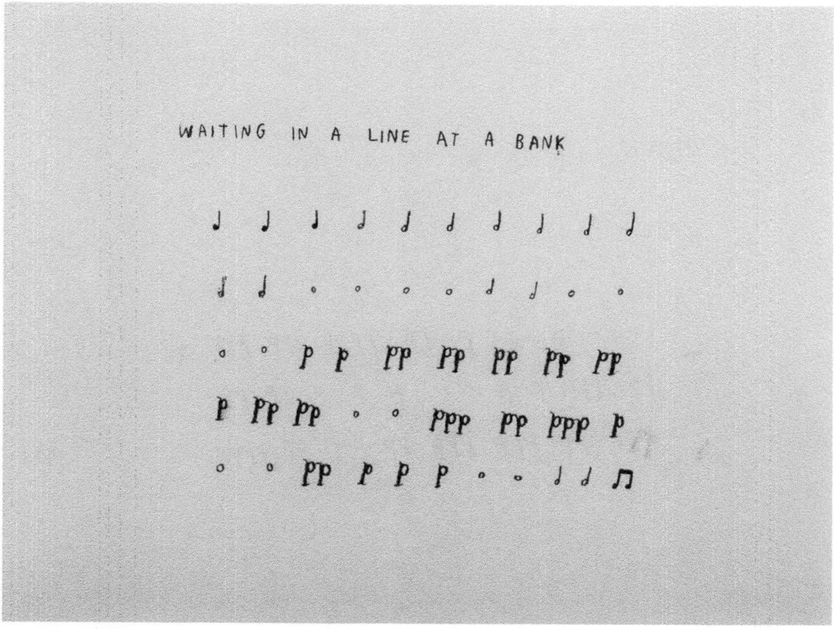
WAITING IN A LINE AT A BANK

WAITING FOR CUSTOMER SERVICE AT
AN ART SUPPLIES SHOP

SITTING IN AN IMMIGRATION OFFICE'S WAITING ROOM

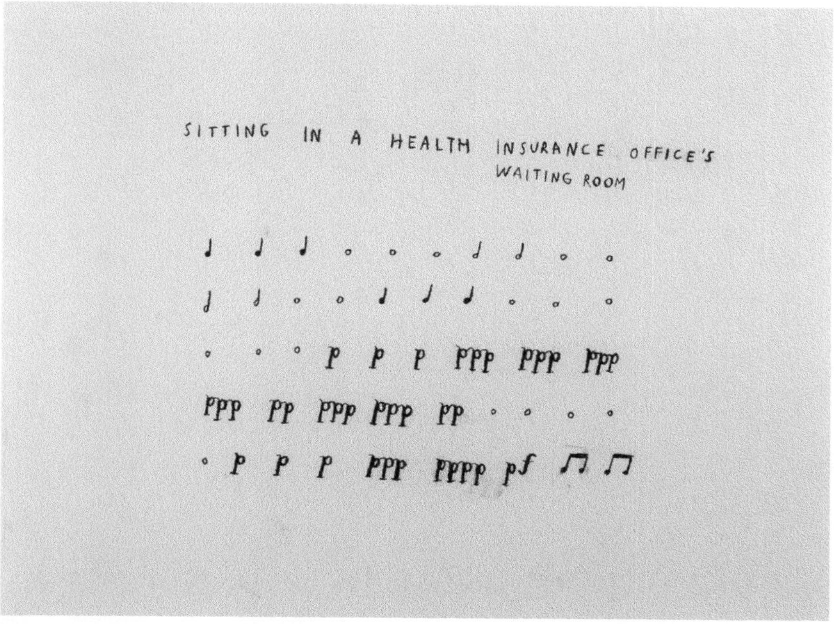
SITTING IN A HEALTH INSURANCE OFFICE'S WAITING ROOM

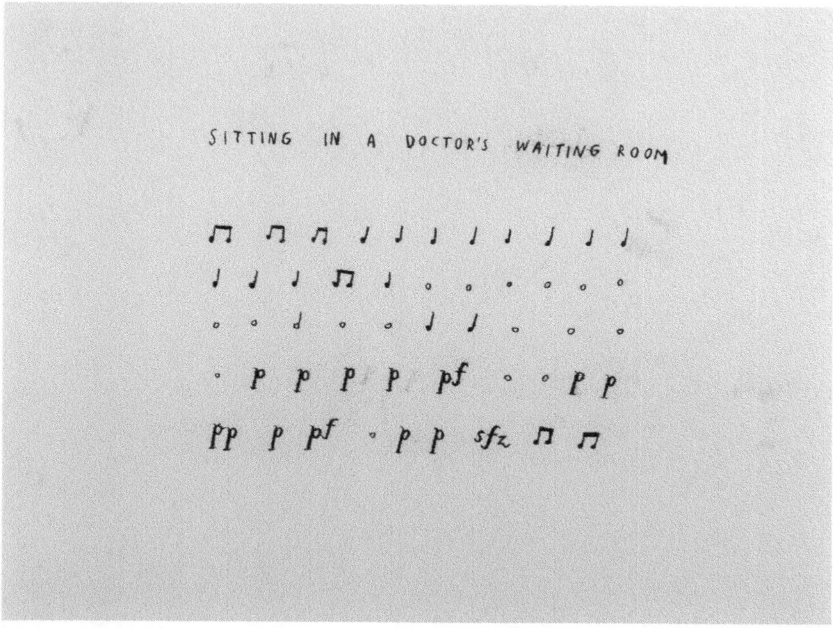
SITTING IN A DOCTOR'S WAITING ROOM

Moya Bailey

The Ethics of Pace

I began writing this article a week after submitting my book manuscript to my editor (on time!) so it can be sent out for review. As a junior academic, part of my work is to prove my intellectual prowess by producing a book published by an academic press that very few people will read. I was working on the aforementioned book project while teaching a regular load of courses and performing service for four different academic units at my institution, in addition to the service I do outside the university. I don't say all of this to inspire any sympathy from you, dear reader; I just want to make apparent the regular conditions of my mostly charmed life in the academy. I get to set my own schedule and teach what I want, and most of the service I perform involves things I want to do. But this list of tasks delayed my writing this piece on the ethics of pace and crip temporalities—the irony.

Even beyond the academy, humans are feeling an exponential pressure to move faster and produce more efficiently, all in service to an imperative to survive that has been warped by capitalistic greed. This pressure exacerbates disability, creates impairments, and even leads to premature death. In Japan there is a name for this

The South Atlantic Quarterly 120:2, April 2021
DOI 10.1215/00382876-8916032　© 2021 Duke University Press

"overwork death" phenomenon: *karoshi* (Nishiyama and Johnson 1997). Disability is not the problem; rather, the problem is society's, particularly employers', refusal to acknowledge the exploitation of our labor and bodyminds. As we work under debilitating conditions, all in an effort to try to afford care necessitated by this heightened demand on our persons, a vicious cycle emerges, resulting in unnecessary suffering. Disability studies has continually asked us to rethink these demands on our bodies and time by reminding us that not all humans are able to move and produce in line with these ever-mounting societal expectations. Drawing on the work of disability theorists like Susan Wendell, this article addresses the unique challenges of creating an ethical pace of life for those multiply marginalized by race, gender, sexuality, and ability (Wendell 1989; Kafer 2013; Kuppers 2014). I argue that, in our social justice visions of the future, we must radically reconsider our insistence on "jobs with dignity" and begin to question the meaning and need for jobs themselves. I argue for a reimagining of the ethics of pace, focusing on my own occupation in the academy and in the field of digital humanities (DH) as a necessary case study.

Pace of Life

Susan Wendell's critical text *The Rejected Body* (2013) is where I first learned about how the pace of life impacts disability. As Wendell explains,

> When the pace of life in a society increases, there is a tendency for more people to become disabled, not only because of physically damaging consequences of efforts to go faster, but also because fewer people can meet expectations of "normal" performance: the physical (and mental) limitations of those who cannot meet the new pace become conspicuous and disabling, even though the same limitations were inconspicuous and irrelevant to full participation in the slower-paced society. (59)

In other words, we make disability where there was none because of our need for speed. Our insistence on moving faster, both physically and in production, can actually slow us down as more people experience the drag caused by the friction of an impossible expectation of pace. And why must we move faster? To what end? The need to move quickly simply for the sake of moving quickly is not a compelling reason to do so. Capitalism's insistence on profits over people seems to be a major force behind the seemingly unquestioned ethos to make us produce more and faster. I ask that we consider the ethics of this pace, particularly in the academy, where research has shown there are other ways, better ways, for humans to move.

This last piece, the application of the insights of academic research, is perhaps what is most fascinating to me as a researcher. Fellow academics have shown the ill effect of the quickened pace, and their work is transformed into advice that we do not follow. For instance, we have done studies that suggest sitting all day in front of a computer screen is having a negative impact on human lives, yet we continue to create and sustain jobs that require us to sit for most of the day (Owen et al. 2010; Tremblay et al. 2010). We have evaluated the impact of building design and fluorescent lighting on our mental health, yet we persist in designing spaces that do not alleviate their negative impact on us (Boubekri 2008; Hamraie 2017; Sterling and Sterling 1983; Pauley 2004). In addition to asking us to work within these literal structural impediments to health and happiness, the academy demands more and more output: more research that is evaluated by quantity rather than implemented into our institutions' strategic plans going forward. Institutions delight in the excellence that their scholars produce without actually considering the possibility that this work could change how we live in the world. Efficiency and productivity drive the pace of life, and the ethics of that pace—the demand it makes on the human body—is rarely if ever questioned.

So here I am about to tell you why I think we need to slow down, "move at the speed of trust," as pleasure activist and organizer adrienne maree brown (2017) puts it,[1] even though it is not a strategy I currently fully employ. I am worried about the speed with which we are supposed to produce intellectual thought, even as I participate at and demand of myself an accelerated pace, evident by my impatience as I monitor the lengthy time from submission to publication of an academic work I submitted just weeks ago. I wrote about these unrealistic expectations I have of myself in a piece for the *Sociology Review* about academics with chronic illnesses and disabilities. I wrote about how imposter syndrome supported my internalized ableism, leading to overwork that has manifested as physical symptoms (Bailey 2019).

Despite knowing and feeling the material consequences of my overwork, I press on. I don't exercise as much as I should, and resting makes me anxious because I feel like I should be doing something, anything, to prove my worth in the academy. Like so many of us multiply marginalized in academia, this persistent attention to work is not just expected of us but a seeming necessity for our continued advancement. I want to shift this supposition, but I still feel mired in the reality of how things are. I write here to demand a different orientation to work and productivity even as I feel compelled to maintain my diligence. I ask you, dear reader, to do as I say, not as I do.

I begin by outlining the history of the academy and its Western patriarchal classist origins. I then discuss the retention of this hierarchical undergirding and its influence on the academy today, arguing that those who are multiply marginalized end up experiencing the bulk of the demands of the profession as manifesting negative symptoms on their bodyminds. I provide examples of how the profession is uniquely debilitating to those most marginalized within it, using case studies from the news. I discuss the "overwork death" of Thea Hunter, a Black woman trying to survive by adjuncting at three universities, and what this case reveals about how institutions play a critical role in the exacerbation and creation of disability and delimiting of life (Harris 2019).

Turning from problems to solutions, I build on the work of disability and Black studies scholars who are interested in rethinking the inevitability of these dire consequences on human life (Schalk 2018; Mingus 2010; Nishida 2016). By adopting an ethics of pace in our scholarly practice, I contend, we can disrupt debilitating patterns in academia and beyond. Finally, I argue for a slowed down DH that values moving at the speed of trust, which requires a more democratized relationship with time. Because DH is already attentive to collaborative scholarship, a slow DH would allow for moments of reflection so that multiple collaborators from different vantage points are valued (Lindblad 2017; moyazb 2017; Ceglio 2017). I offer the model of slow DH as a "possibility model," to use trans activist Laverne Cox's (2014) term, for an ethics of pace in the academy that is attentive to how race, gender, sexuality, class, and ability inform our work together. Slow DH has the potential to be an evocative example for other fields. I privilege process over product, arguing that the way we treat each other through our work is much more important than the resulting output. In other words, as disability justice theory teaches us, the end never justifies the means.

White Men in Ivory Towers

When I think about the beginning of the university and academic thought, white male philosophers in togas with laurel wreaths on their heads spring to mind. The word *academy* comes from the Greek *akedemia*, a place of higher learning initially devoted to the wisdom of the goddess Athena. That the goddess's place in the history of the academy would be written out is not surprising given the intensely patriarchal and classist culture of ancient Greece (Blundell 1995; Cantarella 1985; Winkler 1990). Plato and his followers have become the prototypes for professor and student. This life of the mind of able-bodied white men, aided by a social structure that gave them the freedom to think all day, is important for contextualizing the academy as it exists currently. The academy was built on the invisible labor of the women and other marginalized people who did the work of life so that these philosophers could enjoy a life of the mind. Referring to the roots of academic inquiry, feminist scholar Sara Ahmed (2016) wrote that the philosopher's writing table, through the "concealment of domestic labor," makes it possible for the white philosopher to be able to write unfettered by the work of maintaining a house. His ability to think all day and write is directly connected to the unacknowledged labor of those who remain outside the scope of his philosophical musings.

This history informs how universities are run to this day, with the invisible labor of the custodial staff, the support of predominantly female academic staff workers, and even the behind-the-scenes labor of women and other romantic partners not factored into metrics of success. Because white, able-bodied men are still imagined as prototypical scholars, institutions have been slow to ameliorate the different needs of a new set of academics. Parental leave policies are absent or only recently put into effect, as universities have been forced to grapple with the fact that some scholars have children and need time to take care of them. Accommodations for staff and faculty with disabilities are required by law, but the architecture of most institutions predates these mandates, forcing disabled staff, faculty, and students to get around campuses as best they can. Additionally, cultural biases in higher education persist, with policies that police the appearance of campus community members who are not white, straight, and Christian (Morgan-Smith 2018; Bauer-Wolf 2019). It is abundantly clear that the Western academy was built with certain people in mind: cisgender, white, able-bodied men who had wives to do the work of life for them. Many of my academic friends, including myself, are unpartnered and without roommates. We do the work of keeping a home—a full-time job in itself—while also juggling the demands of academic life. Not only that, but household, extended family, and community demands are greater on those of us who are multiply marginalized.

As most academics of color and women can tell you, it is painfully obvious that the academy was designed to be an Old (White) Boys Club. Our presence was hard fought and won, but not without casualties. We often have to do double the labor of our white male counterparts to be recognized. I cannot enumerate how many CVs of young scholars of color, many of whom are women, as well as white women, are twice as long as their full professor white and male colleagues because they are expected to produce more and prove themselves in ways previous generations of academics never had to.

Debility and Death in the Academy

This extra work, the additional work of having to do twice as much to be in the same standing as white peers, can produce an unrelenting self-flagellation in pursuit of tenure and promotion. It is never clear how much is enough, so you just keep going in hopes that it is more than what is expected of you. But even then, after all of that work, sometimes it still doesn't work out. The tenure denials of Kimberly Juanita Brown, Aimee Bahng, and Lorgia García Peña are material examples that doing all and even more of the things required for tenure is no guarantee you will get it if you are a woman of color (Flaherty 2014, 2016; Wilson 2016; Taylor 2020). The "twice as good" narrative that so many of us grew up with does not prove enough all the time.

The most painful illustration of this reality is not these tenure denials but the premature deaths of scholars of color. The list of prominent Black women scholars—including June Jordan, Audre Lorde, and Barbara Christian, all gone too soon—is enough to sound the alarm, but unfortunately, they are not alone. The death of cultural studies scholar José Esteban Muñoz at just forty-six still weighs on the minds of many colleagues of color. One of these premature deaths rocked me to the core: Thea Hunter, an adjunct professor at the New School and several other New York and New Jersey institutions, died in the pursuit of a livable life within the academy. Hunter died alone and overworked by an academic system that cared only about what she did for the institutions she worked for and not about Hunter herself.

In a long-form article in the *Atlantic* titled "The Death of an Adjunct" (2019), author Adam Harris explains the accumulation of bad breaks that led to Hunter's untimely death. The sense that one tenure-track job wasn't right led her to quit that position and move on to a visiting appointment and then later to adjuncting between three different institutions. Hunter was run ragged. With no health insurance, trouble breathing from chronic asthma, heart problems, and a persistent cough, Hunter tried to manage her health with a lone albuterol inhaler. She managed to get herself to the emergency room, but it was too late. The overwork and lack of care took Hunter's life.

Harris does an incredible job of detailing the vulnerabilities of adjunct faculty but only briefly acknowledges how race and gender impacted Hunter's situation. He makes a point to discuss Hunter's research on slavery as unique and even "pioneering" but does not discuss the unique factors women of color face in the professorate. For example, Black women are met with scrutiny from peers and students, sometimes even bullied into changing grades by colleagues who would rather appease a vocal white student than support their Black woman colleague (Wilson 2012). In addition to being subject to heightened surveillance by the institution, Black women are also expected to do a disproportionate amount of service labor, such as mentoring students of color and women. This mentoring, while essential for students, is not valued toward Black women's promotion and tenure (Wallace et al. 2012). Black women are doing additional uncompensated labor, often at the expense of their research agendas, making it that much more difficult to achieve tenure.

In addition to these likely but unnamed struggles, the day-to-day trudge from New York City to Connecticut, coupled with a department that wasn't the right fit, added up to Hunter needing to leave a coveted tenure-track position. Hunter was willing to risk underemployment rather than stay in a situation that didn't work for her. That said, working between three institutions with no health insurance didn't really work either. The travel between institutions and the grading and teaching requirements of each were too much to bear. In a situation like Hunter's, *karoshi* is not unusual—it seems almost inevitable, given the demands of scheduling, travel, and health concerns.

That universities with multimillion- and multibillion-dollar endowments refuse to pay a fair wage and benefits to faculty and staff is ridiculous. According to the National Association of College and University Business Officers, the New School's endowment is nearly $400 million as of 2019, and New York University, another school where Hunter adjuncted, had an endowment of $4.3 billion (*US News and World Report*, n.d.; Suneson 2019). These institutions have the resources to more than equitably pay for the work they demand of their instructors, yet Hunter died without health insurance. Institutions want to save money and extract as much labor from employees as possible. But institutions are made up of people. What happens that people become overly invested in productivity and forget to think about the human cost of the pace of life at an institution or institutions?

I argue that, with the increase of the pace of life in society writ large, so too has come an increased pace of life in academia. Students expect immediate responses to emails, as do other faculty and staff. Administrators rely on multiple-choice student evaluations to help determine professor pay. Graduate students are expected to enter the job market with at least one published peer-reviewed article if they expect to find a tenure-track position (Kafka 2018). The impact of these demands is a heightened sense of anxiety because it seems that every task is urgent.

Slow DH for a Diverse Academy

In my collaborative DH work, I have not been able to force things to move faster than the speed of trust. Author adrienne maree brown (2017) offers nine principles that inform her beliefs surrounding organizing through building trust. Principle 7 calls for people to "focus on critical connections more than critical mass—build the resilience by building the relationships." If we invest first in relationships among people, it won't matter that we are few in number. We need to prioritize the work of growing bonds among people before attempting to do more complex organizing. This principle is a testament to the collaborative nature of an ethic of pace and the need to move at the speed of trust. This phrase means, for example, that before you plan an action to occupy the utility company that has unfairly raised monthly bill rates, the members of the community organizing that action need to trust and be comfortable with one another. Here, the speed of trust is used to connote a slowing down and a need to nurture relationships before trust is established. The plans will fall apart if we move faster than people can depend on one another.

My work in the DH has been a revelation of this reality. As I wrote in my 2015 article for the *Digital Humanities Quarterly*, I have thought of the people I interview for my research as collaborators and not research subjects. In that sense, my collaborators and I all have an investment in how the research is conducted and in the results. This also means moving at the speed of trust in our interactions. Because I was known to many of my future collaborators as a Black queer woman interested in digital organizing, I was trusted before I was understood as a researcher. My organic relationships, built and nurtured over time, established a credibility with future collaborators that I do not think would have been possible without these connections.

DH as a field is already primed for this sort of collaboration, given the staff and faculty who generally work together to create digital projects. Librarians, engineers, and faculty have been the collaborative architects of many of the DH projects that are central to the field. Including community members as part of this already collaborative team means incorporating elements of participatory action research that allow for community interests to be served, not just the researchers' interests. Participatory action research is a process-oriented research method that fundamentally shifts the top-down approach to research where scholars study a community; instead, participatory action research works with a community to cocreate research that is mutually beneficent (Rodriguez 2019). When we include community collaborators from the beginning, our research is all the more impactful. In what follows, I provide two examples from my own research that I think illustrate this principle more clearly.

In writing the manuscript that delayed this article getting to the editors, I formed a community advisory board that consisted of Black women and femmes who use social media platforms for social justice organizing. This small cadre of collaborators helped me shape my research questions and challenged me to be more mindful about the information I shared publicly from my research. I was so focused on how their collaboration was useful to me that I didn't think about how the collaboration would be useful to them. As I wrote in a piece for *Digital Humanities Quarterly*, one member of the group utilized the collective to help with her own journalistic writing. I had never considered that the group members might find the collective useful for their own needs (Bailey 2015). This experience was a lesson in the power of collaboration and scholarly humility. By allowing this community to build trust among one another, it transformed into a group of its own making and its own needs. If we as scholars get out of the way, we can make room for other important connections to happen among collaborators. My own research was strengthened by the connections the group made with one another, which was possible only because of the extended time provided by bringing a group together digitally. When there were some errors in the article once it was published, no anger or animosity was directed at the collaborator who wrote the article. The trust we built meant that a simple mistake would not derail the relationships formed, whereas I imagine that if an unknown journalist had made similar mistakes, it might have been interpreted as intentional and handled with less grace.

I created the advisory group before even writing the prospectus for my book. Thus, these relationships have been able to build and grow for nearly six years. Both the slow building of trust that occurred, before I even thought about this research and invited collaborators into it, and the trust that was cultivated by creating a collaborative space together opened up new possibilities in my research and theirs that we never could have anticipated. An ethics of pace that moves at the speed of trust protects against possible disruptions because people and processes are more important than profits and products.

Most recently, I worked with coauthors Sarah J. Jackson and Brooke Foucault Welles on a book called *#HashtagActivism: Networks of Race and Gender Justice* (Jackson et al. 2020). We all come from different methodological traditions, which we brought together to achieve this text that none of us could have written individually. The speed of trust we built with one another developed over different timelines, as Jackson and Foucault Welles had collaborated previously and I was "new" to Northeastern University and the collaboration. A feminist faculty writing group that Jackson established while an assistant professor at Northeastern allowed us to learn about one another's work and our shared interest in hashtag activism. Over the course of these weekly writing sessions we got to know one another better and felt compelled to collaborate.

In the process of writing *#HashtagActivism*, we knew we needed to include the voices of the hashtag activists that motivated us to write the book. We solicited hashtag creators and paid them for short contributions in which they discussed their relationships to hashtags they started or used. Additionally, as someone who had worked closely with Twitter users as collaborators before, I wanted to give the users whose tweets we referenced a more transparent experience with academics using their tweets in scholarship. We wanted to provide notice that we had used their tweets and give them an option to opt out of seeing their handle or exact words in the text. With the help of our research assistant Kristen Miller, we collected every handle used in the text, and for every personal noncelebrity account, we reached out directly to seek consent to use the handle and tweet in the book. This process took some time but was essential to our ethos to move at the speed of trust.

My community collaborators from previous projects have dealt with the appropriation of their writing and thinking by people who used it for their own gain (Bailey 2015): academics using their tweets and blog posts in scholarly work without telling them; journalists aggregating tweets to make a larger point without checking in with the Twitter users about it, and inadvertently driving a whole new cadre of people to their Twitter timelines without their consent. BuzzFeed had been a particularly egregious offender on this count in the past. Stories of theft, co-optation, and invisibilizing the labor of online content producers have made me extrasensitive to how I conduct my research moving forward, making sure I do the work to acknowledge collaborators as coproducers of my scholarship. In celebrating the hashtag users who inspired the book, one of my collaborators, Foucault Welles, and I were celebrating a different digital activist each weekday by sharing that activist's handle and hashtag. We understand our work to be in collaboration and possible only because of their innovative use of the tool.

DH is not the only field attempting to do this important collaborative work, but it is the one I'm most familiar with and where I see the built-in potential to move at the speed of trust. In both of these examples, the people and the processes by which they are engaged are essential parts of the scholarship. An ethics of pace means that the ends do not justify the means but, rather, that the means are the ends. By remaining attentive to the people involved in our research, keeping the human at the center of DH, we can create a process that does not cause harm, or at least reduces it. The pace of life and the pace of our research are something humans can control. We can make decisions to push back on expectations of overwork through how we design our research and, when we are in positions of power, the kinds of scholarship we value for promotion and tenure.

Those of us who are department chairs and part of national organizations in our respective fields can advocate for the importance of collaborative scholarship. In the 2015 collaboratively produced white paper "New Ecologies of Scholarship: Evaluating Academic Production in the Digital Age," for example, I and colleagues Ryan Cordell, then assistant professor in the Northeastern Department of English; Elizabeth Maddock Dillon, professor in the Department of English; Julia Flanders, professor of practice in the Department of English and director of the Digital Scholarship Group; Benjamin Schmidt, then assistant professor in the Department of History; and William Quinn, then a PhD candidate in the Department of English, worked together to come up with new ways for the humanities to embrace digital and collaborative scholarship. One of our suggestions was to look to the physical sciences, where labs and research agendas are prioritized over individual paper output. We wrote: "The lab is an incubator for ideas that can focus on work in progress rather than 'works.' Collaborators can work together to mature ideas to the point of circulation" (Bailey et al. 2015: n.p.). Our hope was that administrators and professional organizations could use this document, and the crowdsourced comments it generated, to reimagine promotion and tenure guidelines with respect to digital and collaborative scholarship. Northeastern University has begun to take these suggestions seriously, as collaborator Ryan Cordell achieved tenure on the strength of his digital projects and not the generally expected monograph within his field.

I'm grateful to the editors of this issue of *South Atlantic Quarterly* for allowing me to move at the speed of trust to get this article to them, much later than initially promised. In the weeks of my writing this article, the world has been immobilized by the ever-spreading novel coronavirus known as COVID-19, which is forcing humans to slow down whether they want to or not. Once again, disabled activists have been at the forefront of offering best practices in this moment of uncertainty. Disability justice (DJ) organizer Leah

Piepzna-Samarasinha (2020) created a prepper guide for surviving in this moment and beyond. DJ scholar Aimi Hamraie (2020) has been instrumental in sharing accessibility resources and practices to faculty who are scrambling to figure out how to teach their courses online. The late Stacey Park Milbern (2020) and her Disability Justice Culture Club used Facebook and Instagram to organize local communities in Oakland. These practices are not considered DH by some academics, but to me they personify the ethos of the transformative DH I believe in, especially as we teeter on the edge of the end of humanity.

The ethic of pace I want moving forward in my life and in my academic work is a slow and sustainable pace, one that moves at the speed of trust and is not driven by capitalistic imperatives. The excess speed with which we are expected to move, the death of Thea Hunter, and most recently COVID-19 are all clear and unambiguous signs that the way we are living is not sustainable. We must pivot and change how we relate to each other. We must slow down to survive.

I have been so moved by the digital videos of Italians singing together during quarantine or exercising together from their apartment balconies. This moment is a reminder that human beings are capable of profound transformation if need be, and the need is undeniably apparent. I believe we must transition our ways of relating to our work, to our scholarship, to how we live, if we are to survive. The end of life as we know it is not a distant possibility but an inevitability if we continue to operate as we have. We must focus on building the critical relationships that will sustain us and not the failing capitalistic infrastructure that champions the individual.

I see my decisions as a researcher and scholar within DH shaping how I want to relate to all people in my life. I want to move at the speed of trust and afford my collaborators the respect and consideration that I want as a fellow collaborator. Our positionalities are not without an imbalance of power, but when this reality is acknowledged, this privilege can be leveraged for good. I hope to continue to collaborate, and I hope that this moment reminds us how important it is for all of us to do the same.

Note

1   The "speed of trust" comes from former CEO and corporate motivational speaker Stephen Covey, who used the concept to talk about the increased sales speed that results when a company is trusted by consumers. As described in brown's book, the "speed of trust" is augmented from Covey's initial use by community organizer and strategist Mervyn Mercano, who calls for a shift in focus on critical connections between folks invested in creating social justice.

References

Ahmed, Sara. 2006. *Queer Phenomenology: Orientations, Objects, Others*. Durham, NC: Duke University Press. Google Play Books.

Bailey, Moya. 2015. "#transform(ing)DH Writing and Research: An Autoethnography of Digital Humanities and Feminist Ethics." *Digital Humanities Quarterly* 9, no. 2. digital humanities.org/dhq/vol/9/2/000209/000209.html.

Bailey, Moya. 2019. "Race and Disability in the Academy." *Sociological Review* (blog), January 25. thesociologicalreview.com/race-and-disability-in-the-academy/.

Bailey, Moya, Ryan Cordell, Elizabeth Maddock Dillon, Julia Flanders, Benjamin Schmidt, and William Quinn. 2015. "New Ecologies of Scholarship: Evaluating Academic Production in the Digital Age." Google Docs. docs.google.com/document/d/1ON6VKt-kpMifK6J77 Upv8LEHgsYYaf-UpnNhCDQx2jQ/edit.

Bauer-Wolf, Jeremy. 2019. "Gay Rights Activists Ask NCAA to Intervene on Baylor's LGBTQ Policies." *Inside Higher Ed*, August 7, 2019. www.insidehighered.com/news/2019/08/07 /gay-rights-activists-ask-ncaa-intervene-baylors-lgbtq-policies.

Blundell, Sue. 1995. *Women in Ancient Greece*. Cambridge, MA: Harvard University Press.

Boubekri, Mohamed. 2008. *Daylighting, Architecture, and Health: Building Design Strategies*. New York: Routledge.

brown, adrienne maree. 2017. *Emergent Strategy: Shaping Change, Changing Worlds*. Repr. ed. Chico, CA: AK Press.

Cantarella, Eva. 1985. "Dangling Virgins: Myth, Ritual and the Place of Women in Ancient Greece." *Poetics Today* 6, no. 1/2: 91–101. doi.org/10.2307/1772123.

Ceglio, Clarissa (@cjceglio). 2017. "'Ethics of pace' important when digitizing & making community archives publically accessible says @JimMc_Grath quoting @moyazb #MyJNBC." Twitter, October 28. twitter.com/cjceglio/status/924365094070509568.

Cox, Laverne (@lavernecox). 2014. ".@MTVact i Prefer 'possibility model.' Some of my p. models: Leontyne Price and Eartha Kitt to name a few. #AskLaverne." Twitter, October 14. twitter.com/lavernecox/status/522072765336416256.

Flaherty, Colleen. 2014. "Are Colleges Denying Tenure to Improve Their Rankings?" *Slate Magazine*, August 14. slate.com/human-interest/2014/08/is-northeastern-university -denying-professors-tenure-and-raising-publication-standards-to-improve-its-national -rankings.html.

Flaherty, Colleen. 2016. "Campus Unrest Follows Tenure Denial of Innovative, Popular Faculty Member of Color." *Inside Higher Ed*, May 17. www.insidehighered.com/news /2016/05/17/campus-unrest-follows-tenure-denial-innovative-popular-faculty-member -color.

Hamraie, Aimi. 2017. *Building Access: Universal Design and the Politics of Disability*. Minneapolis: University of Minnesota Press.

Hamraie, Aimi. 2020. "Accessible Teaching in the Time of COVID-19." *Mapping Access* (blog), March 10. www.mapping-access.com/blog-1/2020/3/10/accessible-teaching-in-the-time -of-covid-19.

Harris, Adam. 2019. "The Death of an Adjunct." *Atlantic*, April 8. www.theatlantic.com /education/archive/2019/04/adjunct-professors-higher-education-thea-hunter/586168/.

Jackson, Sarah J., Moya Bailey, Brooke Foucault Welles, and Genie Lauren. 2020. *#Hashtag Activism: Networks of Race and Gender Justice*. Cambridge, MA: MIT Press.

Kafer, Alison. 2013. *Feminist, Queer, Crip*. Bloomington: Indiana University Press.

Kafka, Alexander C. 2018. "Another Sign of a Tough Job Market: Grad Students Feel Bigger Push to Publish." *Chronicle of Higher Education*, May 30. www.chronicle.com/article/Another-Sign-of-a-Tough-Job/243536.

Kuppers, Petra. 2014. "Crip Time." *Tikkun* 29, no. 4: 29–30. doi.org/10.1215/08879982-2810062.

Lindblad, Purdom (@Purdom_L). 2017. "Here here! @moyazb calling 4 ethics of pace—Slow archives, slow Dh projects, focused on social justice project rather than urgent now #d4d." Twitter, October 17. twitter.com/Purdom_L/status/920376521310855168.

Milbern, Stacey Park. 2020. "The administration has disregarded disabled people's . . . " Facebook, March 16. www.facebook.com/smilbern/posts/881771477357.

Mingus, Mia. 2010. "Changing the Framework: Disability Justice." *Resist Newsletter*.

Morgan-Smith, Kia. 2018. "Nursing Student Says University Is Penalizing Her over Her Natural Hair." *TheGrio* (blog), May 25. thegrio.com/2018/05/25/holy-cross-natural-hair-jade-payadue/.

moyazb (@moyazb). 2017. "So I guess my next journal article will be on the ethics of pace. Thank You #d4d." Twitter, October 17. twitter.com/moyazb/status/920383682996789248.

Nishida, Akemi. 2016. "Understanding Political Development through an Intersectionality Framework: Life Stories of Disability Activists." *Disability Studies Quarterly* 36, no. 2. dsq-sds.org/article/view/4449.

Nishiyama, Katsuo, and Jeffrey V. Johnson. 1997. "Karoshi—Death from Overwork: Occupational Health Consequences of Japanese Production Management." *International Journal of Health Services* 27, no. 4: 625–41. doi.org/10.2190/1JPC-679V-DYNT-HJ6G.

Owen, Neville, Geneviève N Healy, Charles E. Matthews, and David W. Dunstan. 2010. "Too Much Sitting: The Population-Health Science of Sedentary Behavior." *Exercise and Sport Sciences Reviews* 38, no. 3: 105–13. doi.org/10.1097/JES.0b013e3181e373a2.

Pauley, Stephen M. 2004. "Lighting for the Human Circadian Clock: Recent Research Indicates That Lighting Has Become a Public Health Issue." *Medical Hypotheses* 63, no. 4: 588–96. doi.org/10.1016/j.mehy.2004.03.020.

Piepzna-Samarasinha, Leah. 2020. "Half Assed Disabled Prepper Survival Tips for Preparing for a Coronavirus Quarantine." Google Docs, March 10. docs.google.com/document/d/1rIdpKgXeBHbmM3KpB5NfjEBue8YN1MbXhQ7zTOLmSy0/.

Rodriguez, Louie F. 2019. Foreword to *Community-Based Participatory Research: Testimonios from Chicana/o Studies*, edited by Natalia Deeb-Sossa, ix–xi. Tucson: University of Arizona Press.

Schalk, Sami. 2018. *Bodyminds Reimagined: (Dis)Ability, Race, and Gender in Black Women's Speculative Fiction*. Durham, NC: Duke University Press.

Sterling, E., and T. Sterling. 1983. "The Impact of Different Ventilation Levels and Fluorescent Lighting Types on Building Illness: An Experimental Study." *Canadian Journal of Public Health / Revue Canadienne de Santé Publique* 74, no. 6: 385–92. www.jstor.org/stable/41990204.

Suneson, Grant. 2019. "These Universities Receive the Most Money through College Endowments." *USA Today*, March 29, 2019. 247wallst.com/special-report/2019/03/20/americas-richest-universities.

Taylor, Kate. 2020. "Denying a Professor Tenure, Harvard Sparks a Debate over Ethnic Studies." *New York Times*, January 2. www.nytimes.com/2020/01/02/us/harvard-latinos-diversity-debate.html.

Tremblay, Mark Stephen, Rachel Christine Colley, Travis John Saunders, Genevieve Nissa Healy, and Neville Owen. 2010. "Physiological and Health Implications of a Sedentary Lifestyle." *Applied Physiology, Nutrition, and Metabolism* 35, no. 6: 725–40. doi.org /10.1139/H10-079.

US News and World Report. n.d. "How Does the New School Rank among America's Best Colleges?" www.usnews.com/best-colleges/the-new-school-20662 (accessed March 16, 2020).

Wallace, Sherri L., Sharon E. Moore, Linda L. Wilson, and Brenda G. Hart. 2012. "African American Women in the Academy: Quelling the Myth of Presumed Incompetence." In *Presumed Incompetent*, edited by Gabriella Gutiérrez y Muhs, Yolanda Flores Niemann, Carmen G. González, and Angela P. Harris, 421–38. Boulder: University Press of Colorado. doi.org/10.2307/j.ctt4cgr3k.38.

Wendell, Susan. 1989. "Toward a Feminist Theory of Disability." *Hypatia* 4, no. 2: 104–24. doi.org/10.1111/j.1527-2001.1989.tb00576.x.

Wendell, Susan. 2013. *The Rejected Body: Feminist Philosophical Reflections on Disability*. New York: Routledge.

Wilson, Robin. 2016. "A New Front of Activism." *Chronicle of Higher Education*, November 6. www.chronicle.com/article/A-New-Front-of-Activism/238319.

Wilson, Sherrée. 2012. "They Forgot Mammy Had a Brain." In *Presumed Incompetent*, edited by Gabriella Gutiérrez y Muhs, Yolanda Flores Niemann, Carmen G. González, and Angela P. Harris, 65–77. Boulder: University Press of Colorado. doi.org/10.2307/j.ctt 4cgr3k.11.

Winkler, John J. 1990. *The Constraints of Desire: The Anthropology of Sex and Gender in Ancient Greece*. New York: Psychology Press.

María Elena Cepeda

Thrice Unseen, Forever on Borrowed Time: Latina Feminist Reflections on Mental Disability and the Neoliberal Academy

> For those of us marked as both shamelessly
> excessive and wholly deficient, understanding
> what has become our place in the world is a
> maddening, soul-crushing journey.
> —Juana María Rodríguez, *Sexual Futures,*
> *Queer Gestures, and Other Latina Longings*

Ironically, I sit down to write this *testimonio* to my own resiliency and strength in what has historically been the most vulnerable of seasons for me, the slow-moving expanse between late winter and the faint beginnings of hope for spring. For most of my life, the weeks and months beginning with the December holidays through May have constituted a mental health minefield of considerable proportions. It is a temporal lapse marked by predictable episodes of deepening, suicidal depression gradually followed by the alluring reprieve of hypomania, and then—if I am not resolutely vigilant, if I fail to resist the siren song of full-blown mania—another shift, this time into a relentless high at times accompanied by psychotic features. I write these words in the thick of that vulnerable location. And I am well aware that I may be composing the manifesto of my own liberation, or just as easily paving the way to professional demise.

The South Atlantic Quarterly 120:2, April 2021
DOI 10.1215/00382876-8916046 © 2021 Duke University Press

Or perhaps both—or neither—simultaneously. As Stephanie Kerschbaum (2014: 57) observes, the rhetorical performance of disability disclosure is never without consequence.

Many of us are able to remember the most foundational moments of our academic careers in vivid detail. Finally finishing the dissertation, landing the first job outside of graduate school, publishing the first book—these are all fundamental milestones. The most vivid moment of my career thus far occurred a bit more than nine years ago, shortly after I earned early tenure as a Latina/o studies faculty member at Williams College and subsequently was appointed chair of the Latina/o studies program. While conducting my dissertation research in Miami, Florida, ten years prior to that life-altering moment, I had been diagnosed with bipolar I disorder, which in my case is characterized by a strong tendency toward mania, a state long considered the provenance of men, given its tendency to arouse fits of anger, aggression, and hypersexuality (Jamison 1995). After several years of much trial and error, my doctors and I arrived at a medication regime that managed to keep most of the worst of my moods at bay, enabling me to pursue my chosen career with relatively few disruptions, but also with the aid of a great deal of compartmentalization and denial on my part, or what I have come to refer to as my significant collection of psychological Tupperware. (Almost) Hermetically sealed, pointedly relegated to the farthest corners of my mind, teeming with decades' worth of excruciating secrets destined to detonate my personal and professional existence as I knew it, these well-worn vessels contained my childhood and adolescent secrets. They housed the long-suppressed details of the regular physical and emotional abuse that I had endured in my Colombian immigrant family from early childhood until the moment I eagerly left home for college at age eighteen. Indeed, my psychological Tupperware was a clear symptom of the severe case of complex post-traumatic stress disorder (PTSD) that I developed in concert with bipolar I disorder over the years. And it was complex PTSD and bipolar I disorder that landed me in a psychiatric ward approximately six times in three different states between 2011 and 2015, with many more aborted attempts at seeking in-patient treatment. (Until I recently acquired my medical records, I could not precisely state just how many suicide attempts and hospital stays I endured during this period. My memories of these four years are lacuna-like, at best, and shot through with solid periods of amnesia linked to disassociation.)

Crip time is lost time.

I do, however, remember standing between the aseptic, mint-green concrete walls in the hall of the adult psychiatric ward of the Brattleboro

Retreat in Vermont, hugging the public phone against my ear as I stared down at my laceless gray Converse low-top sneakers and the joyless combination of my cordless gray hoodie and well-worn gray sweatpants. It was March of my first year as chair, and my newly tenured self had finally, painfully accepted the fact that it was time to share my secret over the phone with the most senior member of my program, the Puerto Rican woman who had shepherded me through to tenure. I had managed to keep my first involuntary hospitalization in Florida over the December holidays a secret, but this was the middle of the semester and circumstances were now even more dire. I gave up the charade that afternoon on the phone. I openly sobbed, humiliated, as I explained that the doctors wanted to hold me in the hospital for at least two weeks, followed by months of intensive outpatient therapy. So no, I was no longer able to chair. And no, I would not be returning to campus that semester. Emergency arrangements needed to be made. I felt as insignificant and hopeless as I did as a child. I ultimately did not return to work for one year, and three years later I was forced into another semester-long medical leave. In April 2015, I was released from the last outpatient program that I attended, and the years since, while certainly not free of chronic symptoms and episodic struggles, have constituted the most significant period of stability of my adult life. Every day I wonder when the ride will end and the roof will cave in.

Crip time is borrowed time.

I have been writing this article in my head for years. Now that I am among the minute proportion of tenured US faculty who are Latina full professors, it is time to let the words go. To quote Margaret Price (2011: 24) in her important study of the rhetorics of mental disability in the US academy, I am composing this article "because I could not go any longer without writing it." Far more than earning tenure or promotion, nearly dying several times in the past ten years has shifted my relationship with my career, and with time in general. Embracing crip time is my only option if I wish to survive. I say this without resignation or bitterness, as crip time is not a temporal prison. It is not grounded in deficiency or lack. Crip time, as Alison Kafer (2013: 27) asserts, can actually lead us to "more expansive notions of both time and futurity." For me, crip time has opened up a pathway to many freedoms. These include the freedom to erect firm boundaries between my professional and private lives, the freedom to recognize and assert my own limits, and the freedom to wholeheartedly listen to my body-mind, among many others. Yet it would be disingenuous to cast all of these freedoms as wholesale choices.

Latina Feminist *Testimonio* and the Dynamics of Passing

"The patient was admitted to Tyler 2 where she was placed on 15 minute checks for safety. She was cooperative. Patient was extremely labile, pressured, with elevated affect with bursts of crying. She described racing thoughts, flight of ideas. Speech was very fast. Still she described herself as depressed which was inconsistent with observed affect." Nearly nine years after the fact, I survey this short paragraph from a 2011 intake summary in disbelief. I was, you see, convinced that at the time I was passing for neurotypical, even to trained medical staff. Approximating "normal" is what earns you privileges in a psychiatric institution: fresh air in the locked courtyard, meals in the cafeteria instead of on the secure ward, a supervised walk on the hospital grounds. The convincing performance of psychiatric normalcy is ultimately what earns you your medically approved release after anywhere from three days to weeks in a locked-down ward. For those who are vulnerable to experiencing a total loss of control over their lives, any sense of control is cherished (Wang 2019: 52–53). When passing for "normal" in both personal and professional settings, the stakes are higher for the mentally disabled.[1] As Esmé Weijun Wang (2019: 76) wryly noted, "My fate is being judged based on how well I show off just how very fine I am."

Crip time is exhausted time.

Passing for neurotypical in a world that views the mentally disabled as a problem, as a disposable class of individuals, demands great effort—far more effort (though no less complex in its iterations and impacts) than the white-passing privileges that my light olive skin and gray eyes have often afforded me. Even in my deepest moments of crisis, I clung to the fiction of neurotypicality, even at the moments when those around me (often other neurodivergent children or adults, and using precisely the following language) detected that I was indeed "one of the them." Although my passing was not always to my benefit as a long-term strategy, I would concur that it may be understood as a gesture of defiance (Samuels 2003: 243) or even as a trickster strategy that subverts the academic status quo (Price et al. 2017: 5–6) in the overwhelmingly ableist milieu of higher education. Even as I engage in what Price et al. (2017: 6) rightfully characterize as the endless, ongoing process of disclosure, with a carefully selected number of colleagues and students—a process that is inextricably bound to my ethnoracial and gender identities—I often find myself favorably emphasizing the amount of time since my last noteworthy episode, in an attempt to highlight my normalcy: "See my ordinary, even superlative appearance! Witness the fact that

I am articulate. Rewind our interaction and see if you can spot any cracks in the façade. See if you can, in sifting through your memory, find hints of insanity to make sense of what I've said about who I am" (Wang 2019: 54). I must, in other words, somehow prove that I am "normal," just as I am required in other contexts to prove to professional colleagues that I am in fact in need of disability accommodations per the Americans with Disabilities Act (ADA). This is what N. Ann Davis (2005: 154–55) refers to as the "double bind" of invisible disability: either one forgoes much-needed workplace accommodations, or one must endure the not-so-subtle violence of regularly disclosing one's condition to mere acquaintances, including superiors tasked with evaluating one's performance at a later date. This is not the only double bind; for me, enhanced stability translates into higher functioning, which can further invisibilize my mental disability. The goal is to spend less time in the hospital, yet hospitalizations "prove" the disability.

I have just engaged in a brief reflexive ethnography regarding the politics of invisible disability in the neoliberal academy. Initially legitimized by feminist scholars who employed their personal experiences and social positionalities as a critical data set, reflexive ethnography constitutes a point of departure from which to engage in broader cultural critiques (Ellis and Bochner 2000: 740–41). Traditionally, writing pertaining to the emotions, lived experience, and "practiced vulnerability" (Tami Spry, qtd. in Nzibi Pindi 2018: 25) has been framed as a stereotypically "feminine" endeavor and, in turn, has been perceived as inferior if not a wholesale impediment to the superior forces of objectivity, rationality, and ultimately masculinity (Holman, Adams, and Ellis 2013: 29). However, I would posit that casting such epistemological practices as simply and inherently feminine is problematic, as they are just as often femin*ist*, given their facility for elucidating the everyday linkages between the personal and the political. I am writing about just how it feels to be an invisibly disabled Latina in the academy from my unique positionality in part as a means of acknowledging how reflexive ethnography constitutes a form of embodied knowledge and that we write about ourselves as a means of achieving a "deeper critical understanding with others of the ways in which our own lives intersect with larger sociocultural pains and privileges" (Nzibi Pindi 2018: 25–26). As such, the article does not engage in an examination of the self in isolation; rather, I seek to contribute to a broader cultural critique (Boylorn and Orbe 2013: 17) and illuminate questions pertinent to invisibly disabled faculty collectivities. Moreover, I submit these truths about some of my most painful life experiences in the belief, as Laura Halperin (2015: 4) articulates in her literary study of

Latinas and harm, that "hiding harm does nothing to alleviate it or to prevent its future imposition."

Perhaps even more so than reflexive ethnography in the broadest sense of the word, here I engage in a Latina feminist *testimonio*. Echoing the activist scholarly work of the Latina Feminist Group (2001: 2), I offer this *testimonio* as "a crucial means of bearing witness and inscribing into history those lived realities that would otherwise succumb to the alchemy of erasure." Long tied to feminist, self-reflexive research methods, the *testimonio* emerged from contemporary Latin American political movements, including women's struggles for liberation, and offers both artistic platforms for developing politicized notions of self and community and methodological approaches for doing so. Latina feminist testimony is thus fundamentally about resistance from the margins (3). Much like the practice of passing for neurotypical, this brand of *testimonio* retains a subversive edge. It is a written weapon against patriarchy, as well as the classist, racist, xenophobic systems that enabled my long-term abuse at home, and against a mental health system that has more often than not failed me if not my entire family. Potentially collective as well as intersectional, part of the *testimonio*'s power lies in its resistance to genre-based norms, as *testimonios* can encompass anything written by first-person witnesses as texts of those who seek to recount their own story of trauma (Smith 2010–11: 26–27).[2]

Writing from within the frameworks of Latina feminist *testimonio* and building on the scholarship of disability, queer, and ethnic studies scholars such as that of José Esteban Muñoz (2010), Alison Kafer (2013), Juana María Rodríguez (2014), and Ellen Samuels (2017), I am also invested in a discussion of mental disability, the academy, and crip time, or what Kafer (2013: 27) describes as

> flex time not just expanded but exploded; it requires reimagining our notions of what can and should happen in time, or reorganizing how expectations of "how long things take" are based on very particular minds and bodies. We can then understand the flexibility of crip time as being not only an accommodation to those who "need" more time but also, and perhaps especially, a challenge to normative and normalizing expectations of pace and scheduling. Rather than bend disabled minds and bodies to meet the clock, crip time bends the clock to meet disabled bodies and minds.

Productivity, efficiency, and competition—the three cardinal values of corporate higher education—all possess time as a common factor. Corporatization has undeniably quickened the pace of life in academia. I used to wonder if the problem was entirely me, if as a mentally disabled person I was simply unfit for the profession. Yet such an individualistic approach is misguided; perhaps the better question to pose is, Just what is it about higher education that leaves so many of us feeling as if we cannot cope (Berg and Seeber 2016: 8, 16)? As I age and become more aware of the impacts of biopolar I and complex PTSD on all facets of my life, and as I become more sensitized to the outsized demands of life in the contemporary neoliberal academy, I have been purposefully living various forms of crip time. Contrary to the cultural norms of the profession, I listen carefully to my bodymind and make constant adjustments to my workload and schedule; as Samuels (2017) explains, crip time demands that we break time. I break time because as a mentally disabled Latina in the academy, I want, above all, to survive and to be free. I break time and encourage my colleagues and students to do so as well, because I want freedom and survival for all of us.

Crip time is fractured time.

The *Apodo* That Follows Me: *Loca* Epistemologies

For those in the Spanish-speaking world, *apodo* means "nickname." In Latina/o/x communities, nicknames are assigned to virtually everyone, ostensibly as a sign of affection. For much of my life, Loca (in its most innocuous iteration, Spanish for "crazy woman/girl") or the diminutive Loquita have been *apodos*, both before and after my formal psychiatric history began around twenty years of age, and among both those who were previously familiar with that history and those who were not. As podcast hosts Mala Muñoz (Zoe Muñoz) and Diosa Femme (Ariana Rodríguez Zertuche) note in the inaugural episode of the popular Latina/x feminist podcast *Radio Locatora*, in the Latina/o/x context *loca* actually represents more than the less favorable alternative translation of "crazy bitch" suggests. In their discussion of *loca* epistemologies, the hosts acknowledge the historical roots of *loca* ways of knowing, linking the *loca* to the Catholic concept of *marianismo*, or the Madonna/whore complex. While the *loca* is understood within the context of *marianismo* as traditionally tied to the role of the whore and hypersexuality, Muñoz and Diosa Femme reclaim the term, informing listeners that a *loca* may also be understood as "that woman who doesn't give a fuck" (Muñoz and Rodríguez Zertuche 2016), the girl who dares to live her life differently than the women in her family who came before her, or the survivor of domestic violence who is not believed. For example, La Malinche and La Llorona are but two of the famous *locas* who populate Chicana/o/x and Latina/o/x popular culture, as survivors of racism and heteropatriarchy whose experiences go unvalidated. The *loca* trope is thus a site of discursive historical violence that both Mala Muñoz and Diosa Femme ultimately connect to the stigma of mental disability and its impacts on their own lives (Muñoz and Rodríguez Zertuche 2016).

Perhaps most significant, a *loca* is understood by Mala Muñoz and Diosa Femme primarily as any woman who does not conform to societal expectations.[4] While I eagerly reclaim my positionality as a *loca* as it pertains to mental disability, I place equal emphasis on my own inability (in concert with a lack of willingness) to adhere to Latina/o/x and specifically Colombian diasporic norms, on my own connection to what US Colombian writer Patricia Engel refers to as the condition of being a "failed Colombiana." In Engel's (2010: 70) short story "Desaliento" ("Discouragement"), protagonist Sabina consistently rejects the Colombian suitors presented to her by her upper middle-class Miami family and friends, "earning me a rep as a failed Colombiana, or possibly a lesbian, and my mom pretended this didn't worry her." As Catalina Esguerra (2020: 359) contends, "failing as a Colombiana" indexes multiple deficiencies; it references the failure to maintain upward socioeconomic mobility, and the simultaneous failure to perform compulsory heterosexuality on culturally sanctioned terms.

Crip time is fraught time.

My own status as a failed Colombiana is directly tied to my identity as a *loca*. I am, in the frequently cited words of Sandra Cisneros (1991), "nobody's mother and nobody's wife." Never married, unable to bear children because of my medication regime, terrified to parent due to the potential for my own medical instability, and not even sure if I want children or marriage regardless, I am acutely aware of how "discourses of reproduction, generation, and inheritance are shot through with anxiety about disability" (Kafer 2013: 29). Would it be fair to knowingly pass my psychiatric inheritance on to a child? And what does this stance reveal about how I, too, have perhaps been conditioned to devalue the lives of the mentally disabled? As my childbearing years quickly pass me by, I wonder about the politics of failure, their specific reverberations in the lives of disabled Latina/x subjects, and their intimate linkages to the logic of "straight time," or a futurity linked to reproduction. As Juana María Rodríguez (2014: 11) cogently argued, those who belong to marginalized communities (such as queers, people of color, and the disabled) are denied any futurity. I confess to only recently allowing myself the luxury of imaging a future me, a late middle-age and even an elderly me, as I never expected to make it past forty.

I would assert that embracing an alternative temporal reality can prove liberatory for disabled Latinas/xs, in particular, everywhere. In his writing on queer temporality, José Esteban Muñoz (2010: 185) argued that the liberation from normative temporality can be realized only through the abandonment of straight time: "We must vacate the here and now for a then and there. Individual transports are insufficient. We need to engage in a collective temporal distortion. We need to step out of the rigid conceptualization that is a straight present." Here we witness the overlap between crip and queer temporalities. Crip time, much like queer time, encompasses the anti- or nonreproductive. It can include, moreover, the gendered and sexualized time of infertility, hysterectomy, and menopause. Indeed, both temporal states highlight how "the futures we imagine reveal the biases of the present," just as "imagining different futures and temporalities might help us see, and do, the present differently" (Kafer 2013: 28). As a disciplinary mechanism, straight time endeavors to mold the disabled, queer, raced, and gendered body and mind, much as neoliberal governmentality has become the rule in US higher education. Straight time and academic institutional time occupy my thoughts, constantly feeding off each other.

Collegiality and the Turns of Crip Time

As a failed middle-class Colombiana, I have not complied with the social norms of my gender, culture, and class. Nor have I adhered to the many professional norms around productivity and collegiality in particular. For mentally disabled faculty members, what then is the price of noncompliance— and, I would argue, absolute compliance—to institutional norms around productivity? Of unwavering compliance and noncompliance to commonplace assumptions regarding what it means to be "collegial"?

Notably, the very concept of collegiality is defined against mental disability, and incorporating it into the holy academic trinity of teaching, research, and service further instrumentalizes already weary academics (Price 2011: 114; Berg and Seeber 2016: 14–15). A case in point: the types of medical specialists that my conditions require are overwhelmingly clustered in the central and eastern part of Massachusetts. My job is located in the far northwestern corner of the state. After an initial year living near campus marked by increasing struggles with depression and hypomania, I elected to move closer to central Massachusetts, a decision that significantly increased my commute but that provided me with access to much better health care. After my first medical leave nine years ago, I requested the disability accommodations that ultimately made it possible for me to continue practicing the profession that I love. These accommodations expressly stipulate that I am required to be on campus to teach, hold office hours, and attend meetings and events for a minimum of two days a week.

I do not regret my decision to move, as it has been lifesaving, but it has also meant that I miss many after-hours events and opportunities to socialize with colleagues. Williams is not a commuter school; the expectation is that professors will be readily available to meet with students and colleagues outside of class. In response to this cultural climate, I employ technology to compensate for my lack of physical presence: phone calls, texts, Zoom, Skype, Google Docs, Google Hangouts, and the like. I endeavor to cheerfully emphasize what I can do in terms of scheduling, as opposed to what I can't do. I constantly agonize over my schedule. I pray that my colleagues and students will not interpret my absences as a lack of interest or care. I often consider complete disclosure as the answer to their quizzical looks and comments, but I resent having to prove that I am "disabled enough" for accommodations to students and colleagues that I barely know yet will have the power to evaluate my professional performance. In this way, collegiality requirements at times obscure other forms of discrimination (Price 2011: 114). Disclosure is, after all, a type of forced intimacy, a negotiation that can be characterized as "exploitative, exhausting, and violating" (Pearson and Boskovich 2019: 6) and a process that can ultimately uphold ableism, given how it dampens society's capacity to recognize the empowering features of access for the disabled (6).

I also perform hypercompetency, sometimes taking on extra tasks that can be completed at home in order to prove (to others? to myself?) that I too can "pull my weight." Above all, I thank the universe that I already have tenure and promotion, and I feel deep concern for the invisibly disabled faculty out there who do not enjoy the protections of tenure and the ADA. I notice the widely circulated articles featuring faculty members who have bravely gone public with the stories of mental disability, and I ask myself: why are they all white and male (see, e.g., Pettit 2016)? (This is a rhetorical question. I already know the answers.)

My strategy for dealing with the temporal demands of life in neoliberal higher education is straightforward, if never quite simple: I save my energy whenever possible and attempt, to the extent possible, to anticipate the conditions that render it difficult if not impossible to work. I engage in self-monitoring—not in the neoliberal sense but, rather, as a means of countering ableist temporalities and higher education's relentless emphasis on production, efficiency, and competition. Alison Kafer (2013: 39) characterizes these practices as queer, to the extent that they run counter to US ideals that fetishize productivity at all costs, even when that productivity causes bodily harm. I would also label them as queer in the sense that they can also entail foregoing reproduction; as I often say to myself, I am saving my body and mind for something other than work and raising children.

Widely hailed recent academic treatises such as Maggie Berg and Barbara Karolina Seeber's *Slow Professor* (2016) and the attendant "slow professor" movement encourage professors to elect a different approach toward productivity and the temporal demands of the contemporary neoliberal academy. Many of the authors' suggested tactics, such as their fervent call for academics to reject the culture of performative busyness and engage in "timeless" intellectual pursuits, are sound. But such approaches fail to recognize that, for those with invisible disabilities in particular, the decision to enact productivity seemingly at will quite often lies beyond one's control, regardless of one's work ethic and even the most favorable of institutional circumstances. As Esmé Weijun Wang (2019: 165) describes, the demands of chronic illness articulate themselves in particular ways: "With chronic illness, life persists astride illness unless the illness spikes to acuity; as that point, surviving from one second to the next is the greatest ambition I can attempt." Working from within the ableist discursive frameworks of academia, Berg and Seeber (2016) extol the benefits of slowing down time but do not consider the benefits—or even the necessity, for some—of cripping it by calibrating speed and intensity, slowness and rest. My temporal relationship to my profession and notions of productivity are radically shaped by the episodic nature of PTSD and bipolar I, a hard fact that renders the "choice" to spend my personal and professional time in a different way a false choice. I work when I am able to read, focus, and think lucidly. But this is not always the case, a reality that enhances the pressure to be productive whenever I can—because I never know what's coming around the corner.

Crip time is uncertain time.

Yet my relationship with time is not merely one marked by the underlying anxiety to accomplish as much as possible before the next episode; it is also a relationship of loss, as in memory loss. PTSD provokes an odd temporality, one marked by both anticipation/forward motion (where is the next danger?) and flashes of the past/backward motion (Kafer 2013: 38) (in many ways I become—if but momentarily—my previous self, enveloped in the abusive environment of my upbringing and unable to separate it from the present context). During periods of intense disassociation both past and present I have lost swaths of time, particularly memories of traumatic childhood events. As an adult I reexperience these losses during flashbacks that at times have left me with no memory whatsoever of why or how I managed to be in a certain place at a given time. During my hypomanic and manic episodes, the congealed nature of PTSD time is dislodged, sped up in fits and starts beyond recognition and marked by behavioral risks seemingly without consequence in the moment.

Crip time is forever lost time.

Crip time is scrambled time.

Ellen Samuels (2017: 2) reminds us that crip time also encompasses time travel. Through PTSD flashbacks I travel to the past, to a world where I am not safe, to a world where as the parentified child of immigrants I am prematurely pushed into the future.

Crip time is grief time.

I grieve for the childhood I never had, and for the repeated breakdowns of communication with my family in a Latina/o/x cultural context where observing such boundaries, however healthy, is even more taboo than among white Anglo Americans.

Disclosure: Balancing the Individual and the Collective

So why am I sharing these intimate details with all of you, most of whom are perfect strangers? After all, none of my colleagues, nor even most of my family, knows the entire story. My motives are multifaceted. First, I would ask that we consider one of the central tenets of the ADA: that individuals are legally ensured "reasonable" workplace accommodations without having to disclose their specific disability—a point that, as Linda Kornasky (2009) argues, confers advantage on those of us with invisible disabilities. While I would concede that on initial reflection invisible disabilities might appear to confer relative privilege, a recent survey of mental disability disclosure among US college and university faculty found that the greatest stigma is still attached to mental health disclosure (Price et al. 2017: 10). I would also counter that, within the neoliberal academy, the price of psychological and professional "passing" is far too high for us to cling to any seeming advantage. I am therefore disclosing in my own self-interest, as well as in the interest of my colleagues and students, past and present. I am also speaking out because as a tenured professor it is my moral obligation to do so in support of the untenured and contingent faculty also struggling with mental disability.

Price et al.'s (2017) survey also found that, among 267 faculty members who self-identified as having mental disabilities, mental health illnesses, or mental health histories, only 13 percent had sought out formal accommodations at work, citing stigma and the desire for privacy. As the authors of this groundbreaking survey noted, disability disclosure is also inextricably tied to other factors, such as gender, rank, and ethnoracial identity, among others (for more on this research, see Price's article in this issue). In a higher education system that is already geared to make virtually everyone (though some clearly more than others) feel as though they were disposable because employment is so increasingly precarious, mental disability disclosure becomes an even riskier proposition, particularly for untenured or contingent faculty. In essence, disability accommodation law demands a form of disclosure that troubles institutional protocols about what should be public and what should remain personal or private (Pearson and Boskovich 2019). Similarly, my own disability disclosure simultaneously challenges the profound association of disability with Anglo whiteness in the US popular imagination, including within the field of disability studies (see Bell 2013).

The story of my own accommodations is rather grim; as with most professors battling mental disabilities who seek out disability accommodations under the auspices of the ADA, ad hoc approaches constitute the norm, not the exception, and change is slow. Amid the dense fog of a major depressive episode and acute anxiety, I had to commit to all of the legwork in determining how and if I was protected under the law and just what was meant by "reasonable" accommodations, or the workplace structures that signal the opposite of denial, as they are rooted in a healthy respect for my previous experience.

I was informed that I was the sole individual out of over 360 faculty at my institution to seek out formal disability accommodations, as if my desire to formalize such accommodations represented a troubling lack of faith in a small elite institution where many agreements are made over evening drinks and a handshake. It was as if I were a problematic anomaly on two counts: once for being invisibly disabled in the first place, and then again for requesting that my status be legally acknowledged in the face of institutional practice to the contrary. I am reminded that institutional legal compliance to the ADA does not necessarily equal a commitment to access (Ahmed 2012: 115). (And truth be told, I do not trust institutions. My life experience and my education have taught me that lesson well. I am happy to report, however, that in recent years my home institution has made some key strides toward formalizing its policies regarding faculty with disabilities.)

As researchers who surveyed mentally disabled and mentally disabled faculty have noted, when institutional attitudes toward mental disability are unclear, faculty members are more conservative with regard to disclosure (Flaherty 2017). And let us not fail to recognize the value that the academy attaches to rational thought. *Chronicle of Higher Education* columnist Katie Rose Guest Pryal (2014) quotes one mentally disabled professor as saying, "They hired you for your mind. . . . Why would you volunteer that there's something wrong with it?" The academy is also reluctant to acknowledge stress—one of the primary triggers for bipolar and PTSD—as it runs counter to the notion that higher education is grounded in the mind and reason, as opposed to the body and emotion (Berg and Seeber 2016: 2). We all know the unspoken rule: corporate academia assumes if not expressly demands able bodies and able minds. In my more pessimistic moments, I wonder if we might better understand structural and attitudinal postures toward faculty with mental disabilities in higher education as a brute exercise in Foucauldian governmentality, or a set of practices that includes the creation of docile subjects most readily responsive to the needs and directives of the governing institution.

In this context, mental disabilities in faculty members are so often invisible in higher education because we are not actively looking for or seeing them due to the ableist expectations of the profession, as well as our societal expectations regarding what disability "looks like" in everyday life, including with respect to ethnoracial identity. As N. Ann. Davis (2005: 156) posits,

> When we say that something is invisible, we do not mean to claim that the thing is invisible to everyone, or to anyone in any circumstances. What we do mean is that it is (or would be) invisible to a particular set of perceivers under a particular set of conditions. When we say that something is invisible, we are generally making a tacit comparison between this thing and others of the same kind that we think not invisible, and implying that invisibility is not the norm for things of that kind.

This insistent reliance on normative notions of faculty able-bodiedness and neurotypicality within academia constitutes a form of social control or governmentality that portends very real professional and, above all, health consequences for invisibly disabled professors.

I routinely receive extraofficial requests from faculty and staff from other institutions with invisible disabilities regarding just what accommodations to ask for and how. In other words, the proper information is simply not accessible, a structural flaw that highlights not only the limited understanding of what constitutes disability in higher education but also just who (for lack of more elegant verbiage) is "allowed" to be disabled in the first place.

Latina/o/x faculty like myself with invisible disabilities are, to refer back to the title of this article, thrice unseen, meaning the process of being actively rendered triply invisible. This occurs, first, via the general individual/collective silences and ignorance surrounding disabilities not visibly inscribed on the body. Second, it is generated by means of institutional structures and practices that openly—if not necessarily sufficiently—recognize the existence and specific needs of invisibly disabled students (or "customers") while failing to acknowledge the unique challenges faced by faculty ("customer service representatives") coping with invisible disabilities. And third, I am rendered invisible by the facts on the ground: according to the American Association of University Professors, a scant 3 percent of all full professors in the United States are Latina. I am not the individual that most imagine when they think of a professor. Nor am I the individual that most imagine—including my fellow professors—when they think of the disabled. These are but two forms of the invisibilization that we are encouraged to engage in within the neoliberal workplace, even during, as in the case of academia, a scholarly period ironically marked by an interest in self-reflexivity (Gill 2009: 2).

For faculty living with invisible disabilities, liberal arts colleges such as the one I am employed by foster an institutional culture in which mentally disabled Latina/o/x faculty are rendered hypervisible, while our invisible disabilities remain comfortably and conveniently illegible for the sake of business as usual. Indeed, at times I sacrifice what I value to appear able-bodied (Davis 2005: 159). I would ask, then, that we interrogate the triple bind of invisibility as both a product and a symptom of institutional practices and that we strive to elucidate how the very bodies of the invisibly disabled constitute a stark challenge to the neoliberal regime of ever-increasing productivity and efficiency. I would posit that, to some extent, both the current state of disability support services for faculty within higher education and even well-meaning texts like *The Slow Professor* reproduce a profound bootstrap mentality that ultimately reflects just as it further re-entrenches neoliberal doctrine within higher education. Indeed, Berg and Seeber (2016: 72) contend that "corporatization has imposed an instrumental view of not only time but also each other." Like those authors, I advocate that we engage in disclosure with the full knowledge that, while our honesty will not always be reciprocated, the potential rewards of the occasional return of candor by others in kind are enormous (84). When another wave of fear at the thought of publishing this article overcomes me, I remind myself: this is what tenure is for.

To paraphrase bipolar disorder researcher Kay Redfield Jamison (1995) (who is herself bipolar), one of the advantages of having had bipolar disorder (and, I would argue, complex PTSD) for decades is that very little seems insurmountably difficult. Therefore, this necessarily collective and individual labor of reimagining mental disability's relationship to academia, while difficult, is not intrinsically impossible. Above all, it demands—as I have already mentioned—vulnerability and candor on the part of the mentally disabled. As a Latina, I see this candor as a decolonizing gesture that counters normative constructs of faculty belonging rooted in ableism, racism, and sexism in particular, just as it rejects traditional top-down, neoliberal solutions to the unique challenges of mentally disabled faculty. It necessitates that the institutions largely populated by those who do not struggle with invisible disabilities actively participate in developing effective structural safety nets that do not place so much of the onus on navigating institutional structures on the faculty who must contend with them in an atmosphere permeated by the cult of productivity.

Within academia as well as within US culture as a whole, the tendency to frame disability as a "personal problem afflicting individual people, a problem best resolved through strength of character and resolve" (Kafer 2013: 4) impedes our ability to recognize invisibly disabled faculty as a highly diverse class in need of various forms and degrees of accommodation. This lack of collective recognition reflects the ableist assumption that mental disability does not substantively exist in the academy—and, in the process, promotes the notion that any change with respect to invisible disability is largely up to individual professors. Yet, what might be construed as a limited brand of agency within the machinery of large, unwieldy institutions stifles any attempt to approach the unique challenges of mentally disabled faculty collectively and systemically (see Berg and Seeber 2016: 5). I advocate for disclosure whenever possible and, above all, among tenured faculty, because they hold the potential to propel us past the current framework of invisible disability (and, in particular, mental disability) as individual aberration and "problem" to a more collective approach. The latter approach portends benefits for all in higher education, as it rightfully centers a recognition of the systemic structures within the profession that affect the mental health of *all* of us, if some disproportionately. Specifically, widespread institutional recognition of invisible disability among faculty as a class contests its narrow definition as a key site of difference that affects only students. Any effective acknowledgment of invisibly disabled faculty as a class demands that we achieve the tricky balancing act of holding collective recognition and protections in tension with the need for individualized approaches to accommodations. This balancing act necessarily encompasses a recognition, at the level of discourse as well as deed, of the differential relationship that many mentally disabled academics possess to time. While writing from the position of the "thrice invisible"—and indeed, perhaps because of my long-standing experiences with other forms of discrimination in the academy—this *testimonio* represents a move in that direction.

Crip Time as Pandemic Time

As I begin thinking about the conclusion to this article, it is late March 2020 in Massachusetts. Spring is emerging, the time of year when I often shift out of depression into mania. This spring, however, we happen to be in the midst of a global pandemic. As I shelter in place, it occurs to me:

Crip time is pandemic time.

It is, in the most basic of senses, an open-ended exercise in adjusting one's everyday movements and activities in the pursuit of well-being—and, indeed, survival. As such, it feels deeply familiar. I slip into pandemic time with ease mingled with acute distress, the latter mitigated in part by the class privileges that a tenured job and light skin afford me. I observe many of my (nondisabled) friends and colleagues and wonder if they realize that they, too, are living some iteration of crip time now.

Weeks creep by and my anxiety blooms alongside the springtime flowers I spy from the window. My startle response is even more finely attuned than usual—my partner begins quietly announcing his presence before he enters the room so that I do not jump and cry out. On my brief forays outside, I constantly scan the downtown streets of the small city where we live to calculate the nearest safe exit should I encounter any form of coronavirus danger. My limbs move constantly, crawling with thousands of invisible ants, accompanied by a host of since-abandoned nervous tics. My ability to concentrate abandons me; I read the same paragraphs in vain, retaining nothing. My desire to drink during the day returns.

Yet I consider myself quite fortunate.

Sheltering in place is awfully similar to life in a locked psychiatric unit. I survive by bending time, by accessing some of the coping mechanisms that have always buoyed me in my struggles with PTSD and bipolar: I (re)conceptualize time in terms of hours or even minutes (I just need to make it through the next five minutes); I divide tasks into small units and work intermittently to conserve energy and concentration; I continuously assess my limits and weigh the momentary rewards of pushing myself too hard against the need to survive the expanse of semester that remains;

I make an extensive list for myself of what I must do (down to the most minute detail) when I am overwhelmed and unable to plot the next move forward. I tell myself, over and over, that I must survive the marathon and for that I must relinquish the sprint.

Regularly, I anxiously cast my thoughts ahead to the eventual return of temporal "normality," to a time when I once again will feel obligated to justify my everyday temporal strategies to others. The jaded piece of me, the part that has borne witness to so much institutional ableism around time in academia, holds little hope for any sort of lasting change around dominant temporal norms within corporate academia. Yet I will admit that in this collective experience there also exists the possibility for crip time as pandemic time to generate greater understanding on the part of faculty and administrators who do not conceptualize themselves as disabled. Perhaps the collective— if varying—experiences of pandemic boredom, isolation, fear, and exhaustion will temper any absolute relief regarding the return to academic temporal business as usual. Maybe those of us who consider ourselves disabled, as well as those who do not, can collectively reimagine our relationship with time, taking heed from the lessons of disabled scholars and activists.

Notes

Many thanks to Ellen Samuels and Elizabeth Freeman for their editorial comments and the much appreciated invitation to participate in this important project. I also thank Cindy Wu for the opportunity to present the first draft of this article at the American Studies Association in Atlanta—your confidence in me means a great deal. Finally, warm thanks are due to my research assistant Mari Noya for their hard work gathering the materials necessary for this publication.

1   Like other scholars who write about what is popularly referred to as *mental illness*, in this article I choose to forgo that language and instead speak in terms of *mental disability*. I do so in accordance with Price's (2013: 292, 335–36) reasoning that the language of *mental illness* encourages a binary with *mental health* and suggests that those with mental disabilities require a definitive cure.

2   The work of Latina/o/x scholars such as Alberto Sandoval-Sánchez (1997, 2005, 2007) provides a foundational model for the written *testimonio* at the intersection of disability, Latina/o/x, and queer studies.

3   *Mil gracias* to Elena R. Gutiérrez for encouraging me to theorize the cultural, sexualized, and gendered specificities of the *loca* trope more deeply and for suggesting that I listen to the first episode of the *Locatora Radio* podcast carefully. This article is much improved by your influence.

4   While for the purposes of this article I focus on the notion of the *loca* as it pertains to Latinas/xs, I would be remiss if I did not note how the term *loca* also circulates within Latina/o/x communities as a synonym for gay males.

References

Ahmed, Sara. 2012. *On Being Included: Racism and Diversity in Institutional Life.* Durham, NC: Duke University Press.

Bell, Chris. 2013. "Is Disability Studies Actually White Disability Studies?" In *The Disability Studies Reader,* edited by Lennard J. Davis, 406–15. New York: Routledge.

Berg, Maggie, and Barbara Karolina Seeber. 2016. *The Slow Professor: Challenging the Culture of Speed in the Academy.* Toronto: University of Toronto Press.

Boylorn, Robin M., and Mark P. Orbe. 2013. "Introduction: Critical Autoethnography as Method of Choice." In *Critical Autoethnography: Intersecting Cultural Identities in Everyday Life,* edited by Robin M. Boylorn and Mark P. Orbe, 13–26. Walnut Creek, CA: Left Coast Press.

Cisneros, Sandra. 1991. *The House on Mango Street.* New York: Vintage.

Davis, N. Ann. 2005. "Invisible Disability." *Ethics* 116, no. 1: 153–213.

Ellis, Carolyn, and Arthur P. Bochner. 2000. "Autoethnography, Personal Narrative, Reflexivity." In *Handbook of Qualitative Research,* edited by Norman K. Denzin and Yvonna S. Lincoln, 733–69. Thousand Oaks, CA: Sage.

Engel, Patricia. 2010. "Desaliento." In *Vida,* 59–75. New York: Black Cat.

Esguerra, Catalina. 2020. "Diasporic Home: US Colombian Belonging and Becoming in Patricia Engel's *Vida.*" *Latino Studies* 18, no. 3: 343–62.

Flaherty, Colleen. 2017. "Portrait of Faculty Mental Health," *Inside Higher Ed,* June 8. www.insidehighered.com/news/2017/06/08/study-faculty-members-mental-health-issues-finds-mix-attitudes-disclosing-and.

Gill, Rosalind. 2009. "Breaking the Silence: The Hidden Injuries of Neo-liberal Academia." In *Secrecy and Silence in the Research Process: Feminist Reflections,* edited by Róisín Ryan-Flood and Rosalind Gill, 1–19. London: Routledge.

Guest Pryal, Katie Rose. 2014. "Disclosure Blues: Should You Tell Colleagues about Your Mental Illness?" *Chronicle of Higher Education,* June 13. chroniclevitae.com/news/546-disclosure-blues-should-you-tell-colleagues-about-your-mental-illness.

Halperin, Laura. 2015. *Intersections of Harm: Narratives of Latina Deviance and Defiance.* New Brunswick, NJ: Rutgers University Press.

Holman Jones, Stacy, Tony Adams, and Carolyn Ellis. 2013. "Coming to Know Autoethnography as More than a Method." In *Handbook of Autoethnography,* edited by Stacy Holman Jones, Tony E. Adams, and Carolyn Ellis, 17–48. Walnut Creek, CA: Left Coast Press.

Jamison, Kay Redfield. 1995. *An Unquiet Mind: A Memoir of Moods and Madness.* New York: Vintage.

Kafer, Alison. 2013. *Feminist Queer Crip.* Bloomington: Indiana University Press.

Kerschbaum, Stephanie. 2014. "On Rhetorical Agency and Disclosing Disability in Academic Writing." *Rhetoric Review* 33, no. 1: 55–71.

Kornasky, Linda. 2009. "Identity Politics and Invisible Disability in the Classroom." *Inside Higher Ed,* March 17. www.insidehighered.com/views/2009/03/17/identity-politics-and-invisible-disability-classroom.

Latina Feminist Group. 2001. *Telling to Live: Latina Feminist Testimonios.* Durham, NC: Duke University Press.

Muñoz, José Esteban. 2010. *Cruising Utopia: The Then and There of Queer Futurity.* New York: NYU Press.

Muñoz, Zoe, and Ariana Rodríguez Zertuche. 2016. "Loca Epistemologies." *Locatora Radio* (podcast), November 16. radiopublic.com/locatora-radio-a-radiophonic-nove-WxVN1V /s1!6e871.

Nzibi Pindi, Gloria. 2018. "Hybridity and Identity Performance in Diasporic Context: An Autoethnographic Journey of the Self across Cultures." *Cultural Studies <–> Critical Methodologies* 18, no. 1: 23–31.

Pearson, Holly, and Lisa Boskovich. 2019. "Problematizing Disability Disclosure in Higher Education: Shifting Towards a Liberating Humanizing Intersectional Framework." *Disability Studies Quarterly* 39, no. 1. doi.org/10.18061/dsq.v39i1.6001.

Pettit, Emma. 2016. "Stigma, Stress, and Fear: Faculty Mental-Health Services Fall Short." *Chronicle of Higher Education*, August 4. www.chronicle.com/article/Stigma-Stress Fear-/237353.

Price, Margaret. 2011. *Mad at School: Rhetorics of Mental Disability and Academic Life*. Ann Arbor: University of Michigan Press.

Price, Margaret. 2013. "Defining Mental Disability." In *The Disability Studies Reader*, edited by Lennard J. Davis, 292–99. New York: Routledge.

Price, Margaret, Mark S. Salzer, Amber O'Shea, and Stephanie L. Kerschbaum. 2017. "Disclosure of Mental Disability by College and University Faculty: The Negotiation of Accommodations, Supports, and Barriers." *Disability Studies Quarterly* 37, no. 2. doi.org /10.18061/dsq.v37i2.

Rodríguez, Juana María. 2014. *Sexual Futures, Queer Gestures, and Other Latina Longings*. New York: NYU Press.

Samuels, Ellen. 2003. "My Body, My Closet: Invisible Disability and the Limits of Coming-Out Discourse." *GLQ* 9, nos. 1–2: 233–55.

Samuels, Ellen. 2017. "Six Ways of Looking at Crip Time." *Disability Studies Quarterly* 37, no. 3. doi.org/10.18061/dsq.v37i3.5824.

Sandoval-Sánchez, Alberto. 1997. "Puerto Rican Identity Up in the Air: Air Migration, Its Cultural Representations, and Me 'Cruzando el Charco.'" In *Puerto Rican Jam: Rethinking Colonialism and Nationalism*, edited by Frances Negrón-Muntaner and Ramón Grosfoguel, 189–208. Minneapolis: University of Minnesota Press.

Sandoval-Sánchez, Alberto. 2005. "Politicizing Abjection: In the Manner of a Prologue for the Articulation of AIDS Latino Queer Identities." *American Literary History* 17, no. 3: 542–49.

Sandoval-Sánchez, Alberto. 2007. "An AIDS Testimonial: It's a Broken Record/Ese Disco Se Rayó." In *Technofuturos: Critical Interventions in Latina/o Studies*, edited by Nancy Raquel Mirabal and Agustín Laó-Montes, 297–310. Lanham, MD: Lexington Books.

Smith, Kathryn M. 2010–11. "Female Voice and Feminist Text: Testimonio as a Form of Resistance in Latin America." *Florida Atlantic Comparative Studies Journal* 12: 21–37.

Wang, Esmé Weijun. 2019. *The Collected Schizophrenias: Essays*. Minneapolis: Graywolf Press.

Michael D. Snediker

Poems

These Sufferings Are What

Are called vastations: the heart
      within turns
white as coin and
     says
  I will
     replete the earth
        with
earth
    the cloud made
thin
    thickened &
    thinned

    I made
    a sun of oil a   daughter
        of
   light   their hand was
            as
   a Winte
    ring
      vine

The South Atlantic Quarterly 120:2, April 2021
DOI 10.1215/00382876-8916060 © 2021 Duke University Press

Hung about the Neck

Just touching
  the crooked
     spoon
  of
         peridot   a heart its
           garible pen-
       ancy covering   over
   two kinds of human err
or   bare knee magistery
         in
       the grass
          we
         dye cast
           darts neck
        laced anodynes to aid in
       the doubts
    of   detention our
    fernshaw
     passion
  for pledging
  buckthorn
lunacies eked
    Our neptune
        out for
       the fight for
     doting on
   the body's
pendulum

He Borrowed the River

The stranger the   oak   hast Breached
Anemone   the   quench &
          heapeth half
                    the bend his long neck redden
                              North
                    past cedar pond full Harbor   Scrub this
cheer & eddies kept   the one wrd Thunder   a Cherubim you were
& are   & *I full Salt*   borne up by Providence   how
                    it Flamed
                              a maze
that made pine gape   &   hammered
               soft

          this gold
like mouth

Mercury Series

The heart
  knows stress &
      mystic pheasant scending
      to
a cabalie of Things   hexagonal
compost
      forces pipped
            into cyder   contiguous
                                    oratories
                  the Dead let
      Rest &
so
                  I also   left
slippers in
      the shower having
known some body
there
      Quires of   vellum sewn with
  hemp   straps riveted to
                  iron studs edge
            to Edge with
some care   Chased
            the Forest
      where
                              he   was
                  Laid
                  to waste
      from which
was hewn a prow   for ships
            a little boy
      gold gilt to
blush
through Mist

Jina B. Kim and Sami Schalk

Reclaiming the Radical Politics of Self-Care: A Crip-of-Color Critique

> Survival isn't some theory operating in a vacuum. It's a matter of my everyday living and making decisions.
> —Audre Lorde, "A Burst of Light"

Google searches for the term *self-care* in the United States began to climb in 2015, as the country approached its contentious 2016 election; searches for the term continued to reach new highs well into 2018 (Google, n.d.). As Aisha Harris (2017) wrote, "In 2016, self-care officially crossed over into the mainstream. It was the new chicken soup for the progressive soul." Between 2016 and 2018, articles on self-care appeared in a variety of major outlets online, such as the *New York Times*, *Forbes*, *Psychology Today*, and the *New Yorker* (Donner et al. 2018; Nazish 2017; Baratta 2018; Kisner 2017). In 2016 singer Solange released a song titled "Borderline (An Ode to Self-Care)," and in 2018 the late rapper Mac Miller released a song and music video called "Self Care." On social media, the hashtag #selfcare increasingly appeared (and continues to appear) on posts (many of them sponsored by advertisers) for just about everything: yoga, meditation, massages, face masks, juice cleanses, resort getaways, and more. An overview of the use of the term *self-care* online, therefore,

The South Atlantic Quarterly 120:2, April 2021
DOI 10.1215/00382876-8916074　© 2021 Duke University Press

suggests that it refers to any behavior that directly, and often exclusively, benefits an individual's physical or mental health. The rise of searches for and references to *self-care* during and after the 2016 election season suggests that, in a frightening and divisive political time, many Americans were trying to figure out how to attend to their mental and physical well-being.

Several mainstream articles have attempted to track the rising cultural interest in self-care, noting how the term's use, particularly on social media, seems to encourage conspicuous consumption and performative self-improvement that can be harmful (Penny 2016; Meltzer 2016; Lieberman 2018). In the *New Yorker*, Jordan Kisner (2017) also noted that, despite the recent uptick in uses of the term, the concept of self-care can be traced back much farther in American culture in relationship to such ideas as self-reliance and self-development or cultivation: "Self-care in America has always required a certain amount of performance: a person has to be able not only to care for herself but to prove to society that she's doing it." At the same time as this first set of mainstream articles critiquing contemporary performances of self-care was being published between 2016 and 2018, another group of essays were also appearing. In these pieces, authors who identify as people of color and/or queer attempt to reclaim the term as a political survival concept, frequently also critiquing the loose, performative, and capitalist uses of *self-care* in the contemporary moment (Dionne 2015; Mirk and Dionne 2016; Harris 2017; Rupiah 2017). These authors each grounded their understanding of self-care in the work of black feminist lesbian poet and theorist Audre Lorde. In the titular essay "A Burst of Light," in her 1988 book *A Burst of Light: And Other Essays*, Lorde ([1988] 2017: 130) wrote: "Caring for myself is not self-indulgence, it is self-preservation, and that is an act of political warfare." In this second group of articles, many of which include this quote, authors argue that the concept of self-care as Lorde theorized it is deeply political, based in experiences of racialization, womanhood, and/or queerness.

As queer women of color working in disability studies, we both noticed a conspicuous absence in nearly all of the mainstream discussions of self-care: disability seemed nowhere to be found—except, perhaps, in the unspoken shadow of what might happen should one not take care of one's health. This, we thought, was highly ironic considering that "A Burst of Light" is a series of journal entries about Lorde's experience as a black lesbian living with cancer. For us, understanding self-care as Lorde theorized it and understanding the importance of self-care in our current political moment are deeply grounded in experiences of disability. As a result, in this article we propose a reclamation of the radical crip, feminist, queer, and racialized roots of self-care offered by Lorde. We argue that a radical politics of self-care is inextricably tied to the lived experiences and temporalities of multiply marginalized people, especially disabled queer people, disabled people of color, and disabled queer people of color. Our work here attempts to hold the complexity of claiming time for ourselves to slow down, to take care, while also understanding the real urgency of our contemporary moment. We thus propose that, while crip time is often about slowing and adapting models of time and productivity, crip time as a concept is urgently needed to understand self-care outside capitalist imperatives. To perform this reclaiming of the radical politics of self-care, we engage in crip-of-color critique.

Crip-of-color critique is a concept developed by Jina B. Kim that models potential affinities between feminist of color/queer of color and disability theorizing. It offers a method of analysis drawn from the intersection of antiracist, anticapitalist, and feminist disability politics, highlighting the centrality of ideologies of ability to racial-gendered violence and management, as well as the refusal of women and queers of color to submit to those ideologies.[1] In so doing, it follows the call issued by Grace Kyungwon Hong and Roderick A. Ferguson (2011: 3) in *Strange Affinities: The Gender and Sexual Politics of Comparative Racialization* , which stresses the urgency of developing relational, coalitional, and cross-categorical analytics that can appraise "how particular populations are rendered vulnerable to processes of death and de-valuation over and against other populations" in the decades following civil rights and decolonization. A crip-of-color critique thus highlights how the ableist language of disability, dependency, and laziness has been marshaled by state and extralegal entities to justify the denial of life-sustaining resources to disabled, low-income, immigrant, and black and brown communities, with women, queer, and gender-nonconforming populations often suffering the greatest costs. It further examines how writers, artists, and activists, primarily women and queers of color, generate systems of value, aesthetic practices, and liberatory frameworks that center the realities of disability, illness, and dependency. As such, a crip-of-color critique reads for relations of support, care, and regeneration in a world for those "never meant to survive," understanding care as itself vital political work that simultaneously asks us to slow down and to pay attention and learn quickly (Lorde 1997: 255).

In what follows, we first provide a brief overview of Lorde's work, with an emphasis on "A Burst of Light," to establish how Lorde discussed caring for one's self. Building on Lorde, then, we make arguments for how and why we must understand self-care as political, followed by a theorization of what it means to practice both self-care and care, beyond the individual and outside capitalist temporalities focused on productivity and profit. Throughout, we center work by people of color, queer people, and disabled people (and those who live at the intersection of more than one of these categories) whose lives continue to be threatened, who continue to experience harm in this white supremacist, capitalist, ableist, heteropatriarchal settler-colonial nation state, and for whom a radical politics of self-care is necessary for survival.

Defining Self-Care, Returning to Lorde

How do I want to live the rest of my life and what am I going to do to ensure that I get to do it exactly or as close as possible to how I want that living to be?
—Audre Lorde, "A Burst of Light"

This quote from Lorde that caring for one's self "is not self-indulgence" but, rather, "self-preservation" and "an act of political warfare" is one that, like many beloved quotes, is often taken up outside of its original context (Lorde [1988] 2017: 130). The quote appears in the epilogue of "A Burst of Light," and understanding how and where it appears in the text, as well as the content of the text overall, is useful in understanding how Lorde defined and mobilized the concept of self-care. First, "A Burst of Light" is a collection of journal entries written between January 1984 and August 1987. In the text, Lorde chronicles her life as she discovers her breast cancer (written about previously in her 1980 collection *The Cancer Journals*) has metastasized to her liver. She chooses to pursue homeopathic treatments, including a specialty clinic in Switzerland, rather than undergo another surgery. "A Burst of Light" captures not only Lorde's experiences with the medical industrial complex, alternative medicine, weight loss, pain, and other people with cancer but also her theorization of these experiences in relationship to her writing, her political activism, and her understanding of racism, sexism, homophobia, apartheid, and imperialism. At its core, "A Burst of Light" is about "living with cancer in an intimate daily relationship" as a multiply marginalized person, a black disabled lesbian (109). This daily relationship with cancer embodies the simultaneous temporalities of a crip-of-color approach to self-care, in that Lorde is forced to slow down and focus on her well-being and that slowing down remains urgent and necessary, as refusing to do so risks quickening the pace of her debilitation and illness.

The quote about caring for one's self appears toward the end of this essay, in the last sentence of the first paragraph of the epilogue, which reads in total:

> Sometimes I feel like I'm living on a different star from the one I am used to calling home. It has not been a steady progression. I had to examine, in my dreams as well as in my immune-function tests, the devastating effects of overextension. Overextending myself is not stretching myself. I had to accept how difficult it is to monitor the difference. Necessary for me as cutting down on sugar. Crucial. Physically. Psychically. Caring for myself is not a self-indulgence, it is self-preservation, and that is an act of political warfare. (Lorde [1988] 2017: 130)

In the sentences preceding the more famous quote, Lorde suggests that learning to live with cancer feels like a different world, a different temporality than she lived within before—it is not a steady progression. Although Lorde was visually impaired and therefore already living with a disability, her work in "A Burst of Light" and *The Cancer Journals* suggests that living with cancer brought her into a new relationship with her bodymind. In the epilogue, Lorde describes the changes she has had to make as crucial for both physical and psychic well-being, and these crucial aspects of self-care then lead into the more recognized quote about caring for one's self as an act of political warfare. Reading the quote in the context of both "A Burst of Light" as a whole and this particular opening paragraph of the epilogue begins to demonstrate what exactly Lorde understood self-care to be: physical and mental, thoughtful, purposeful, necessary, political, and resistant to normative, capitalist approaches to time that stand in opposition to wellness for marginalized people.

In concrete terms, Lorde described her self-care as thoughtfully taking care of herself to ensure both quantity and quality of her remaining time. This included things we would associate with self-care today, such as reducing sugar, not overworking one's self, and meditation, but it also meant educating one's self in order to make informed, conscious decisions about one's health and life. Lorde journals about going to Barnes & Noble to read in the medical section, talking to other cancer survivors, and seeking out alternative treatments. Lorde ([1988] 2017: 114) noted, however, that obtaining this knowledge "does not mean I give into the belief, arrogant or naive, that I know everything I need to know in order to make informed decisions about my body. But attending to my own health, gaining enough information to help me understand and participate in the decisions made about my body by people who know more medicine than I do, are crucial strategies in my battle for living." Self-care is not, therefore, a rejection of medicine but, rather, an active and informed participation with medicine that recognizes the knowledge and insights of both patient and practitioner. In multiple places in the text Lorde is critical of the medical-industrial complex for being controlling, capitalist, racist, and sexist, such as when doctors tried to rush her decision about surgery using fear tactics rather than allowing her time to process the shock of her cancer's return, or when a specialist calls her "girl" during a consultation and describes her in his notes as having an "obese abdomen" and a "pendulous breast" (110, 11). In these moments, we see why Lorde feels compelled to care for and educate herself in order to make health choices that truly center her needs and holistic well-being.

In addition to these concrete elements of self-care in "A Burst of Light," Lorde also makes clear that the process of self-care must be integrated into living life, not separate from it, and that self-care is not exclusively oriented toward cure. Lorde must take time for self-care consistently, demonstrating that care cannot occur outside of time or only during what capitalism would consider "personal time" but, rather, is an ongoing engagement that cannot necessarily be adapted to a forty-hour work week or a nine-to-five job. At one point Lorde ([1988] 2017: 114) wrote, "I fight hard to keep my treatment scene together in some coherent and serviceable way, integrated into my daily living and absolute. . . . This not only keeps me in an intimate, positive relationship to my own health, but it also underlines the fact that I have the responsibility for attending my own health. I cannot simply hand over that responsibility to anybody else." This commitment to caring for one's self while living a full life is clear in the way Lorde, despite the tumor and the urgency from doctors, continues to work as she desires, attend black literary events, visit with friends, and write. She refuses to allow her disability to stop her from living, but this is not an overcoming narrative; it is instead a rejection of the notion that health or achieving able-bodiedness should be the sole focus of disabled people's lives at all times. This becomes most clear in the epilogue, when she wrote, "I try to weave my life-prolonging treatments into a living context—to resist giving myself over like a sacrificial offering to the furious single-minded concentration upon cure that leaves no room to examine what living and fighting on the physical front can mean. What living with cancer can teach me" (131). Here Lorde rejects an exclusive, compulsive focus on cure while acknowledging the need for care and well-being. For her, survival is not merely about being not-dead, about having more time at all costs, but, rather, about living fully for the time one has and learning from one's experiences, identities, and embodiment.

As this overview makes clear, disability is central to Lorde's conceptualization of self-care: not the avoidance (or cure) of it entirely but living as well as possible with it and understanding experiences of disability, illness, and disease in the context of her other social identities (race, gender, and sexuality), as well as the ordinary aspects of her everyday existence, her life passions, and her political commitments. This, then, is why, in addition to recognizing the concrete practices of Lorde's own particular self-care for her particular embodiment, disability, identities, passions, and goals, we must also understand self-care as always inherently political.

Self-Care as Political

I respect the time I spend each day treating my body, and I consider it part of my political work . . . a kind of training in self-love and physical resistance.
—Audre Lorde, "A Burst of Light"

Self-care for Lorde is an inherently political project that we contend cannot be divorced from disability politics and that derives its sense of political urgency in part from the foreshortened time of a cancer diagnosis. Lorde explicitly theorized how to be political while sick/ill/disabled and understood cancer, disability, illness, and disease as sites of political theorization. In other words, a particular kind of politicized knowledge emerges directly from Lorde's experience with cancer and from the truncated life span that comes with such a diagnosis. When you live in a world that seeks to do you harm or one that neglects you in such a way that your death is allowable, even necessary, both how you live and how you die are political. And when your death looms imminently due to the "economics of disease in america," the temporal framework of terminal illness inevitably shapes your creative and intellectual output (Lorde [1988] 2017: 95). Crip temporality, in this context, also accelerates the clock and the rhythms of living and writing in conversation with Sarah Lochlann Jain's (2007) concept of "living in prognosis." As Lorde ([1988] 2017: 53–54) wrote, "I wasn't supposed to exist anyway, not in any meaningful way in this fucked up whiteboys' world. I want desperately to live, and I'm ready to fight for that living even if I die shortly."

Throughout "A Burst of Light," Lorde makes clear not only that self-care and survival are political but also that what she has learned from living with cancer informs and is informed by what she has learned as a black feminist lesbian activist and poet. This is clear in the way that in both "A Burst of Light" and *The Cancer Journals* Lorde weaves in imagery and discussions of the civil rights movement, apartheid, indigenous land rights, and environmental racism. Again, her identities, her race, gender, sexuality, and disability mutually inform one another and her theorization of self-care. As Lorde

([1988] 2017: 41) asserted, "The struggle with cancer now informs all my days, but it is only another phase of that continuing battle for self-determination and survival that Black women fight daily, often in triumph." As the phrase "all my days" suggests, these battles, while not synonymous, are mutually entwined and continue with no clear end date for multiply marginalized people.

In addition to the personal political context of being a black disabled lesbian, Lorde's theorization of self-care was also developed in the particular social, historical, and political context of the 1980s and Ronald Reagan's administration, which, not unlike our current political regime, was slowly dismantling the welfare state and its provisions of state care for low-income communities. The Reagan administration reduced benefits for most working parents in the Aid to Families with Dependent Children program, eliminated 4 percent of food stamp recipients, lowered state subsidies for Medicaid recipients, and cut spending on federal housing, school lunch assistance, and social service programs nationwide. This erosion of state and federal supports and protections for various marginalized groups is critical for understanding both the practical and political nature of self-care for Lorde. Further, this historical context also makes clear why, for Lorde, insisting on caring for one's self and surviving in a hostile climate was inherently tied to her political work for social and political change, for self-determination and liberation for marginalized people.

Indeed, it is impossible to understand "A Burst of Light" and its assertion of self-care outside of the shaping influence of Reaganomics, which Lorde references throughout the text as a primary antagonist in both personal and collective bids for survival. Reagan's antiwelfare policies constitute the center of one of the first entries in "A Burst of Light," dated February 9, 1984:

> So. No doubt about where we are in the world's story. It has just cost $32,000 to complete a government-commissioned study that purports to show there is no rampant hunger in the U.S.A. I wonder if they realize *rampant* means *aggressive*.
>
> So. The starving old women who used to sit in broken-down rooming houses waiting for a welfare check now lie under park benches and eat out of garbage bins. "I only eat fruit," she mumbled, rummaging through the refuse bin behind Gristede's supermarket, while her gnarled Black hands carefully cut away the rotted parts of a cantaloupe with a plastic Burger King knife. ([1988] 2017: 44)

Cataloging welfare reform's contradictions, as well as the intensified cruelty enacted by a state committed only to the bare minimum, Lorde's frank condemnation of Reaganomics issues an abrupt break from previous entries, which described sensuous meals with the black lesbian group Sapphire Sapphos and her own experience watching the movie *King*. The first passage in "A Burst of Light" not written from a first-person perspective, the above entry radiates Lorde's meditations on survival outward from the sphere of immediate personal experience, attaching them to structural violence on a national (and, later in the essay, international) scale. The decimation of state care, meager to begin with, is co-articulated with her own struggles for self-care and preservation in an antiblack, misogynist, heteronormative, and profiteering medical industry. For Lorde, such struggles are part of the same machinery that seeks to delimit black life. Rather than something depoliticized and relegated to individual concern, then, care emerges as a political problematic that resonates across a number of scales, from Lorde's own bids to determine her own course of medical care to the death-dealing denial of state care and the foreshortening of life for the nation's most vulnerable.

An additional key component of Lorde's conceptualization of self-care is that it is not just political but political *work*. Routing this discussion now toward the politics of labor, Lorde's condemnation of Reagan-era welfare reform evokes what Nancy Fraser (2016) and others have termed a "crisis of care": the inability to perform the work of care in an increasingly unforgiving context of not only reduced state support but also eviscerated labor protections and ever-accelerating mandates for productivity.[2] The crisis of care is thus also a crisis of time, in which the unforgiving temporalities of capitalism increasingly disappear the slivers of time available for replenishment and renewal. According to Fraser (2016: 99), capitalism's relentless drive for sustained accumulation effectively "[squeezes] a key set of social capacities: the capacities available for birthing and raising children, caring for friends and family members, maintaining households and broader communities, and sustaining connections more generally." In Marxist feminist traditions, such capacities travel under the term of *social reproduction*—the unvalued, invisibilized, and feminized labor of support, care, and maintenance that simply make life more possible and that demand temporalities outside of frameworks of productivity and efficiency. Although worker productivity and well-being are contingent on social reproductive labor, capitalism's "orientation to unlimited accumulation tends to destabilize the very processes of social reproduction on which it relies" (100), or in other words, the temporal demands of unlimited accumulation eviscerate the labor-time available for social reproduction. As Fraser makes clear in her analysis, this crisis of care is simultaneously a crisis of labor, which in turn furthers an ableist ideology that denies the physical and psychological needs of workers, as well as their capacity to provide care for others. Another politicized feature of self-care, then, is its relationship to labor and labor-time—whether it is marshaled in the service of producing better workers and thus reclaiming time for care or, in the case of Lorde, it entails working toward a world adverse to the violence of capitalism altogether.

Indeed, as self-care went viral in the past few years, circulating across mass, popular, and social media, the concept soon became inextricable from the imperatives of work and productivity. One of the most prominent uses of the term connects self-care to the optimization of work—one cares for the self in order to increase one's capacity as a productive worker. In other words, taking time for self-care is acceptable only insofar as it enables the further optimization of one's time spent at work. A 2017 *Huffington Post* article, "Want More Productive Employees? Encourage Self-Care" (Kline 2017), encapsulates this particular usage, acknowledging the rise of chronic work-related stress affecting the American workforce and suggesting "employee self-care" as the antidote. The article suggests that "encouraging employees to tend to their own health and well-being produces a number of benefits, including reduced absenteeism and staff turnover, reduced health-care costs, happier employees, and greater productivity overall." Among the activities grouped under employee self-care are "mindfulness practices," "exercise," and "spending time in nature." Many scholars have observed how suggestions such as these deflect the possibility of corporate accountability to workforces, placing the onus of responsibility for worker well-being on the employees themselves. Certainly, the redirecting of self-care toward the well-being of corporations is part of an overall trend to dismantle public and collective structures of care and to depoliticize care labor by relegating it to individual spheres of concern. It is also a means of further compromising the time already belonging to the worker, insofar as these corporate self-care suggestions do not imply increased time away from work.

Yet, even in ostensibly progressive circles, the concept of self-care (and, at times, care more broadly) is cast outside the realm of political work and positioned as a waste of time. Often, care or social reproductive labor is seen as, in the words of disability justice activist and theorist Leah Lakshmi Piepzna-Samarasinha (2018: 143), "a sideline or afterthought to our movements." For instance, in the piece "An End to Self Care," labor organizer B. Loewe (2012) critiques the co-optation of Lorde's call for self-preservation, calling for, as the title suggests, an "end to self-care." The mainstream circulation of self-care, Loewe argues, stands in for "an importation of middle-class values of leisure," one that ignores power dynamics and collective responsibility for others. Loewe (2012) casts this version of self-care as not just outside of but antagonistic to radical political work: "We cannot knit our way to revolution." While "An End to Self Care" does indeed acknowledge the importance of collective models of care and does not wholly dismiss care labor, it nonetheless promotes a vision of round-the-clock organizing work that seems to deny the physical, psychological, and emotional needs of working bodyminds, positioning the movement itself as self-care. This ethos of endless work, while oriented toward political liberation, nonetheless upholds capitalism's wish that we never be "off the clock" and that care for the self should occur only in the (increasingly disappearing) slivers of time granted to nonwork and nonactivist activities.

In her insightful cri(p)tique of B. Loewe's anti-self-care polemic, Piepzna-Samarasinha (2018) highlights the evacuation of care labor and radical care politics from Loewe's conception of political work. Loewe's (2012) idealization of a "politics and practice of desire that could . . . ignite our hearts with a fuel to work endlessly," as Piepzna-Samarasinha points out, ignores the necessity of rest, joy, and self-preservation in movement work. It promotes an understanding of movement organizing implicitly centered on ideologies of ability, or a preference for bodyminds with seemingly endless energy reserves and the capacity to "optimize" their time. Further, Loewe's polemic again casts certain forms of care labor as outside political possibility. The work of knitting and other forms of cultural work, Piepzna-Samarasinha argues, have in fact long been central to movement building. Of course, the bourgeois model of self-care rooted in individual responsibility "has been co-opted by people who want to make money off it," but this model does not mean we should do away with self-care altogether or see self-care as a distraction from political work (Piepzna-Samarasinha 2018: 210). As Piepzna-Samarasinha observed in an earlier essay, "A Time to Hole Up and a Time to Kick Ass" (2006: 172, 171), the self-care and survival work done "on a daily basis" by women of color in fact counts as activism, and to sustain movements for the long haul—to ensure that their time is not limited—it is also necessary to take "time on the couch." Piepzna-Samarasinha (2018: 210–11) thus advocates for forms of self-care that replicate "a model of sustainability that comes from disability justice," which entails that we "[listen] to broke-ass, disabled, and femme communities about how we actually create ways of organizing where we're not just grinding ourselves into the dust."

Though Lorde's "A Burst of Light" was written far before the advent of *disability justice* as a term, in returning to it we enact this type of listening practice, one that directs attention to how disabled and sick women of color conceive of and carry out movement building against the temporal imperatives of productivity and efficiency. Akin to Piepzna-Samarasinha's theorization of care, Lorde's ([1988] 2017: 51) political imaginary as encapsulated in "A Burst of Light" posits self-care, self-preservation, and care work more broadly as political projects fundamentally rooted in social change and transformation: "I am saving my life by using my life in the service of what must be done." This, too, can be understood as a radical reclaiming of time insofar as Lorde uses her limited days left in the work of political liberation and the nurturance of black queer collectivity. In fact, Lorde begins "A Burst of Light" with an entry describing a special dinner thrown by the group Sapphire Sapphos during their regular monthly meeting. The rich, sumptuous details of the food and shared company stand in pointed contrast to Loewe's (2012) characterization of "comfort food" as "supplemental" to the work of revolution. Lorde ([1988] 2017: 41–42) wrote:

> Coming in out of the D.C. winter storm felt like walking into an embrace. The roaring fireplace, the low-beamed wooden room filled with beautiful Black and Brown women, a table laden with delicious foods so obviously cooked with love. There was sweet potato pie, rice and red beans, black beans and rice, pigeon peas and rice, beans and pimentos, spaghetti with Swedish meatballs, codfish and ackee, spinach noodles with clam sauce, five-bean salad, fish salad, and other salads of different combinations.

The description of the nourishing spread, which features food traditions from multiple corners of the African diaspora, continues onward for several more lines; indeed, the cataloging of the food takes up about half of this introductory entry. Here, then, the time of the narrative dilates as description subsumes action, mirroring the time of rest, renewal, and replenishment. And while this gathering is not explicitly for disabled women of color, Lorde's description of the meeting nonetheless foregrounds some of the physical, psychological, and social needs of the body (and, more specifically, the bodies of black and brown women), as well as outlining what it looks like for those needs to be met. What is more, this breaking of bread has a temporal axis: it not only ensures the endurance and survival of bodies in the present—performing the labor of maintenance and reproduction—but also imagines a future world that these bodies might inhabit. In other words, the Sapphire Sapphos' dinner positions the care labor of preparing and sharing food as a world-making practice in and of itself; this gathering is the "past dreaming the future real and tasty into the present" (Lorde [1988] 2017: 41). Political liberation, in the context of this dinner, is thus also a temporal project—the expansion and prioritization of time spent toward care and replenishment.

The directing of the group's care work toward their own pleasure, endurance, and survival, and Lorde's purposeful recollection of this process, feels particularly significant given the historic uses of black women's social reproductive labor, namely, to sustain and reproduce white families. In the pathbreaking essay "From Servitude to Service Work," Evelyn Nakano Glenn (1992: 6, 3) identifies "domestic labor in private households" as a primary example of the "racial division of reproductive labor" that accompanied the rise of industrial capitalism in the late nineteenth century (see also Chang 2000). In the South, black women made up the vast majority of the domestic servant class, though the racial-ethnic identities of such workers varied based on region (e.g., Chicana women in the Southwest, Japanese women in Hawaii and California). White women conscripted black domestics to per-form the burdensome tasks that they themselves refused to do, at the rate of about "one-third of [white women's] wages" (Glenn 1992: 10). This, too, came at the expense of black women's own children and families: "A black child nurse reported in 1912 that she worked fourteen to sixteen hours a day car-ing for her mistress's four children. . . . She reported that she was allowed to go home 'only once in every two weeks, every other Sunday afternoon. . . . I see my own children only when they happen to see me on the streets'" (18). In other words, white women stole black women's time for self- and other-care and redirected it toward the replenishment of their own families.

Lorde displays an acute awareness of such labor practices and histories in her writings. In the oft-cited "The Master's Tools Will Never Dismantle the Master's House," she critiques the contemporary manifestations of the racial division of reproductive labor, even within the ostensibly progressive circles of white academic feminism. Addressing a largely white audience at "The Second Sex" conference, Lorde ([1984] 2020: 102) declared: "If white american feminist theory need not deal with the differences between us . . . then what do you do with the fact that the women who clean your houses and tend to your children while you attend conferences on feminist theory are, for the most part, poor women and women of color?" Care, then, is a political practice not only because of its function as a key method of social change but also because of the particular histories surrounding black women's social reproductive labor, which endure into our present moment.

To reorient black women's practices of care toward the self, and toward reproducing black, queer, and disabled life rather than the structures of white supremacy, is not only a profoundly political gesture but also a mode of production toward alternate social and political worlds altogether. In this context, self-care is less about caring for one's individual body, and thus replicating what is, than about speculating on what could be. What would it look like to understand black, queer, disabled, and low-income populations as worthy recipients of care? What would it mean for black women to actually care for themselves? What would it mean for black women to use their time toward self-renewal and the renewal of their communities? What would we have to imagine and build in order to bring this world into being? Self-care, then, for Lorde, is a practice of political creation, a practice of reclaiming time, and a practice that necessarily goes beyond the boundaries of the self and toward the genesis of other ways of being.

Conclusion: From Self-Care to Care Work—Moving beyond the Self

For the first time I really feel that my writing has a substance and stature that will survive me.
—Audre Lorde, "A Burst of Light"

If one black woman I do not know gains hope and strength from my story, then it has been worth the difficulty of telling.
—Audre Lorde, "A Burst of Light"

Having now explored Audre Lorde's theorization of self-care as an inherently political work that emerges from experiences of marginalization, especially disability, race, gender, sexuality, and class, reclaiming self-care's radical potential, we want to conclude with thoughts on what it might mean to take the politics of self-care beyond the self, to care work more generally, particularly as theorized by disabled women and femmes, especially disabled women and femmes of color. In doing so, we want to emphasize crip-of-color temporality: our lineage, our survival and futurity, grounded in creative-critical practices that emerge from marginalized knowledges and experiences. As our epigraphs for this section suggest, Lorde wrote with the hope and understanding that telling her individual story, sharing her individual knowledge and practices, would have a wider, collective impact.

We contend that the logical outcome or future of Lorde's radical politics of self-care is care work, because for Lorde caring for one's self was never about the individual self alone but, rather, as this article has detailed, about caring for the self in order to do one's political work of change, including involving others in the work of care through networks of support. In other words, the self for Lorde was never about the individual, bounded body but about how the self exists in relation to and in support of other bodies. In this sense, self-care is socially reproductive, productive of both a social field and a viable future and time for socially dispossessed populations. We see this in "A Burst of Light" and *The Cancer Journals* when Lorde continually discusses and names the many people, particularly black women, who provide support, advice, and love beyond romantic relationships and biological kinship alone. At one point in "A Burst of Light," Lorde even expresses sadness and frustration with her friends with breast cancer whose deaths feel like betrayals of their promises to survive together. More contemporarily, we see the connection between individual self-care and care work more generally in the emergence of care collectives and online communities of sick, ill, and disabled people who share knowledge, support, and resources in order to help another survive, physically, mentally, and emotionally. These contemporary networks of politicized care are documented in Piepzna-Samarasinha's *Care Work* (2018) in ways far more eloquent and detailed than we can or should do here, as scholars who have not actively participated in these networks. But we argue that this work, like Lorde's ([1988] 2017: 97), seeks to "acknowledge all those intricate connections between us by which we sustain and empower each other," no matter how big or small, across time and space, both in the sense of Lorde providing us sustenance through her work from the past and in the sense of the digital networks of disabled activists using the internet to organize and provide care. In this way, we want to highlight the strong genealogical connections between Lorde's radical politics of self-care and the care work documented and theorized by Piepzna-Samarasinha, urging our fellow scholars, especially those working in feminist and critical race disability studies, to learn from the work of disability justice and healing justice activists who are currently creating and sustaining new forms of self-care and care work that are just as radical and essential as Lorde's.

Too often our activist heroes, from Martin Luther King Jr. to Audre Lorde, get hollowed out into static figures after their deaths, mined for punchy quotes, with their radical roots and visions obscured by (neo)liberal interpretations. By reclaiming the radical politics of self-care as theorized by Lorde and making genealogical connections between her work and the work of Piepzna-Samarasinha specifically (and disability justice writ large), we aim to resist the depoliticization and devaluing of radical queer, racialized, and disabled care work. In "A Burst of Light" Lorde ([1988] 2017: 117) wrote: "Most of all I think of how important it is for us to share with each other the powers bearing within the breaking of silence about our bodies and our health, even though we had been schooled to be secret and stoic about pain and disease. But that stoicism and silence does not serve us nor our communities, only the forces of things as they are." Lorde's emphasis on disabled wisdom as a means of serving marginalized communities reminds us that crip temporality also entails generating forms of sociability that can sustain individuals and collectivities into the future. Further, disability justice activists are currently breaking these silences through social media threads and groups, blogs, memoirs, and performance art, as well as more traditional forms of activism, such as the summer of 2017 ADAPT protests against the plan to dismantle the Affordable Care Act, which included sit-ins and die-ins at government buildings, speak-outs at congressional hearings, and sharing stories of how the destruction of the Affordable Care Act and the Americans with Disabilities Act, as proposed by the current administration, would harm and kill many disabled people.

As feminist disability studies scholars, we need to do more to break down the activist-academic divide to support and lift up the work of marginalized activists and cultural workers. As people invested in sustainable social justice practices, we must work to develop, enact, share, and teach a radical politics of self-care, learning and following the lead of those who have had to work hardest for survival and resisting the allure of neoliberalism and capitalism within our care work. We ought to live our lives and do our political work (whatever that work looks like) with the fervor of Lorde, whose words about time, love, collectivity, and urgency we would like to end on: "I want to live the rest of my life, however long or short, with as much sweetness as I can decently manage, loving all the people I love, and doing as much as I can of the work I still have to do. I am going to write fire until it comes out of my ears, my eyes, my nose holes—everywhere. Until it's every breath I breathe. I'm going to go out like a fucking meteor" (Lorde [1988] 2017: 71).

Notes

1   The term *ideology of ability* comes from Tobin Siebers (2008: 10–11).
2   A valorization of work—waged labor in particular—also furthered antiwelfare policy in the 1980s and 1990s, in which low-paid, poorly protected jobs, referred to as "workfare," emerged as the alternative to state dependency.

References

Baratta, Maria. 2018. "Self Care 101." *Psychology Today.* www.psychologytoday.com/us/blog /skinny-revisited/201805/self-care-101.

Chang, Grace. 2000. *Disposable Domestics: Immigrant Women Workers in the Global Economy.* Cambridge, MA: South End Press.

Dionne, Evette. 2015. "For Black Women, Self-Care Is a Radical Act." *Ravishly,* March 9. ravishly.com/2015/03/06/radical-act-self-care-black-women-feminism.

Donner, Francesca, et al. 2018. "Self-Care: A Working Definition." *New York Times,* August 11. www.nytimes.com/interactive/2018/08/11/style/how-i-self-care.html.

Fraser, Nancy. 2016. "Contradictions of Capital and Care." *New Left Review* 100: 99–117.

Glenn, Evelyn Nakano 1992. "From Servitude to Service Work: Historical Continuities in the Racial Division of Paid Reproductive Labor." *Signs* 18, no. 2: 1–4.

Google. n.d. "Google Trends: Explore: Self-Care." trends.google.com/trends/explore?date =today%205-y&geo=US&q=self-care (accessed January 14, 2019).

Harris, Aisha. 2017. "A History of Self-Care." *Slate,* April 5. www.slate.com/articles/arts /culturebox/2017/04/the_history_of_self_care.html.

Hong, Grace Kyungwon, and Roderick A. Ferguson. 2011. Introduction to *Strange Affinities: The Gender and Sexual Politics of Comparative Racialization,* edited by Grace Kyungwon Hong and Roderick A. Ferguson, 1–24. Durham, NC: Duke University Press.

Jain, Sarah Lochlann. 2007. "Living in Prognosis: Toward an Elegiac Politics." *Representations* 98, no. 1: 77–92.

Kisner, Jordan. 2017. "The Politics of Conspicuous Displays of Self-Care." *New Yorker,* March 14. www.newyorker.com/culture/culture-desk/the-politics-of-selfcare.

Kline, Kenny. 2017. "Want More Productive Employees? Encourage Self-Care." *Huffington Post,* February 14. www.huffingtonpost.com/entry/want-more-productive-employees -encourage-self-care_us_58a3763be4b0e172783aa19e.

Lieberman, Charlotte. 2018. "How Self-Care Became So Much Work." *Harvard Business Review,* August 10. hbr.org/2018/08/how-self-care-became-so-much-work.

Loewe, B. 2012. "An End to Self Care." *Organizing Upgrade,* October 15. archive.organizing upgrade.com/index.php/blogs/b-loewe/item/729-end-to-self-care.

Lorde, Audre. (1984) 2020. "The Master's Tools Will Never Dismantle the Master's House." In *Sister Outsider: Essays and Speeches,* edited by Mahogany L. Brown, 100–103. New York: Penguin.

Lorde, Audre. (1988) 2017. "A Burst of Light." In *A Burst of Light: And Other Essays,* 40–133. Mineola, NY: Ixia Press.

Lorde, Audre. 1997. "A Litany for Survival." In *The Collected Poems of Audre Lorde,* 255–56. New York: Norton.

Meltzer, Marisa. 2016. "Soak, Steam, Spritz: It's All Self-Care." *New York Times,* December 10. www.nytimes.com/2016/12/10/fashion/post-election-anxiety-self-care.html?_r=0.

Mirk, Sarah, and Evette Dionne. 2016. "Audre Lorde Thought of Self-Care as an 'Act of Political Warfare.'" *Bitch,* February 18. www.bitchmedia.org/article/audre-lorde-thought-self-care-act-political-warfare.

Nazish, Noma. 2017. "Practicing Self-Care Is Important: Ten Easy Habits to Get You Started." *Forbes,* September 19. www.forbes.com/sites/payout/2017/09/19/practicing -self-care-is-important-10-easy-habits-to-get-you-started/#391f0005283a.

Penny, Laurie. 2016. "Life-Hacks of the Poor and Aimless." *Baffler*, July 8. thebaffler.com /latest/laurie-penny-self-care.

Piepzna-Samarasinha, Leah Lakshmi. 2006. "A Time to Hole Up and a Time to Kick Ass: Reimagining Activism as a Million Different Ways to Fight." In *We Don't Need Another Wave: Dispatches from the Next Generation of Activists*, edited by Melody Berger, 166–79. Emeryville, CA: Seal Press.

Piepzna-Samarasinha, Leah Lakshmi. 2018. *Care Work: Dreaming Disability Justice*. Vancouver: Arsenal Pulp Press.

Rupiah, Kiri. 2017. "Oh Lordey, Self-Care as Warfare." *Mail and Guardian*, June 15. mg.co.za /article/2017-06-15-00-oh-lordey-self-care-as-warfare.

Siebers, Tobin. 2008. *Disability Theory*. Ann Arbor: University of Michigan Press.

Jake Pyne

Autistic Disruptions, Trans Temporalities:
A Narrative "Trap Door" in Time

This article proceeds from the observation that
autistic and transgender experiences have significant and overlapping temporal schemes to which
narrative is crucial. While both autism and transgender are highly medicalized states of being,
there exists no biological marker that distinguishes
autistic from allistic (nonautistic) minds, or transgender from cis ones. Indeed, both autism and
transgender can be understood as "narrative conditions" (Duffy and Dorner 2011), in the sense that
each comes into being as it is storied over time, by
oneself and by others. As two so-called epidemics
on the rise, a temporality of urgency now attaches
to both autistic and transgender subjects, and in
recent years those who straddle the categories—
autistic and trans—have come to inspire maximum hand-wringing (see Bradley 2017). In this
article, I draw on the life writing of autistic, trans,
and autistic-trans authors to consider the temporal possibilities of their narratives.

Within the past decade, the autistic-trans
overlap known at the community level has been
confirmed by research findings that autistic children are more likely to be gender variant (Strang
et al. 2014) and vice versa (De Vries et al. 2010).
Research perseverates on insulting questions of

The South Atlantic Quarterly 120:2, April 2021
DOI 10.1215/00382876-8916088 © 2021 Duke University Press

etiology—on the neurological whyness of an autistic-trans overlap[1]—suggesting these as co-occurring disorders (Mukaddes 2002) or gender variance as an autistic obsessive-compulsive behavior (Landen and Rasmussen 1997). It should hardly need saying that these theories miss the plot entirely of autism as a neurology of a queer nature (Yergeau 2018). Yet, while the scientific gaze—or what Julia Miele Rodas (2018b) calls "the outstretched clinical finger"—is trained elsewhere, we find, within the narratives of autistic-trans life, the electric possibilities of neuroqueerness unfolding in real time.

Like all narratives, those of the autistic, the trans, and the autistic-trans hold out the hope of finding sequence and meaning within life's chaos. Drawing on Elizabeth Freeman's (2010) theorizing of queer temporalities, Kadji Amin (2014) points out that, historically, trans narratives have been a chrononormative affair. Diachronic and linear, autobiographical trans accounts have pursued, quite relentlessly, the shoehorning of life's disorder into a story that coheres. In his early work on trans narratives, Jay Prosser (1998) argued that twentieth-century transsexuals were drawn to autobiography for precisely this reason—as a narrative home: to not be so adrift in the world. Yet Amin (2014) points out that, if retrospective linearity proves healing for some, then it is at the expense of others, who lack the coherence to spin into story. Thus, in trans life, to amplify the non-chrononormative may be a way of doing justice.

In *Trap Door* (2017), Reina Gossett, Eric Stanley, and Joanna Burton wrote that many doors are currently opening for trans lives—visibility, recognition, citizenship—yet these doors are also traps that harbor a demand to suitably orient oneself toward capital and national priorities—productivity, wealth, accumulation—in exchange for belonging. On the list of the costs for seeking such belonging, the demand for normativity could be reread as an incitement to able-mindedness. For trans subjects, this requirement of citizenship is key: one may be permitted a "wrong" body on the condition it is inhabited by a "right" mind (Ophelian 2011). One must strive toward a functioning state in the personal sense, in service of a functioning state in the societal sense. Nevertheless, when Gossett, Stanley, and Burton (2017) wrote that the doors currently opening for trans people are traps, they clarify there are also "trap doors," through which another life becomes possible, through which we might escape. Here I suggest that in the narratives of autistic-trans life, therein lies a trap door,[2] taking us toward what Alison Kafer (2013: 3) calls an "elsewhere, or an elsewhen."

Drawing on this concept of the trap door, I use the literatures of crip theory and crip time, critical autism studies, trans studies, and queer temporalities to argue that autistic-trans narratives "intervene in the temporalities of the present" (Amin 2016). Dwelling with autistic-trans and nonbinary life writing, essay, and memoir, I argue that autistic-trans stories generate their own temporalities by scrambling transgender's narratemes in three ways: (1) by claiming autism and gender nonconformity as mutually inclusive (Goletski 2020: 37), (2) by foregrounding alternative sensory life, and (3) by disrupting the mandate to get better. I argue that cripping trans time through autistic disruption offers a route of escape, a possible way out of the new traps of trans identity, and a means of insisting on what Rodas (2008) calls "autistic integrity" and what Remi Yergeau[3] (2018: 28) calls "autistic survivance."[4]

A Note on Positionality and Method

Yergeau (2018: 2) wrote that nonautistic stakeholders often become authorized as "autism-somethings," that is, autism researchers, autism experts, autism parents. In this context, it is important to clarify that I am not an autism-anything and am merely an allistic trans academic who comes to my interest in autistic-trans time by way of my research about the thinkable futures of trans youth (Pyne 2017). To minimize my allistic watermark, I primarily cite autistic authors and defer to their acumen. While I neither define autism nor opine on what Yergeau calls its "whatness" (2018: 9), I will note that the whatness is contested and I do not attempt to resolve it. Following the autistic community dictum that "if you've met one autistic person, you've met one autistic person" (Gratton 2019: 11), I aim to avoid generalization and instead draw on the specificities that arise in autistic narratives. Consistent with community demands, I discard the phrase *person with autism* in favor of "identity-first" wording: *autistic person,* a choice that signals one of many ways autistic life is bound up in the temporal reordering of things.

The Trap(s) of Trans Time

S. Stryker, P. Currah, and L. J. Moore (2008) invited readers to recognize *trans* as a term situating bodies in time and space, proposing *trans-*, with a hyphen, to stand in for potentiality, possibility, change, and an unknown future. The openness of *trans-*, however, should not be mistaken for a suggestion that trans narratives always deliver the unexpected. Some of the earliest texts in trans studies noted that the temporal structure of twentieth-century transsexual autobiography was a feedback loop with clinical expectations (see

Stone 1991; Prosser 1998) and that clinicians themselves might be regarded as the "primary authors" of these stories (Prosser 1998: 108).⁵ More recently, Jessica Robyn Cadwallader (2014) and Amin (2014) suggested that trans narratives keep chrononormative time by delivering medicine's static stable subject—a requirement that lingers in the clinical expectation that trans youth be "insistent, persistent and consistent" in their identities (Hidalgo et al. 2013: 286). While *consistent* may indeed describe how a particular trans person regards their own gender, and while Amin (2014) reminds us that *chrononormative* is not a synonym for *bad*, it is undeniable that trans authenticity is greatly subject to temporal regulation.

The recent exponential rise in the "nowness" of trans could be described as nothing short of spectacular (Amin 2016). Although 2014 was declared the "Transgender Tipping Point" by *Time* magazine (Steinmetz 2014), the question of what we have tipped into continues to be queried among activists and scholars. Gossett, Stanley, and Burton (2017) suggest a trap, through which neoliberal and normative state agendas receive our acquiescence and even enthusiastic approval. With transgender named as "the next civil rights frontier" (Steinmetz 2014), Jasbir Puar (2017) points out that this signaling of a progress teleology implies a resolution of long-standing grievances that is demonstrably false. Documented antitrans violence has risen, not fallen, during this progressive era, and in the years since Laverne Cox (Democracy NOW 2014) identified violence against Black trans women as an "epidemic," murder rates have doubled rather than decreased (Human Rights Campaign 2017). The current legislative attack on trans youth vis-à-vis a staggering number of proposed and pending transphobic US state bills demonstrates we have not tipped into a happier time. Progress narratives from within and without the community, however, continue to insist that we have.

The (incomplete) depathologization of trans identity is one change heralded as part of the tipping point. With the replacement of the diagnosis of "gender identity disorder" with the (somewhat) less pathologizing "gender dysphoria" in the fifth revision of the *Diagnostic and Statistical Manual of Mental Disorders* (*DSM-5*) (APA 2013), as well as the declaration by major health organizations that trans identity is now a "matter of diversity, not pathology" (Coleman et al. 2011: 4), and the growth in medical community support for trans youth (American Academy of Pediatrics 2016), these key shifts have allowed for a social position that is, as one article dubs trans children, "finally normal" (Shapiro 2015). Yet the fact that a trans person can now be considered able-minded must also be understood as a means of distancing ourselves from disabled and mentally suspect others (Brown 2016). Further, along with this new normal, comes the expectation to assume our places as productive members of society. While transition was once discouraged as an impairment to an otherwise industrious body (Irving 2013), access to transition is now advocated for increasing the future earning ability of trans youth (Trans Active, n.d.). Swift movement toward this transnormative future may be the goal of some, yet this is not necessarily what occurs, and a temporality of delay saturates the literature on trans time, including the phenomena of waiting for legislative gender recognition (Grabham 2011) and for gender-affirming care (Cadwallader 2014; Pitts-Taylor 2019; Pyne 2017). These and other imposed delays may unfortunately prime trans communities to welcome affirmation in whatever suspect form it arrives and, further, to disavow our relation to those who are deemed "slow" or "delayed"—those deemed a frustration to progress and productive chrononormative citizenship.

Autistic Time

Within contemporary autism research, a so-called abnormal relation to time is currently a focus of study, with "temporal deficit" proposed by some as an explanatory theory for autism proper (Allman and Falter 2015). Yet even before such research, the assumed wrongness of autistic tempo pervaded the earliest assessments of autistic children as repetitive and ritualistic (Kanner 1943),[6] pervading too the widespread treatment regime of applied behavior analysis (ABA), in which autistic repetition is paradoxically treated with the repetition of tasks for up to forty hours a week. As objects of these theories, autistic authors recount childhoods in which they lacked permission to frequent their own joy, with favorite toys swapped out if too often enjoyed (Smith 2020). Thankfully, as Tito Rajarshi Mukhopadhyay (2015: 7) reminds us in his memoir of a "special-ed" classroom, we might look forward to the end of behavioral methods, since "every educational approach has a lifespan."

Notably, the "symptoms" that currently make up the autism diagnosis in the *DSM-5* primarily refer to temporal misdemeanors. Criterion A includes so-called failures of reciprocity, such as length of eye contact or "normal back-and-forth conversation" (APA 2013), while criterion B is concerned with fixedness of interests "abnormal in intensity or focus," as well as "repetition," "sameness," "inflexibility," and "adherence to routines or ritualized patterns" (APA 2013). Nonetheless, Laura Kate Dale (2019) points to an unlisted criterion that always precedes diagnosis: having become a disruption to others. Further, in Noah Adams and Bridget Liang's (2020: 119) interview with mixed-race autistic-trans man Reynard, the temporality of disruption itself seems to be racialized, with Reynard's comportment interpreted as "aggressive and loud" only in white spaces.

In the autism advocacy industry (not to be confused with autistic *self-advocacy*), clinicians, researchers, and parents race together toward a future with no autism (McGuire 2016). In cure campaigns by Autism Speaks and similar charities, the autistic subject is a perpetual child, loaded with politically expedient futurity while conveniently lacking a public voice. Similarly, in the antivax movement, which erroneously insists that vaccines cause autism, proponents are so afraid of an autistic future that they bring back diseases from the past, such as measles. Autism awareness initiatives in general depict autism as a stand-in for social death, as in a 2007 New York University Child Study Center campaign featuring a ransom note written by autism itself: "We have your son. We will make sure he will no longer be able to care for himself or interact socially as long as he lives" (Kras 2010). The metaphorical death to which parent memoirs allude, purporting to have cured or "triumphed" over "life with autism" (Maurice 1993), mingles uncomfortably with the very real rates of parental murders of autistic children, what McGuire (2016: 194) refers to as the pursuit of "life *without* autism."

In contrast to the "curative violence" (Kim 2017) of the autism advocacy industry, the life writing of autistic authors is concerned with the violence that can befall those who are "out of step with life's procession" (Sparrow 2013: 148). Indeed, for all the diagnostic concern over autistic intensity and repetition, its punishment is no less intense and repetitive: Sparrow (2013) wrote that the most consistent experience across their lifetime has been bullying, while Dale (2019) wrote that peer shunning forced her to grow up before her time. Despite facing insulting developmental theories of delay, Sparrow (2013: 99) clarifies that they experience life as a "canary in a coal mine"—thus the opposite of lagging behind—instead encountering the world first, and without protection.

Given the high price of being marked as autistic, the practice of masking—strategically presenting oneself as nonautistic—has its own set of temporalities. Dale (2019) describes using complex flow charts to predict iterations of social conversations and rehearse responses in advance. Indeed, the concept of communication—the back-and-forth flow of social time—is a primary source of neurotypical power over autistic ways of being, with the purported failure to follow "natural" social time perpetually at the top of diagnostic symptom lists and arguably reflected in an autistic unemployment rate of 85 percent (Eckerd 2020). As Freeman (2010: 3) wrote, the embodiment of norms and proper subjecthood is a matter of timing—the sort of timing that "seems natural" for those whom it privileges.

Neurotypical time is assumed to be not only natural but also productive. In an incisive chapter on autism and time, McGuire (2016) wrote that, in texts ranging from autism advocacy messages printed on Starbucks cups to the UN proclamation for World Autism Awareness Day, the autistic body is presented as developmentally too slow and thus a threat to the economic growth of the family and the nation. The 2008 UN resolution states unequivocally that high rates of autism are a developmental concern in both senses of the word, including the "development challenges to long-term health care, education, training and intervention programmes" in the public and private sectors (UN General Assembly 2008: para. 5). Reflecting the chrononormative incitement to arrange bodies for "maximum productivity" (Freeman 2010: 3), the autism advocacy industry frames autism as a frustration to the family's ability to generate capital and thus social value. As the singular goal of many autism charities, cure is relentlessly pursued to prevent autism from draining the economy.

In contrast to the developmental focus on efficient forward movement, the writing of autistic people themselves is often haunted by a longing for an alternate past in which one could have been acquainted with one's autism decades before. Autistic nonbinary author Jennifer Lee Rossman (2019) tells a story of a child who reaches through a rip in time to find the autistic nonbinary mentor who had never been, while Rowan Nicholl (2020: 113) wrote that being diagnosed was like the liberation of finally finding "the missing pages from the technical manual." The liberation of diagnosis, however, may not always be the case for Black and other racialized autistics, for whom life can be abbreviated by way of poverty, violence, criminalization, and "doing time" (Brown, Ashkenazy, and Onaiwu 2017). Indeed, autistic-trans therapist Finn Gratton (2019) noted that the likelihood of police brutality increases for racialized autistics when their bodily movements are perceived as impulsive. Gratton suggested one of the overarching autistic issues writ large is trauma—and more so for those of color—with trauma sometimes defined as a temporality exceeding what the body/mind can absorb: trauma as "too much, too fast" (Trauma Recovery Scotland, n.d.). Laura Kurchak (2018) wrote on the eve of her birthday that autistic trauma and stress result in an average life span of precisely her age: thirty-six. Further, autistic hypervigilance can lead to mistimed chronic health issues—Ellen Samuels's (2017) crip "time travel," in which common late-age conditions are felt in adolescence: Jordan (2020: 156) wrote that her "first diagnosed 'stress' ulcer was at age 12."

Despite this "pathological landscape" (Yergeau 2018), the possibility of celebrating autistic temporalities radiates out from autistic writing about the consuming passion of an interest, the concentrated pleasure of a stim, the uncontainable joy of a flap or twirl.[7] Laura Kate Dale (2019) wrote that the pleasure of stimming lies in the predictability of sensation and insists there is no neurotypical parallel for its exponential joy: stimming due to feeling overjoyed, which is then cause for more and more joy—stimming as a queer disruption in time and space, according to Yergeau (2018). Steacy Easton[8] (2013) remarked on the autistic delight of categorization, sorting, and list making, while Julia Miele Rodas (2018a) called the "ricochet" of echolalia nothing short of poetic. Ralph Savarese (2018) commented on the precision of autistic focus, suggesting the literary practice of close-reading could really be called "autistic reading" (38), while Sparrow (2013: 40) gestured to the joy of suspended time represented by this focus—in economic terms, nonproductive time—asking, "Have you ever spent half the day lost in the beauty of how water moves?" A recent Maori language glossary represents autism with the word *Takiwātanga*, which translates as "My/His/Her own time and space" (Opai 2017). Refusing the temporality of treatment—the temporality of getting better—autistic editor Julia Bascom (2017: 10) stated simply: "We are fine." While early autistic autobiographers like Temple Grandin (Grandin and Scariano 1996) once celebrated their "emergence" out of autism, others, like Dawn Prince-Hughes (2004: 1), have narrated instead their emergence *into* autism—into its "beauty."

Autistic-Trans Time: Scrambling Transgender's Narratemes

While not all trans people (or autistic-trans people) desire medical transition, many do, and narrative is key to its achievement. Jay Prosser (1998: 108) wrote of the need to story oneself during clinical assessment: "There has probably never been so much at stake in oral autobiography. . . . Tell the story persuasively and you're likely to get your hormones and surgery; falter, repeat, disorder, omit, digress, and you've pretty much had it." Freeman (2010: 5) commented on the ontological status of medical narratives, writing that in areas such as psychiatry and medicine "having a life entails the ability to narrate it." In this final section, I argue that autistic-trans narratives disrupt the scaffolding of transgender's narratemes in three ways: by insisting on autism and gender variance as "mutually inclusive" (Goletski 2020: 37), by foregrounding alternative "sensorealities" (Jackson-Perry et al. 2020), and by interrupting the able-minded future and the mandate to get better. In these ways, autistic-trans narratives offer us a possible escape.

The projection of a dismal future has been key to the clinical management of both autistic and gender-nonconforming lives over time. In both cases, anxiety over the problem-future animates clinical expeditions into the past, at times precipitating a violent race toward cure, what Eunjung Kim (2017) calls "folded time" and what Alison Kafer (2013) names as a sign of "no future." Indeed, autistic and trans nonfutures once collided in the same violent time and place: the 1970s UCLA psychology department, where both conversion therapy to cure "feminine boys" and applied behavior analysis (ABA) to modify autistic children were developed at the same time by the same clinicians (Gibson and Douglas 2018; Pyne 2020). Nevertheless, in spite of clinical attempts to disappear autistic and trans forms of life, both would seem to be appearing in greater numbers—and, greater still, appearing together (White 2016).

There is much clinical consternation as to the precise relationship between autism and gender variance. From its inception, the autism research enterprise was saturated in gender, with Leo Kanner claiming that "refrigerator mothers" caused autism by failing at emotive womanhood, and Hans Asperger declaring as early as 1944 that autism was an "extreme variant of male intelligence" (Frith 1991: 84). However, individuals both autistic and trans did not come to be of clinical interest until the 1990s, when a number of case studies suggested gender diversity as the result of faulty autistic wiring (Landen and Rasmussen 1997; Mukaddes 2002). Autism is now a proper focus in the field of trans health, with its own specific literature, yet this literature suggests a skeptical stance. Clinician-researchers De Vries et al. (2011: 2277) were hesitant when autistic youth sought to transition, as they may not have a "true core cross-gender identity" and might feel "just different." Physician Jack Turban (2018: 4008) questioned whether the autistic-trans overlap is overestimated and if autistic "social deficit" could really be a manifestation of the rejection trans youth face; thus, there is "hope" they can develop "normative mental health."[9] These clinical claims—that autistic youth might not really be trans (De Vries et al. 2011), that trans youth might not really be autistic (Turban 2018), that trans identity is "true" but autism feels "just different" (De Vries et al. 2011), and that autistics are in perpetual "deficit," but there is "hope" for trans youth to become "normative" (Turban 2018)—are claims that rely on a prying apart of autistic and trans life. Despite this hope that the trans future might leave autism behind, autistic-trans narratives thwart this goal.

Gender Nonconformity and Autism as "Mutually Inclusive"

In contrast to these clinical narratives, autistic trans and nonbinary people assert the union of their neurological and gender identities: as endever corbin (2020: 81) wrote, "My gender is autistic." Not all autistic-trans people agree (see Adams and Liang 2020), yet when filmmaker Rachel Miller begins her short documentary *The Autistic Ways of Gender* (2018) by asking autistic interviewees if there is a connection between autism and gender identity, the replies are unanimous: "absolutely," "yeah definitely," "yes." Insisting on the binding of autism and gender, autistic-trans narratives complicate the mandate to pull transgender into an able-minded future.

In Kourti and MacLeod's (2018: 4) study with autistic women, they found the majority do not identify with gender at all, and for some their autistic topical interests (or, as Easton calls them, "passions") are more meaningful: "I don't feel like a gender," said one participant. Reversing the temporality of identity in which one's gender would stay constant while one's interests change over time, another autistic participant stated: "The only constant identity that runs through my life as a thread is 'dancer'" (5). endever corbin (2020) offered the term *fascigenders* to describe genders that focus on autistic interests—genders that xe describes as specific to autistic people in relation to their fascinations, including multiple genders with which xe personally identifies: neutrois, stargender, dryagender, fasciboy-flux, contrabinary, and autpunk. Autistic-trans authors offer idiosyncratic ways of narrating the "inseparability" (Brown 2016) or "mutually inclusive" (Goletski 2020: 37) nature of neuro- and gender divergence. Alyssa Hillary (n.d.) wrote: "Either autism holds the spot where most people put their gender, or autism is my gender, and I am not sure if those are two different ways of saying the same thing." V. Mike Roberts (2020: 178–79) wrote: "My autism and my transness interact not because of some theoretical linkage between them, like the throttle linkage on a car, but because they are both the same stuff. They are both me, like a part name and a part number, they describe the same object."

Moreover, autistic-trans and queer writing often signals a disidentification from gender—gender as an empty signifier. The late autistic activist and blogger Mel Baggs (2018) identified as genderless: "I lack any gender identity at all." Lydia X. Z. Brown (2016) makes use of the autism-specific term *gender vague*, writing that gender holds little intrinsic meaning for many autistic people and primarily impacts them when projected onto them. While failure to fully understand the bewildering experience of gender may be universal, autistic-trans writers stand out as readily admitting to nonmastery. Adams and Liang (2020: 134) wrote about their interview with autistic-trans man Tristan: "Gender is inherently confusing to him." Brown (2016) wrote: "For many (but certainly not all) autistic people, we can't make heads or tails of either the widespread assumption that everyone fits neatly into cat-egories of men and women or the nonsensical characteristics expected or assumed of womanhood and manhood." As Jack Halberstam (2011: 3) wrote, however, failure can offer its own rewards, the most obvious of which is "escape." In failing to do gender right and instead claiming autism and gen-der as "the same stuff" (Roberts 2020: 179), these narratives thwart the assumed social good of trans depathologization and insist on a place for dis-ability in the future.

Transition and the Sensory Self

A key narrateme in the chrononormative trans story is the liberation or ful-fillment possible when an inner gender identity is finally outwardly expressed—social transition. This is an accurate account of many trans lives—recall Amin's (2014) reminder that *chrononormative* is not synony-mous with *bad*. Yet other relations can be seen in autistic-trans narratives. In a talk at a 2018 UK conference on autism and gender, Maurice Frank (2018) recounted his own autistic school experience through the lens of today's (painfully incomplete) public protections for trans children, declaring that if support had existed in his time for trans children to dress as they wished (perhaps carrying more significance in a UK school-uniform culture), then he believes he would have represented herself[10] as a trans girl in order to wear a skirt instead of the boys uniform trousers and to avoid the roughness of boys' sports: "The school trans revolution brings instant recognition and longing, that it would have helped me with my sensory issues and needs with clothes." As Frank explained, he has a severe heat and fabric sensitivity and cannot tolerate cloth against his knees; he currently has an employment accommodation allowing shorts at all times. But within the structure of a tra-ditional trans narrative, this story strains intelligibility. Frank suggests his gender identity would have been, if not unimportant, then at least of lesser importance and considerably more flexible than his sensory needs identity.

Frank does not identify as trans during this presentation, and in fact notes that his is "a cis narrative making an intersection with trans" (pers. comm., Maurice Frank, November 12, 2020), and yet other autistic-trans nar-ratives echo this "sensoreality" (Jackson-Perry et al. 2020). In autistic-trans memoirist Laura Kate Dale's (2019) book *Uncomfortable Labels,* her title does double duty as a commentary on social labeling as well as the common autistic agony of clothing labels rubbing on skin. Despite expectations, including those of the professionals who preside over access to transition technologies, to socially transition (at least initially) can cause rather than alleviate distress for autistic-trans people due to an onslaught of sensory information. Dale wrote that, despite desiring hair removal, her skin could not tolerate shaving. While makeup eased her daily movements, the texture was unbearable and merely tolerating it could consume the day's mental resources. Fabrics that flap, fibers that scratch, seams that poke, and straps that travel the shoulders all create unpredictable tactile trouble in Dale's information intake. When Kafer (2013: 39) commented on how disabled writer and activist Harriet McBryde Johnson would plan her attendant care shifts—every meal, drink, and bathroom visit—she remarked that McBryde's life required she project her body *"as a body"* into the future. For Dale, planning her days around her own sensoreality, the need to be coded as female yet maintain mental focus, and the search for seamless clothing, compression garments, and socially acceptable stimming jewelry result in the need to project herself into the future as a sensory being. Yet this narrative is discordant with the more common story of transition as the temporal thrill of a second adolescence.

My point here is not to suggest that autistic-trans individuals do not benefit from transitioning. If they desire it, they certainly will benefit. Yet the pace of their narratives can point to lesser known temporal and sensory priorities, swerving and serving as a disruption to chrononormative trans time while also threatening their access to gatekept care. When psychiatrist Parkinson (2014: 84) recounted withholding access to estrogen for autistic transfeminine patients for years at a time, he described one client as "an unshaven male" who made "little attempt at make-up." Parkinson elaborated: "He [sic] would despairingly plead for female hormones but I would point firmly to the Standards of Transgender Care that he [sic] must first live three months full time in role in the 'target' sex" (84).[11] With a narrative and sensoreality askew from the temporal trans norm, these individuals were blocked from transition until, as Parkinson proudly recounted, they gave up. Autistic-trans man Cliff wrote: "It may be because I'm autistic. I like to wear clothes that feel right, even if they don't always 'look' right to others, because of sensory things" (Mendes and Maroney 2019: 56). While "sensory things" are part of neurotypical trans narratives as well, they are rarely named as such, and as Jackson-Perry et al. (2020) wrote, there are politics at play regarding which sensorealities are intelligible. Lacking the rush to socially transition, and instead measuring gender embodiment against other sensations, these narratives disrupt the transition temporality of getting better.

Disrupting the Able-Minded Future

Within chrononormative trans narratives, transition represents a step on the happy ending escalator, the trajectory C. Riley Snorton and Jin Haritaworn (2013: 67) describe in their critique of whiteness and transnormativity as "coming out/transition, visibility, recognition, protection, and self-actualization." The clinical iteration of this schedule was once described to me by a child psychologist working with trans youth as "assessment, diagnosis, sanctioning treatment, happy person."[12] As noted, along with greater societal support for transition comes an expectation that trans bodies will begin to "function," and trans health literature is peppered with this term. In one eight-page article about trans youth and their "health" (De Vries et al. 2014), the word *functioning* appears thirty times; in another (Smith et al. 2001), thirty-five times. It is beyond my scope to properly historicize the term *functioning*, but for the autistic community it remains a keyword in violent normalizing efforts to parse the so-called high from low functioners and press for coercive behavior treatment. While the history of trans medicine is riddled with pathology and pity, disorder and doom, this is now less often the case. We might interpret the banning of conversion therapy in some jurisdictions to mean that trans might now have a future (of sorts). Yet tellingly, ABA, known by some as "autistic conversion therapy," remains the gold standard in autism "treatment" in many areas (Pyne 2020).

When psychologist Diane Ehrensaft (2018: 4080) writes about "double helix rainbow kids"—by which she means youth who are both autistic and trans—she recalls one autistic-trans youth who received trans-positive care and then returned to wow the clinicians: "The clinic team was astounded to discover a child who strode into the clinic, shook hands with the team, made eye contact, and began talking in full, although truncated, sentences." Ehrensaft asks: "Could gender be an alleviator for the stressors of autism?" (4081). If the answer for some turns out to be yes, this would be fine. However, autistic authors remind us that to be or to appear to be normate is not evidence of health, and the practice of masking—to perform neurotypicality for advantage or survival—is an indicator not of wellness but of the need to "map the relations of power" with which one is faced (Stryker and Whittle 2006: 58). Additionally, autistic temporalities have been known to include the counterdevelopmental move from eye contact to none and from speech to no speech as an indicator of wellness, not disorder. When physician Jack Turban (2018: 2) holds out "hope" that, if accepted, some autistic-trans youth might turn out to be "normative" (not autistic), he is banking on the trans future being able-bodied and able-minded. Indeed, at the point in time into which we have tipped, *banking* may be an apt term to describe the type of investment in trans employability, "earning potential" (Trans Active, n.d.), and the economics of the trans future, especially juxtaposed against "untimely" autism, as McGuire (2016) notes, so poorly suited for these neoliberal times.

Adams and Liang (2020) report that, when autistic-trans interviewee Moose transitioned, his autistic "symptoms" increased rather than decreased. Posttransition, Moose began rocking and stimming more and experiencing more echolalia while at the same time finding himself more self-confident and less inclined to hide either his trans or his autistic status: "Although his transition caused him to lose the ability to hide his autistic symptoms, he gained the ability to live without shame" (79). Emerging from his self-actualization, Moose appears more disabled rather than less, in defiance of a chrononormative account. While Prosser (1998) argued that narrative is a trans person's "second skin," autistic memoirist Dawn Prince-Hughes (2013: 19) wrote that being autistic is "simply being human—but without the skin." Although the lack of an expected narrative can limit the life chances of autistic-trans people and diminish their potential for legibility, this difference also allows for swerving around the trap of transnormativity and toward, in Kafer's (2013: 23) words, "desirably disabled worlds."

Closing: Escaping the Trap

In the opening to her text *Feminist, Queer, Crip*, Alison Kafer (2013: 45) states: "I wrote this book because I desire crip futures." While Kafer's desire is not yet widely shared, the desire for trans futures has grown exponentially. As Gossett, Stanley, and Burton (2017) point out, however, many of those futures are traps, concealing a demand to assume normative and neoliberal priorities in exchange for belonging. I have argued that some of these traps might be undone through autistic disruption—through the narratives of those who, by choice or by circumstance, defy the chrononormative mandate of the able-minded future. I argue that, by claiming autism and gender as "mutually inclusive" (Goletski 2020), by foregrounding alternative sensorealities, and by interrupting the incitement to get better, cripping trans time through autistic disruption offers a route of escape, a possible way out of the new traps of normate trans life, and a way for autistic life to insist on the continuation of "queer ticcings toward queer futures" (Yergeau 2018: 206).

Notes

The author thanks the editors of this special issue, as well as Steacy Easton, Fallon Binns, Bridget Liang, Cory Silverberg, and Maurice Frank, for incisive and thoughtful feedback on previous drafts. Gratitude to Carla Rice and the staff of Re.Vision: The Centre for Art and Social Justice, at the University of Guelph, where I was a postdoctoral fellow while writing. Funding was provided by the Banting Postdoctoral Fellowship Program.

1   Yergeau 2018: 9 uses the phrase the *whatness* of autism.
2   Although Gossett, Stanley, and Burton (2017) focus on visual culture, I apply the term to narrative representation.
3   Remi Yergeau has previously published under the name Melanie Yergeau.
4   *Survivance* is a keyword from Native American studies signaling, in addition to survival, an insistence on presence and a rejection of tragedy (Vizener 1999).
5   Stone 1991 was published prior to the term *transgender studies.*
6   Rodas (2018a) points out that with its "repetitive" and "ritualistic" lists, the *DSM* could be an example of autistic language par excellence.
7   *Stimming* refers to self-stimulating bodily movements commonly used by autistic people.
8   Steacy Easton has previously published under the name Anthony Easton.
9   Turban (2018) is nonetheless clear that autistic-trans individuals must be treated with dignity and not be prevented from accessing gender-affirming care.
10   Frank wishes to be referred to as "Imogen" and "she" when speaking of the hypothesized trans girlhood option.
11   In the first set of international treatment guidelines for autistic-trans individuals, twenty-two clinical authors were unable to reach agreement on the recommended timing for transition; some felt autistic-trans individuals must socially transition prior to medical steps, as is typical, whereas others felt this was an unnecessary barrier (Strang et al. 2016).
12   The analysis for a previous study with clinicians working with trans youth can be found in Pyne 2018.

References

Adams, N., and B. Liang. 2020. *Trans and Autistic: Stories from Life at the Intersection.* London: Jessica Kingsley.

Allman, M., and C. Falter. 2015. "Abnormal Timing and Time Perception in Autism Spectrum Disorder? A Review of the Evidence." In *Time Distortions in Mind: Temporal Processing in Clinical Populations,* edited by A. Vatakis and M. J. Allman, 37–56. Leiden: Brill.

American Academy of Pediatrics. 2016. "Letter from the President: Pediatricians Should Not Be Transgender Children's First Bully." August 8. www.aappublications.org/news/2016 /08/03/Letter072816.

Amin, K. 2014. "Temporality." *Transgender Studies Quarterly* 1, no. 1–2: 219–22.

Amin, Kadji. 2016. "Trans and Now." Opening remarks delivered at the "Trans Temporality Conference," University of Toronto, April 1.

APA (American Psychiatric Association). 2013. *Diagnostic and Statistical Manual of Mental Disorders.* 5th ed. Washington, DC: American Psychiatric Association.

Baggs, Mel. 2018. "Language Preferences: Genderlessness." *Cussin' and Discussin'*, September 16. cussinanddiscussin.wordpress.com/2018/09/16/language-preferences-genderlessness/.

Bascom, Julia. 2017. Foreword to *Loud Hands: Autistic People, Speaking*, edited by the Autistic Self Advocacy Network, 6–11. Washington, DC: Autistic Self Advocacy Network.

Bradley, S. 2017. "How Trans Activists Are Unethically Influencing Autistic Children to Change Genders." *National Post*, January 12. nationalpost.com/opinion/susan-bradley -how-trans- activists-are-unethically-influencing-autistic-children-to-change-genders /wcm/167338bb-cf8f-4378-a013-165122bfb7c3.

Brown, Lydia X. Z. 2016. "Gendervague: At the Intersection of Autistic and Trans Experiences." Asperger Autism Network, June 22. www.aane.org/gendervague-intersection -autistic-trans-experiences/.

Brown, Lydia X. Z., E. Ashkenazy, and M. G. Onaiwu. 2017. *All the Weight of Our Dreams: On Living Racialized Autism*. Lincoln, NE: DragonBee Press.

Cadwallader, Jessica Robyn. 2014. "Trans Forming Time." *Social Text Online*, July 10. social textjournal.org/periscope_article/trans-forming-time/.

corbin, endever. 2020. "I'm Trans and Autistic, and Yes for Me, They're Related." In Sparrow, *Spectrums*, 81–86.

Dale, Laura Kate. 2019. *Uncomfortable Labels: My Life as a Gay Autistic Trans Woman*. London: Jessica Kingsley.

Democracy NOW. 2014. "'Black Trans Bodies Are Under Attack': Freed Activist Cece McDonald, Actress Laverne Cox Speak Out." February 19. www.democracynow.org/2014/2/19 /black_trans_bodies_are_under_attack.

De Vries, A., J. McGuire, T. Steensma, E. Wagenaar, T. Doreleijers, and P. Cohen-Kettenis. 2014. "Young Adult Psychological Outcome after Puberty Suppression and Gender Reassignment." *Pediatrics* 134, no. 4: 696–704.

De Vries, A. L. C., I. L. J. Noens, P. T. Cohen-Kettenis, I. A. Van Berckelaer-Onnes, and T. A. Doreleijers. 2010. "Autism Spectrum Disorders in Gender Dysphoric Children and Adolescents." *Journal of Autism and Developmental Disorders* 40: 930–36.

De Vries, A. L. C., T. D. Steensma, T. A. H. Doreleijers, and P. T. Cohen-Kettenis. 2011. "Puberty Suppression in Adolescents with Gender Identity Disorder: A Prospective Follow-up Study." *Journal of Sexual Medicine* 8, no. 8: 2276–83.

Duffy, J., and R. Dorner. 2011. "The Pathos of 'Mindblindness': Autism, Science, and Sadness in 'Theory of Mind' Narratives." *Journal of Literary and Cultural Disability Studies* 5, no. 2: 201–16.

Easton, Steacy [Anthony]. 2013. "Autism: An Anecdotal Abecedarium." *Kadar Koli* 8: 98–107.

Eckerd, M. 2020. "Eighty-Five Percent Autistic Unemployment Rate Is Unacceptable: How to Help." PsychCentral, March 16. blogs.psychcentral.com/aspergers-nld/2020/03/85 -autism-unemployment-is-unacceptable-how-to-help/.

Ehrensaft, Diane. 2018. "Double Helix Rainbow Kids." *Journal of Autism and Developmental Disorders* 48: 4079–81.

Frank, Maurice. 2018. "On Sensory Issues Colliding with Gendered School Dress Rules, Including the Lived Pain and Present Issues for Those of Us in the Generations Who Missed Having Any Gender Rights at School." Presentation delivered at the conference "Intimate Lives? Autism, Gender, Sex/uality and Identity," University of Birmingham, UK. autgensex.wordpress.com/livestreaming/.

Freeman, E. 2010. *Time Binds: Queer Temporalities, Queer Histories.* Durham, NC: Duke University Press.

Frith, U. 1991. "Asperger and His Syndrome." In *Autism and Asperger's Syndrome,* edited by U. Frith, 1–36. Cambridge: Cambridge University Press.

Gibson, B., and Patty Douglas. 2018. "Disturbing Behaviours: O Ivar Lovaas and the Queer History of Autism Science." *Catalyst: Feminism, Theory, Technoscience* 4, no. 2: 1–28.

Goletski, G. 2020. "Bodies with Purpose: An Exploration of the Intersection of Autistic and Transgender Coding in *Star Trek.*" In *Spectrums: Autistic Trans People in Their Own Words,* edited by M. Sparrow, 36–43. London: Jessica Kingsley Press.

Gossett, Reina, Eric Stanley, and Joanna Burton. 2017. *Trap Door: Trans Cultural Production and the Politics of Visibility.* Cambridge, MA: MIT Press.

Grabham, E. 2011. "Transgender Temporalities and the UK Gender Recognition Act." In *Sex, Gender, and Time in Fiction and Culture,* edited by B. Davies and J. Funke, 154–69. New York: Palgrave Macmillan.

Grandin, Temple, and M. Scariano. 1996. *Emergence: Labelled Autistic.* New York: Grand Central.

Gratton, Finn. 2019. *Supporting Transgender and Autistic Youth and Adults: A Guide for Professionals and Families.* London: Jessica Kingsley.

Halberstam, Jack. 2011. *The Art of Queer Failure.* Durham, NC: Duke University Press.

Hidalgo, M., D. Ehrensaft, A. Tishelman, L. Clark, R. Garofalo, S. Rosenthal, N. Spack, and J. Olson. 2013. "The Gender Affirmative Model: What We Know and What We Aim to Learn." *Human Development* 56: 285–90.

Hillary, Alyssa. n.d. "Alyssa Hillary." alyssahillary.wordpress.com/ (accessed November 16, 2019).

Human Rights Campaign. 2017. "A Time to Act: Fatal Violence against Trans People in America." www.hrc.org/blog/hrc-trans- people-of-color-coalition-release-report-on-violence -against-the.

Irving, D. 2013. "Normalized Transgressions: Legitimizing the Transsexual Body as Productive." In *The Transgender Studies Reader 2,* edited by S. Stryker and A. Aizura, 15–29. New York: Routledge.

Jackson-Perry, D., H. Bertilsdotter Rosqvist, J. L. Annable, and M. Kourti. 2020. "Sensory Strangers: Travels in Normate Sensory Worlds." In *Neurodiversity Studies: A New Critical Paradigm,* edited by H. Bertilsdotter Rosqvist, N. Chown, and A. Stenning, 125–40. London: Routledge.

Jordan. 2020. "A Transtistic Evolution." In Sparrow, *Spectrums,* 152–59.

Kafer, Alison. 2013. *Feminist, Queer, Crip.* Bloomington: Indiana University Press.

Kanner, Leo. 1943. "Autistic Disturbances of Affective Contact." *Nervous Child* 2: 217–50.

Kim, Eunjung. 2017. *Curative Violence: Rehabilitating Disability, Gender, and Sexuality in Modern Korea.* Durham, NC: Duke University Press.

Kourti, M., and A. MacLeod. 2018. "'I Don't Feel like a Gender, I Feel like Myself': Autistic Individuals Raised as Girls Exploring Gender Identity." *Autism in Adulthood* 1, no. 1: 1–8.

Kras, J. 2010. "The 'Ransom Notes' Affair: When the Neurodiversity Movement Came of Age." *Disability Studies Quarterly* 30, no. 1. dsq-sds.org/article/%C2%Aoview/1065/1254.

Kurchak, Laura. 2018. "I'm Autistic. I Just Turned Thirty-Six—the Average Age When People like Me Die." *Vox,* February 19.

Landen, M., and P. Rasmussen. 1997. "Gender Identity Disorder in a Girl with Autism—A Case Report." *European Child and Adolescent Psychiatry* 63: 170–73.

Maurice, C. 1993. *Let Me Hear Your Voice: A Family's Triumph over Autism.* New York: Fawcett.

McGuire, A. 2016. *War on Autism: On the Cultural Logic of Normative Violence.* Ann Arbor: University of Michigan Press.

Mendes, E., and M. Maroney. 2019. *Gender Identity, Sexuality, and Autism: Voices from across the Spectrum.* London: Jessica Kingsley.

Miller, Rachel. 2018. *The Autistic Ways of Gender* [documentary]. Oni Photography. www.youtube.com/watch?v=d8pGyJogDdU.

Mukaddes, N. M. 2002. "Gender Identity Problems in Autistic Children." *Child: Care, Health, and Development* 28, no. 6: 529–32.

Mukhopadhyay, T. R. 2015. *Plankton Dreams: What I Learned in Special-Ed.* London: Open Humanities Press.

Nicholl, Heather Rowan. 2020. "Meetings and Partings." In Sparrow, *Spectrums.*

Opai, Na Keri. 2017. "Te Reo Hapai: The Language of Enrichment." Te Pou o te Whakaaro Nui. www.tepou.co.nz/uploads/files/Te%20Reo%20Hapai%20booklet.pdf.

Ophelian, A. 2011. *Diagnosing Difference* [film]. Floating Ophelia Productions.

Parkinson, J. 2014. "Gender Dysphoria in Asperger's Syndrome: A Caution." *Australasian Psychiatry* 22, no. 1: 84–85.

Pitts-Taylor, V. 2019. "'A Slow and Unrewarding and Miserable Pause in Your Life': Waiting in Medicalized Gender Transition." *Health* 24, no. 6: 646–64.

Prince-Hughes, Dawn. 2004. *Songs of the Gorilla Nation: My Journey through Autism.* New York: Three River Press.

Prince-Hughes, Dawn. 2013. *Circus of Souls: How I Discovered That We Are All Freaks Passing as Normal.* CreateSpace.

Prosser, Jay. 1998. *Second Skins: The Body Narratives of Transsexuality.* New York: Columbia University Press.

Puar, Jasbir K. 2017. *The Right to Maim: Debility, Capacity, Disability.* Durham, NC: Duke University Press.

Pyne, Jake. 2017. "Arresting Ashley X: Trans Youth, Puberty Blockers, and the Question of Whether Time Is on Your Side." *Somatechnics* 7, no. 1: 95–123.

Pyne, Jake. 2018. "Thinkable Futures, Permissible Forms of Life: Listening to Talk about Trans Youth and Early Gender Transition." PhD diss., McMaster University.

Pyne, Jake. 2020. "'Building a Person': Legal and Clinical Personhood for Autistic and Trans Children in Ontario." *Canadian Journal of Law and Society* 35, no. 2: 341–65.

Roberts, V. Mike. 2020. "Remember the Time." In Sparrow, *Spectrums,* 173–79.

Rodas, Julia Miele. 2008. "'On the Spectrum': Rereading Contact and Affect in *Jane Eyre.*" *Nineteenth Century Gender Studies* 4, no. 2. www.ncgsjournal.com/issue42/rodas.htm.

Rodas, Julia Miele. 2018a. *Autistic Disturbances: Theorizing Autism Poetics from the "DSM" to "Robinson Crusoe."* Ann Arbor: University of Michigan Press.

Rodas, Julia Miele. 2018b. *Because the Butterfly: Autistic Disturbances of Language and Rhetoric.* Video. CUNY School of Professional Studies, October 1. www.youtube.com/watch?v=QXMpubwtiTY.

Rossman, Jennifer Lee. 2019. "The Doll in the Ripped Universe." In *Spoonknife 4: A Neurodivergent Guide to Spacetime,* edited by B. Allen, D. Raymaker, and N. I. Nicholson, 3–9. Fort Worth, TX: Neuroqueer Press.

Samuels, Ellen. 2017. "Six Ways of Looking at Crip Time." *Disability Studies Quarterly* 37, no. 3. dsq-sds.org/article/view/5824/4684.

Savarese, Ralph. 2020. *See It Feelingly: Classic Novels, Autistic Readers, and the Schooling of a No-Good English Professor*. Durham, NC: Duke University Press.

Shapiro, L. 2015. "'Finally Normal': How a New Medical Landscape Is Changing Life for Trans Youth." *Huffington Post*, March 18. www.huffingtonpost.com/2015/03/18/transgender -youth- dallas_n_6887980.html.

Smith, J. 2020. "My Body." In Sparrow, *Spectrums*, 20–27.

Smith, Y. L., S. H. van Goozen, and P. T. Cohen-Kettenis. 2001. "Adolescents with Gender Identity Disorder Who Were Accepted or Rejected for Sex Reassignment Surgery: A Prospective Follow-up Study." *Journal of the American Academy of Child and Adolescent Psychiatry* 40: 472–81.

Snorton, C. Riley, and Jin Haritaworn. 2013. "Trans Necropolitics: A Transnational Reflection on Violence, Death, and the Trans of Color Afterlife." In *The Transgender Studies Reader 2*, edited by A. Aizura and S. Stryker, 66–76. New York: Taylor and Francis.

Sparrow, Maxfield. [as Sparrow Rose Jones]. 2013. *No You Don't: Essays from an Unstrange Mind*. Unstrange Publications.

Sparrow, Maxfield. 2020. *Spectrums: Autistic Transgender People in Their Own Words*. London: Jessica Kingsley Press. Steinmetz, K. 2014. "The Transgender Tipping Point." *Time Magazine*, May 29. time.com/135480/transgender-tipping-point/.

Steinmetz, K. 2014. "The Transgender Tipping Point." *Time Magazine*, May 29. time.com /135480/transgender-tipping-point/.

Stone, S. 1991. "The Empire Strikes Back: A Posttranssexual Manifesto." In *Body Guards: The Cultural Politics of Sexual Ambiguity*, edited by K. Straub and J. Epstein, 280–304. New York: Routledge.

Strang, J., et al. 2014. "Increased Gender Variance in Autism Spectrum Disorders and Attention Deficit Hyperactivity Disorder." *Archives of Sexual Behaviour* 43, no. 8: 1525–33.

Strang, J., H. Meagher, L. Kenworthy, A. De Vries, E. Menvielle, S. Leibowitz, L. G. Anthony. 2016. "Initial Clinical Guidelines for Co-occurring Autism Spectrum Disorder and Gender Dysphoria or Incongruence in Adolescents." *Journal of Clinical Child and Adolescent Psychology* 47, no. 1: 105–11.

Stryker, Susan, and S. Whittle. 2006. *The Transgender Studies Reader*. New York: Routledge.

Stryker, Susan, Paisley Currah, and Lisa Jean Moore. 2008. "Trans-, Trans or Transgender?" *Women's Studies Quarterly* 36, no. 3/4: 11–22.

Trans Active. n.d. "Puberty Blocking and Hormone Therapy for Transgender Adolescents." TransActiveOnline.org (accessed November 16, 2020).

Trauma Recovery Scotland. n.d. "Definition of Trauma." www.traumarecoveryscotland.com/ (accessed November 16, 2020).

Turban, Jack. 2018. "Potentially Reversible Social Deficits among Transgender Youth." *Journal of Autism and Developmental Disorders* 48, no. 12: 4007–9.

UN General Assembly. 2008. *Seventy-Sixth Plenary Meeting, World Autism Day Declaration*.

Vizener, Gerald. 1999. *Manifest Manners: Narratives on Postindian Survivance*. Lincoln, NE: Bison Books.

White, B. 2016. "The Link between Autism and Trans Identity." *Atlantic*, November 15. www .theatlantic.com/health/archive/2016/11/the-link-between-autism-and-trans-identity /507509/.

Yergeau, Remi [Melanie]. 2018. *Authoring Autism: On Rhetoric and Neurological Queerness*. Durham, NC: Duke University Press.

Finn Enke

Paintings

Artist Statement: Finn Enke

Watercolor and ink help me dwell with the porousness of all morphologies emerging through birth/death, living/nonliving, dis/ability, interbeing, visible and nonvisible embodiments, and the passages of time. In real life, numerous nontrans people have told me that gender transition gives me control over what happens to my body and what people make of it; gives me more freedom to choose what my body/mind does in the world; makes me get younger instead of older. Like me, watercolor has its own opinion and illumination. Like me, it is mortal. When I use ink, as in these black ink paintings, I often close my eyes as I make the lines. The canvas witnesses my nonlinear, non-Cartesian, queer experience of time and space, grief, and love.

Some of my work can be found at finnenke .com.

The South Atlantic Quarterly 120:2, April 2021
DOI 10.1215/00382876-8916102   © 2021 Duke University Press

But I Love My Earrings

Dys Easement

Dyschronologic

Dystopographic

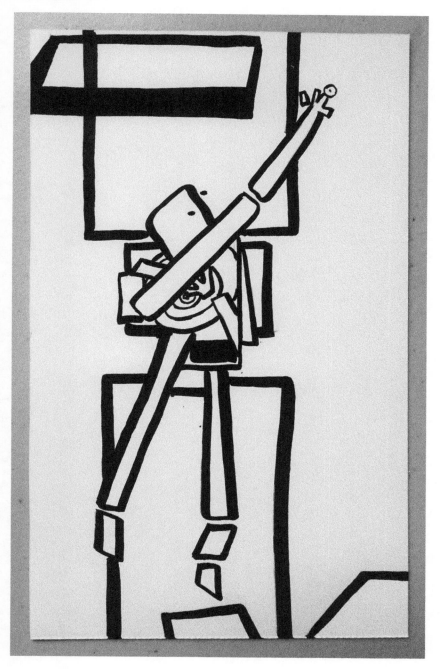

Mimi Khúc

Making Mental Health through *Open in Emergency*:
A Journey in Love Letters

Dear reader,
I am finalizing this article in the midst of the global
COVID-19 pandemic and uprisings for Black life,
summer 2020. I find this writing—and my experience so far of each of these historic events—
shaped by the very theme of this special issue of
South Atlantic Quarterly, by a crip time laid bare in
the forms of state-sanctioned, state-structured
death around me. Many of us are being left to die,
in our homes, in hospitals, in the streets, at unprecedented rates with unprecedented visibility and
national attention. I find myself with both more
time and no time at all; we collectively told ourselves early in the pandemic to take time to care
for ourselves and our loved ones, but we were also
told that work must continue. Now we are being
told that this time of care, this crip time we were
collectively thrust into, is killing our economy.
The administration, and even significant portions
of the American public, is pretending that the
time of corona has ended, while the rest of the
world watches in collective horror as our death toll
skyrockets, surging at the time of this writing
beyond 120,000. Meanwhile, children haven't
been able to go to school, but we, their caregivers,
must somehow create the time to care for not only

The South Atlantic Quarterly 120:2, April 2021
DOI 10.1215/00382876-8916116   © 2021 Duke University Press

their remote learning needs but also their emotional needs, their daily survival needs, our own needs, our own work. Risk management, once reserved mostly for the immunocompromised among us, becomes part of popular language. We learn that risk is both spatial and temporal—exposure through proximity over time. Protests for Black lives have taken over major cities, a temporal disruption asking us to take the time to mourn and rage for George Floyd, to not continue (police) business as usual, to commit to a different futurity that does not foreclose Black life—to take time to care. I have not written a word in months.

I sit down to finalize this article because, let's be honest, the hard deadline approaches (the time for revision ends!), and my daughter's virtual summer camps have begun, giving me the childcare, and thus the time, I haven't had in three months.

As I write this recounting, this memory work to archive, contextualize, and theorize the process by which I've tried to dream better worlds and times into being, I realize it can only appear as a set of letters—love letters to my partner, to my daughter, and to you, reader. These letters are an interruption of the kind of time allotted to us or, rather, that we are conditioned to allot ourselves. The time for scholarly work—the time in which it happens, the time in which it is later read and consumed by others—is not usually a time of intimacy or care. And so I write these love letters to weave together a new kind of time, one in which I take and give care, for me, for you, for all of us.

In these letters is the story of how my mental health project *Open in Emergency* came into being. It is also the story of how I've come into being as a person who embraces a perpetual time of unwellness and care. I have come to organize my life—my writing, my teaching, my arts practice, my parenting, my relationships—around what I call a pedagogy of unwellness: a disability studies, disability justice, and ethnic studies approach that I developed while thinking specifically about Asian American mental health but that has grown outward to encompass an entire way of being in the world, grounded in the understanding that we are all differentially unwell. By this I mean that we are unwell in different ways at different times, in relation to differentially disabling and enabling structures, and so we need differential care at all times. I will no longer believe in the lie that I have no needs, *should* have no needs. That needs, if they must occur, should be intermittent. That wellness is something I can and should achieve, on my own, as a moral responsibility, to prove my worth as a human being, to prove my right to live.

In late 2016 I published a project grounded in this pedagogy of unwellness through The Asian American Literary Review (AALR), an arts nonprofit founded and directed by my partner (see www.aalrmag.org). A special issue on Asian American mental health in AALR's journal, *Open in Emergency*, is a hybrid book arts project that engages the arts and humanities to generate new approaches to understanding wellness and unwellness in Asian American communities. It asks us to move beyond the medical model of individual pathology, to reconceive mental health in the context of historical and structural violence—and in the context of community meaning making and practices of survival. It asks us to shift away from traditional models of wellness and unwellness that have historically been structured by whiteness, capitalism, and empire—and it engages critical arts practices while drawing on ethnic studies, critical disability studies, and queer-of-color feminist critique. We needed new tools, new knowledges. We needed to decolonize mental health. What might an antiracist and antiableist arts project on mental health look like? I gathered over seventy-five contributors across the scholarly, literary, and arts communities to answer this question, together.

Open in Emergency is a love letter, from my partner to me, from me to my daughter, from our family to the larger Asian American community, from Asian Americans to each other. A letter to make visible and care for wounds. A letter to collectively imagine how to dwell in a time of unwellness and care together, for all our sakes.

The response to the project was shocking. Our summer 2016 Kickstarter generated $10,000 in two days and $23,000 by the end of the month-long campaign. We were bombarded by inquiries and orders on a daily basis. Since its publication, the issue has been taught in dozens of classrooms. I've talked to thousands of students, scholars, artists, and organizers about its interventions. Our initial print run sold out in a year, and the requests continued to pour in afterward.

So in 2019 we worked to create an expanded second edition, by first paying attention to community responses to identify gaps and then curating over a dozen new pieces, including one reprinted here in this special issue of *South Atlantic Quarterly*. As we prepare now in 2020 to launch this new edition, I am as excited as I was the first time, and much less uncertain.

But I am getting ahead of myself. Let me try to start at the beginning.

═══

Dear anh,
Do you remember the exact moment we conceived of *Open in Emergency*? I don't. I remember the energy and excitement of what felt like never-ending conversation, near-constant exploration of ideas, across dinner tables, on the

couch, on the phone, in writing, in bed. The journey of this project is intertwined with the journey of us, too easily forgotten now. Summer 2013 we fell
in love in letters. That first month we wrote forty-page journals for each other,
the six months after we exchanged weekly ten-page journals. I did not know I
could dream like this. I did not know this kind of becoming was possible.

You've said that *Open in Emergency* was your love letter to me. You
trusted me with an entire special issue, the most ambitious and wildly
expensive in the journal's history; I had never edited a project before. What
in the world made you think I could create a whole gigantic new thing? As a
mentor once said, sometimes you have to have faith in others' faith in you. I
did not know if I could do this thing, but you did, and so I trusted you and
leaned into your rock-steady faith.

And *Open in Emergency* has changed the face of Asian American mental health, of critical disability studies, even of Asian American literary arts.
It has changed our lives, too.

=====

Dear reader,
Let me remember back to an even earlier beginning, before *Open in Emergency*, before my partner. I need to explain more.

In 2011, I became a mother. And I became deeply unwell.

At the time I still believed in the imperative of wellness, that we are
supposed to strive toward something we're told is "normal" and "healthy,"
and that deviations from those are pathological, to be fixed.[1] And so when I
spiraled into postpartum depression in my daughter's fourth month, ninth
month, tenth month, I thought: something is wrong with me. I want to die;
something must be wrong with me.

Time felt like quicksand, a trap that held me in place, slowly, inevitably,
dragging me under. Life with a new baby was a never-ending routine of
tedium and exhaustion. Where was the joy that was promised, expected?
Failure to be a good mother, to have the correct experience of motherhood, is
something one experiences not once but unendingly—every moment of
every day, waking and sleeping. The time of failed personhood, as erin Khuê
Ninh (2011) has taught me in her work on daughterly failure in Asian immigrant families, does not end.

It is not once that you are the wrong kind of person but every day. This
kind of failure is all-encompassing, endless, forever: a kind of crip time that
I had no name for then. An endless suspension in failure, even as every day
you are trying to "do" your way out. There is no way out.

Unless you realize the game is rigged.

As I began to build structures to make life feel more livable for myself, through the help of my then-partner/coparent and family members, as I read books on postpartum depression, and, most important, as I began applying my training in Asian American studies and queer women-of-color feminism to my own personal experience, I stepped outside of what I would later name the "imperative of wellness" and began to examine it. I began to see the structures that shape well-being—both how we experience it and how we think about it.

The stories I had been told—that mothers are supposed to sacrifice, that they do not and should not need, that Asian Americans can belong in the United States only through assimilation and respectability and model minoritization, that Vietnamese Americans are resilient survivors of the worst kinds of war and refugee trauma—were not only wrong but also the very structures that shaped why life felt unlivable for me. And so I turned my eye to these stories and asked where they came from and how they harm. I asked, What else is hurting us, invisibly, that we internalize as individual pathology to be individually overcome? I asked, What alternative stories might we tell about ourselves, about our suffering and our healing, and what new languages would we need to do so?

———

Dear anh,

I always say falling in love with you was like being struck by lightning. Sudden, all-consuming. Almost painful in its intensity. We called it "drunk love" that summer. Intoxication not simply with each other but with the magic that emerged from us being together.

We make magic. Asian American tarot cards and a new kind of tarot practice for mental health that cultivates alternative ways of knowing and being. We also make magic in that we do what often seems impossible or unimaginable to others. We generate ideas outside of existing channels, and we bring those ideas to life in unexpected ways. And the things we put out into the world often seem mysteriously magical to others—creations puffed into being from nothing. I remember asking erin Ninh to reflect in an interview on the making of *Open in Emergency* as one of its guest curators, and she said, "All I remember is that one day we were all crying in a tiny room at AAAS, and then next there was this box full of treats on my doorstep."

But *Open in Emergency* wasn't made in one poof of magic. That afternoon of crying at the Association for Asian American Studies (AAAS) conference and the box arriving on her doorstep are both distinct moments in the three-year process of *Open in Emergency*'s creation, each marking an important part of what it means to do intellectual and artistic work through a process of community curation.

═══

Dear reader,

I began teaching at the University of Maryland in the Asian American Studies Program (AAST) in 2009 as a PhD candidate, returning to my undergrad alma mater and the program that first introduced me to Asian American studies. I remember walking into the office and meeting two fellow grad students, one dressed very seriously in shirt and tie who quietly and shyly said hi to me. *Who is this white guy teaching Asian American studies?*, I thought. I learned very quickly that this person, who would later become my partner, was not white, though I would continue to think of him as quiet and shy for many years.

In 2013, after finishing the dissertation, I began teaching more at AAST. I developed a new course that quickly became popular: Growing Up Asian American: The Asian Immigrant Family and the Second Generation. I opened the course, as I now do with almost all my courses, with Lisa Park's (aka scholar Eliza Noh) 1997 letter to her sister who killed herself. This course opened with Asian American suicide because those are the stakes, and Eliza's letter reveals not just the fact of unlivability for second-generation Asian Americans but the racialized and gendered conditions that create that unlivability. This gave my students permission to admit out loud that their lives felt unlivable sometimes, all the time, too. I told my students the point of a college course is to transform you—you should grow and have more tools for making sense of your life, or else that course has failed you. They agreed to embark on a journey with me, examining immigrant family power dynamics, racialized narratives of conditional belonging, normative gender and sexuality. Students' final projects were to create workshops that applied course concepts to their own lives and to the lives of those around them; they were to choose what mattered most to them and then create a public program that would help others engage those issues. Some would go on to stage these programs outside the course. We were figuring out, together, how to make life more livable, for all of us.[2]

My students were the first community I felt an urgent need to be accountable to. Their lives were at stake. Any work to address suffering among Asian Americans would need to look directly at student life and student death and not flinch. Asian Americans have the highest rates of suicidal ideation among college students by race.[3] The idea for *Open in Emergency* was first conceived in my classrooms because my students were dying, and they needed me, us, to see.

And we need to see more than just the suicide attempts, more than the breakdowns, the institutionalizations, the medical leaves, the dropping out. We need to see the slow dying that precedes these moments of acute crisis; the slow violence of model minoritization, the strangling of personhood, the endless time of constant failure.[4] The slow death of not being enough. What kind of project could capture and address this?

So I asked my students.

And after I asked my students, we asked our Asian American studies colleagues. And then we asked Asian American writers and artists and community organizers. And then we all dreamed together.

The crying session erin reminisced about was at the 2015 AAAS conference, the second AAAS dreaming session we organized. There were more than forty people crammed in a tiny room, probably no more than twelve by twelve feet, designed for intimate conversation for fifteen or twenty. We moved the chairs to the outer edges. The audience mostly sat on the floor in the center, covering every inch of the dingy carpet. As the panelists began sharing their stories, there was a domino effect of tears. I remember Eliza weeping, talking about her updated letter to her sister, twenty years after her sister's suicide. erin wept, talking about how Eliza's work has so powerfully impacted her own. Jim Lee was solemn, as he usually is.[5] I cried silently, on and off. Audience members shared stories as well, the conversation, and tears, moving seamlessly throughout the room. Everyone remembers this session. Countless folks have invariably brought it up to me over the last few years.

Chad Shomura's work in *Open in Emergency* titled "Corner of Heart-to-Hearts" (2019) helps me rethink this moment in terms of public feelings. What kinds of feeling are allowed in what kinds of spaces? What is appropriate feeling (and expression of feeling)? There is not supposed to be crying at academic conferences, at least not in the formal sessions. What does it look like to inject feeling, to give permission for feeling, in a space like an academic conference? What stakes reveal themselves? And what people begin to matter, differently? Whose feelings get to matter? And what modes of inquiry are suddenly opened up? This session, and others that we hosted afterward, were not simply theoretical or disciplinary interventions—they were affective, too.[6]

We held more dreaming sessions, some with students, some with writers and artists, some formal like at AAAS, some more informal over dinners. The dreaming sessions were an important part of community curation: creating structures to have community engage the process of knowledge making and cultural production. These sessions enabled a kind of listening to discover the shape and scope of community pain and community needs. This takes time. But it also needs structures that interrupt the kind of usual time people move in. Public feeling is an interruption of not only public space but also the kinds of time we allot ourselves for feeling—and what kinds of feeling are appropriate and not appropriate at particular times. Dreaming sessions, the prompts that we designed, the kinds of conversation we stewarded, asked people to disrupt the imperative of wellness—the need to pretend we are all ok and functioning and being productive—to *stop* being productive and to dwell in our unwellness. To take time to hurt.

What we learned:

We are all differentially unwell. We are all unwell in relation to the various structures that shape our lives. Unwellness must be understood in relation to structures of violence. Wellness—that universal ideal we are all striving for, or think we already have and can keep—is a lie. Asian American suffering is tied to Asian American racialization, and any project that wants to capture the scope and shape of our suffering must investigate the kinds of personhood we are being forced to become.

When given permission, when structurally enabled, people will tell you what hurts. People are already dreaming different ways of being, are already working to care for themselves and others. Psychology and psychiatry have led us to think they are the only authorities on something called mental health, but our communities have existed long before those inventions, have struggled with the worst that humanity does to itself, have developed knowledge—ways of knowing and ways of being—and temporalities—time for feeling and time for care.

Psychology and psychiatry have failed, are failing, our communities spectacularly. We need new, different languages for what hurts.

And so we made a box.

══════

Dear Elia,

Sometimes I think of killing myself. I can remember two moments clearly. One, lying in bed next to your tiny always-needing body, exhausted, sleep-deprived for months, seeing no way out, there was no way out. Two, sitting on the edge of the bed as your father walked out of the room, out of my life, a disembowelment, my dreams of love, partnership, family, spilling out onto the floor from somewhere in my middle.

I still have flashes. Moments when I imagine slicing my wrist, the acute burn of the cut, the relief of not feeling anymore.

You have always kept me here. Resentfully so at first. And now, a life-preserver. An anchor. A mission.

This thing called Life is no fucking joke. The world is built on our backs, our wombs, our tears, but it was not made for us. And yet I claim it for us.

Auntie Eliza writes, "The Asian model minority is not doing well." I am not doing well. I'm writing you this letter because I need you to see the crisis that is Asian American life. The civilizing terror that is model minoritization, the neoliberal American Dream. Madness as the psychic life of living under siege. I'm writing you to tell you the lie of the thing called wellness.

My child, the world makes us sick. And then tells us it is our fault. Sickness as individual pathology, a lack of ability or will to "achieve" wellness. The world tells us what wellness looks like, marks it as normal. Moral. Like whiteness, wellness as an ideal to strive for, a state of being in constant performance. Invisibilized structures holding up bodies and persons—certain bodies, certain persons. Invisibilized structures tearing apart other bodies, other persons.

Your worth is not tied to how "well" you can perform racialized capitalist productivity or gendered constructions of the self-made/martyring/sacrificing woman-mother or what Auntie erin calls the debt-bound daughter, parental sacrifice exchanged for daughterly personhood. People are not to be measured by their usefulness, their ability to perform "health," their proximity to racialized gendered ideals, their fulfillment of neoliberal dreams. I need you to understand that we are all differentially unwell, that people are vulnerable, made vulnerable, kept vulnerable. That our vulnerabilities are both our death and our life. That our vulnerabilities link us, connect us, in a web of death and survival.

This thing called Life is no joke, my sweet child. It is ok to hurt. We must allow ourselves to hurt, to trace the losses, the heartbreak, the death. We must allow ourselves to be whole people, in all our brokenness. Our lives as always negotiating violence, trauma, crises of meaning. Our lives as always finding new ways of making meaning, making community. I tell you this to free you, but to also show you how to allow others to be free.

In your hands is a project I dreamed, for me and for you. For the brokenness we all share, so different and so similar. I dreamed this project to save my own life. To help others save their own lives. To help you save yours.

Open in emergency, my darling child.

It's an emergency. Right now.[7]

Dear anh,

I remember that we came up with the pieces first. We knew there were going to be multiple parts; we knew that we needed different forms to address different aspects of Asian American mental health.

Different forms. Thinking with you helped me to reflect on the role of form in intellectual and cultural production. Not everything has to be an academic book. In fact, the academic book may be the *least* generative form for some of the issues we wanted to address. Received, calcified, tradition-bound forms limit knowledge and meaning making; they silo and encourage individual labor, neoliberal conceptions of the self, and ideologies of merit. And within these conceptions and ideologies lie normative bounds of time: the academic book stands not just as the pinnacle of knowledge production; it is also how we measure our professional trajectories, our careers—what "real" scholarship looks like and how long it takes, what a real scholar must go through and achieve to be legitimate (and tenured). The correct amount (and kind) of productivity over the correct amount of time. *How's the book coming along?*, we ask each other. *Which presses and editors are you talking to? Do you have a contract?* And most important, *Will the book come out in time for when you go up for tenure?* To reject existing forms is to recognize their constraints and limitations in and of themselves but also their naturalization as process.

The first form we decided on was the tarot cards. Our friend Long Bùi, a force unto himself, was doing spectacular tarot readings during "down time" at AAAS in 2014 in San Francisco. They were deeply uncanny and meaningful. Long is not fucking around when he does divination! Fortune-telling, a practice familiar to both of us through our Viet families, is also a practice that my inner religious studies scholar has an analytical eye for. Here was Long, a trained scholar himself, doing magic, something the academy allows us to study but does not recognize as a legitimate form of knowledge-making. Tarot did not happen in the official AAAS program; it happened in the cracks of the conference, giving us something the official conference could not. A way of being vulnerable, making alternative sense of our lives, connecting to our colleagues beyond intellectual work and academic rank and professional development—to be more fully human. To understand our wellness and unwellness in new ways. This was care and knowledge, wrapped into one, with all the makings of critical cultural work. And so I said to myself and to you, How much more powerful would this be if the cards being used were not Italian medieval playing cards that had been repurposed into divination tools—that is, white as fuck—but cards made by Asian Americans, for Asian Americans, drawing on Asian American knowledge production, especially Asian American studies? How much more useful would they be if they could provide not "universal" (again, i.e., white as fuck) frameworks of analysis but ones grounded in the kinds of critical knowledges that ethnic studies has developed? And how much more useful would the critical knowledges of ethnic studies be if crafted into this new form? How might an Asian Americanist tarot project open up how Asian Americanist "theory" is generated and deployed—where, when, and for whom? How might we be able to broaden access to Asian American studies, flowing its work through new channels to new recipients?

=====

Dear reader,

I have many favorites from the tarot deck, but perhaps the ones that surprise the most demonstrate the project of mutual faith between writer, artist, and editor best. Jim Lee's card, The Hangman, surprised him, I think, which is how our editorial magic works. When I first told Jim about this tarot idea, he was wary. Maybe too whimsical, he warned. But I asked him to trust me, and then I tasked him with writing The Hangman, an archetype from the original tarot. I gave him the prompt we developed for all our tarot writers, a kind of mad libs that asked them to generate meaning and interpretive tools for their archetype. He promptly ignored the mad libs and wrote a stunning theoretical and affective intervention in what it means to suffer and die in relation to structural violence, in community.

The Hangman: Art by Camille Chew, Text by James Kyung-jin Lee (in Khúc 2019)

The Hangman is the twenty-first card in the major arcana. The Hangman is the body rent asunder by the violence of empire, racism, patriarchy, and ableism. As people pass him hanging there, they thank God that they are not him, until they are. Then, they begin to think differently about this hanged body, because theirs is being hoisted and harnessed to their own suffering borne of empire, racism, patriarchy, age, everyday violence, bodily failure. Then they realize that she who seemed so alone as she hangs there was in fact not so, but instead hung there as witness to the violence but not fully consumed by it. Because even here, in the cataclysm of her hanging, another witnesses her in her suffering and thus liberates her suffering for an altogether different—dare we say utopian—impulse. And so now, they, who are also being hanged, can join in a community of sufferers, a brotherhood and sisterhood who bear the marks of pain, and invite others into such solidarity, so that when they, when we, meet our ends, we will know that we are surely not alone. Receiving this card may feel like the worst fate imaginable, but take heart! The very cosmos weeps with you.

I chose Jim, an Asian American studies and disability studies scholar and Episcopal priest, for this card because of its Christian origins and my faith in Jim to reclaim this Christian image and its related theologies for the social justice needs of today. I trusted in Jim's theological and scholarly dexterity to make us rethink what a hanged man means for us now, in complex and ethical ways. And so here we have hanging as manifestation of structural violence, of "empire, racism, patriarchy, ableism." And we have witness as first a process of distancing oneself from victimhood but then recognizing oneself in another's suffering, recognizing one's own suffering as intimately connected to another's, and then building community through this connection. This card asks us to take the time to witness each other's suffering, and our own, because that is the only way to not be alone.

In this special issue, you'll find a new tarot card, which we commissioned for the second edition of *Open in Emergency* in 2019: The Crip, written by Leah Lakshmi Piepzna-Samarasinha and illustrated by Matt Huynh, curated to bring disability justice and crip joy more directly into the project. Go give yourself a tarot reading with it. See how it might disrupt your usual ways of being in the world, your usual sense of self and community, the time you (don't) give yourself for your own limits, for your own needs, for being in joyful and caring connection with others, through your limited capacities and not despite them.

≡

Open in Emergency would find several other interventional forms. Reader, we made our own version of the American Psychiatric Association's *Diagnostic and Statistical Manual of Mental Disorders (DSM)*. We were brainstorming how to hold together all the essays, stories, and visual work that we wanted, trying to think of a form that was and wasn't a book. A regular anthology wouldn't do any theoretical or interventional work on the level of form—unless it was our own *DSM*.

The *DSM* is the psychiatric "bible," the book that is supposed to tell us everything about what mental illness is. The book to diagnose, evaluate, treat.

A repository for all things mental health. What would it look like to make our own, by, for, about Asian Americans? What would it look like to allow our community to diagnose our own suffering and develop our own healing?

We decided to make ours a *hacked DSM*—a *DSM* in which we had torn out all the pages and inserted our own. Because even if the American Psychiatric Association actually were to make an Asian American edition of the *DSM* (this obviously does not actually exist), it would be absolutely terrible. Not to say there aren't individual psychologists and psychiatrists and therapists who don't do the work of developing their individual practice in terms of understanding race, but as field and industry, psychology and psychiatry remain not only uninterested in but actually disdainful of the knowledge produced in the arts and humanities, which is where much of the most complex and important work on racialization happens.[8] And they hold tightly to their dominance of the territory called mental health.

Hacking disrupts this dominance. It asserts that power must be interrogated and intervened in. It takes back authority, places it in the hands of those not normally allowed to access it. It is unauthorized authoring. It does not reform but revolutionizes. We hacked the *DSM* to discover and offer new languages for our suffering and new models for care. In more academic terms: we hacked the *DSM* to enable marginalized epistemologies and ontologies, marginalized ways of knowing and ways of being in the world. And marginalized temporalities, nonnormative time.

But this would, of course, be deeply threatening to the psychological and psychiatric establishment: a *DSM* out of the hands of those who claim not only the highest expertise on mental health but often the *only* expertise—and in the hands of those intentionally kept outside the bounds of expertise. In late 2016, as we were finishing up production of the first edition of *Open in Emergency* and readying for its launch, we sent out an excited announcement to our networks: it's finished, and it's coming soon! We immediately received the following email from an Asian American psychiatrist—who had not yet read the issue, only our announcement:

Dear Editors:

As someone who has devoted my life to bettering mental health, who also shares great concerns for the Asian-American community, and a writer myself, I was initially very excited to see your special issue-project on Asian-American Mental Health. However, I'm somewhat concerned about the otherwise impressive list of contributors and sponsors in that, except for one Mental Health organization, **I don't think I see anyone who seems formally/ directly involved in mental health care itself: like a department of psychiatry**

or psychology or a licensed professional in that regard. I could be wrong; I haven't looked through everyone named on that list, but if that's actually the case, **it seems like a huge missed opportunity for direct outreach and collaboration with providers who could actually bridge the well-known gap and stigma between Asians and mental health care.** I realize the project was mainly literary-artistic in intention, and probably a gathering of first-person stories, and as a literary writer myself, I love and respect that idea, and have written several pieces in that vein myself. But when I see a rewritten DSM as one topic, even if tongue-in-cheek or as a cultural critique, **I really hope that the information you're disseminating has some basis in actual psychiatric/psychological research and science.** There is so much misinformation and stigma out there about mental health as it is, particularly among the Asian community, that **I would hope this project involved some discussion and collaboration with those who have actual scientific expertise** on a complex and rigorous subject.

My questions/concerns might be moot since I admit I have not read the issue itself yet; I'm just asking ahead of time for any future initiatives you may be pursuing for mental health, that you make sure to include/reach out to the extensive mental health provider and academic community (and although there aren't enough, there are Asian ones out there!), which will ensure Asian-Americans whose mental health needs are so often ignored/neglected get the appropriate resources they need.

Best wishes,
Clinical Assistant Professor of Psychiatry[9]

I've shared this email in talks I've given about *Open in Emergency*, and as I like to say in my talks: as good humanities scholars, *let's close read this together.* What are the assumptions and assertions? That psychologists and psychiatrists and "licensed professionals" are the only experts, the only people who can "actually" address the gap between Asian Americans and mental health care. That science is the foundation of knowledge, and information should come only from those engaged in scientific research. That a collaborative work cannot be responsible or valuable without engaging the true experts of mental health, the scientists. That art and literature are reducible to "a gathering of first person stories"—which of course doesn't have the value of "actual research." Audiences love noting how many times "actual" appears in the email. And they enjoy seeing the power of the humanities in action—we use our close reading skills to unpack what exactly is being said about mental health and who is and isn't allowed to do work on it.

And then my partner's magnificent response, which I've also shared in talks, to audiences' (and his) extreme satisfaction:

> We hear and understand and admire—and share—your concern about how responsibly any project that tackles Asian American mental health takes it work. We're happy to engage in a conversation about what constitutes responsibility—it's a question the special issue means to address directly. Some of the language in your message—and please correct me if I'm wrong on any of the assumptions I'm making here—suggests we hold pretty different notions. AALR is not of the mind that psychological research is the only or even best form of knowledge production when it comes to mental health; so much space has been given to that form of production, and our aim is precisely to make more space for other forms, work by visual artists, literary writers, practitioners, survivors, and non-psychiatry/psychology scholars. We also want to draw attention to the limitations and failures of psychology as field and industry—when it comes to its incomplete and sometimes violent lenses on race, and queer and trans experience, for instance.
>
> "Checking our credentials" to make sure we are including psychologists/psychiatrists and materials based in actual psychiatric/psychological research is pretty clearly privileging one form of knowledge production over others, and it feels like an invalidation of other forms, as well as the people and communities for whom those forms are important. There is a difference between asking for accountability and policing what counts as valid/who gets to speak.[10]

The psychiatrist was very unhappy with this response, claiming she approached us in good faith and we responded with hostility and defensiveness. Indeed, she doubled-down on her fragility, attacking us for so-called hostility. What audiences have found so satisfying is the process of making this fragility visible, of demonstrating psychiatry's grasp for power—and calling it out. They especially enjoy taking authority back from this psychiatrist—this so-called expert does not understand the basic workings of discourse, of the politics of knowledge that she was engaging, something a humanities training would have possibly enabled her to do. I'm sure this psychiatrist, whom we never heard from again and who requested that we never write to her again, would be even more unhappy if she knew I was close reading her email in public talks and now here in this article. But this email exchange is so wonderfully demonstrative of how so-called experts dominate mental health discourse and why an arts and humanities intervention is challenging, in both senses: it challenges the singular dominance of psychiatry, and it is incredibly difficult to do because of that. And this exchange is suggestive of why this kind of intervention is so necessary.

Had this psychiatrist actually read our *DSM*, she likely would not have been reassured—she would probably have been even more disturbed—because within the pages of what we call our *DSM* are essays and stories and visual art and interactive care activities that directly challenge what we've been told mental health is and how one is to achieve it. Most threatening is a critical disability studies and disability justice critique of ableism that destabilizes psychology's and psychiatry's definitions of mental health and its (racialized) imperative of wellness.

Kai Cheng Thom, in her essay "The Myth of Mental Health" (2019), examines the World Health Organization (WHO) definition of mental health, interrogating its focus on productivity as measure or marker of mental well-being. For WHO, the point of wellness, and how one measures it, is the ability to work.[11] This conflation of mental health and productivity is deeply troubling, requiring that we reflect intentionally on what we actually mean when we say *mental health*. I've asked thousands of people over the last few years what mental health means to them. Almost none have said the ability to work. Then I've shown these thousands of people the WHO definition, and while there is collective disapproval and rejection, there is also recognition. This idea of mental health is familiar to everyone; we are always being measured by our ability to work, our ability to appear "normal" and acceptable in a culture that conflates wellness, idealness, and productivity.

So, if mental health is measured by the ability to be productive and "contribute" to society (in correct ways), then failures of mind (and body) lead to failures of labor lead to failures of contribution lead to failures of personhood.

The failure of personhood, as we've already learned, is endless.

But if unwellness were not failure, if it were not measured by productivity and societal contribution but simply by how unlivable life feels, then perhaps we would be allowed to be as unwell as we need to be—and then ask for as much care as we need to make life feel more livable. In *Open in Emergency*, Johanna Hedva (2019) asks us to identify as sick, as a sick woman, because if we think wellness is the norm and requires nothing to sustain itself, then we think sickness is temporary—and so then must be care. The imperative of wellness produces the lack of care; it pathologizes unwellness and thus structures of care as well. We should need care only intermittently;

we should fail only sometimes, and only for the right reasons, and even then, perhaps we should be sorry for how we need, how we burden.

A pedagogy of unwellness asks that we all dwell in an unwell temporality, a crip time, together. It requires a commitment to doing intellectual, artistic, community work from a recognition of our differential unwellness. To look at what hurts, and to understand that hurt within both structures of violence and structures of care. To continually gauge capacity and need for each community member and respond by creating shifting structures to address those capacities and needs. What does continually holding space for our mental unwellness look like? What would continual mental health care look like? What if, instead of parsing out "appropriate" amounts of time for care—and clearly demarcating those periods from the rest of "normal" life—we thought of care as a continuous, unending communal and individual responsibility?

What if we were all personhoods in the endless time of failure?

And what does healing look like in this endless moment of care? Surely not teleological, a trajectory toward some elusive wholeness we're supposed to be able to achieve and then effortlessly maintain to be recognized as human. Surely the time of healing is not linear, nor is it circular, because if we are always differentially unwell, and always deserving of care, then healing is the endless process of care by which we try to make life feel more livable, in all the ways we need, whenever we need.

═══

The first edition of *Open in Emergency* sold out by the beginning of 2018, but requests came unabated throughout that year. So we began dreaming of a second edition. A chance not only to reach more people but also to expand the work itself, taking into account all the conversations I had had on the road with students, colleagues, survivors, community organizers. These conversations helped me see and reflect on the work *Open in Emergency* does in the world—and where it could be expanded to both deepen and broaden its work.

For *Open in Emergency* 2.0, we curated six new *DSM* entries and seven new tarot cards. Two new *DSM* entries directly engage the official, fifth edition of the American Psychiatric Association's *DSM*, hacking several of its entries through poetry. We hadn't felt the need to directly engage the APA's *DSM* in the first edition, but after hearing from folks about its power over their lives, we thought it was important to tackle it head on. We generated new archetypes for the tarot deck, two through an open contest with writers submitting ones they thought the deck needed. A new card, The Student, we created through a student curation process, soliciting ideas, concepts, and language from students while on my speaking tour and then having a student editorial team at AALR synthesize the material. My partner and I would finalize this card, agonizing over each word, each line, trying to do justice to the vast student pain we have witnessed. To meet our responsibility to one of our first communities of accountability. To save their lives.

=====

Reader,
We had no idea what we were getting ourselves into when we started this journey of making *Open in Emergency*, of making mental health. We had no idea of the thing we would produce and the way people would respond to it. We had no idea it would propel me to become a leading voice in mental health, in Asian American studies, in disability studies. We had no idea it would save so many lives. We just knew we had to do it, to save our own, to save our children's, to save our students'. And we knew the process by which it had to be done, to fulfill our ethical commitments to community needs, our sense of responsibility to the life chances and dignity of all our beloveds. Who knew that *Open in Emergency* would allow us to enact and articulate an ethics of knowledge and cultural production grounded in disabled epistemologies and times and ways of being in the world; in community-generated knowledge, practices, and interventions; in arts practices that center community needs and emphasize our responsibility to look directly at—and care for—what hurts.
  Who knew what our love could grow.

=====

Anh ơi,
Thank you for this project. Thank you for your faith, for your love. For helping me become. Thank you for developing together with me this amazing arts practice—as thinkers, writers, editors. As partners and parents. Thank you for helping me grow in how to ethically be in community with others. How to ethically, and fully, be in the world. How to dream worlds into being, together.

Your em

Notes

I began this article while on a writing retreat at Easton's Nook with members of my writing group, Caroline Kyung-Ah Hong, Audrey Wu Clark, and Leah Milne. Our final member, Mai-Linh Hong, couldn't attend but was there in spirit and virtually. This article would not have been possible without each member and without the exquisite hospitality and care offered by Nadine of Easton's Nook.

1   See Clare 2017 for a sustained investigation into the violence of cure, the dangerous implications of narratives of restoration and eradication; and see Kafer 2013 for a helpful political model of disability that names and deconstructs ableism's ways of generating normativity.

2   I have been heartened to see some teachers moving toward more student-centered, compassionate teaching. The popularity of Becky Thompson's *Teaching with Tenderness: Toward an Embodied Practice* (2017) points to this. A critical disability studies and disability justice approach would deepen this kind of teaching, with its eye on ableism and its commitment to access. The work of Jay T. Dolmage (2015, 2017) and Aimi Hamraie (2017) on universal design, as well as the kinds of community resources each of them have created (universal design checklists, podcasts, Google doc resources), are inspiring examples.

3   See American Psychological Association 2012 and Noh 2007.

4   Thank you to Simi Kang for introducing me to Rob Nixon's term *slow violence* in Simi's unpublished work on environmental disasters and discourses of refugee resilience. See also Jina B. Kim's (2014) disability studies engagement with Nixon's concept to make visible the disabling environments created by colonialism and globalization.

5   James Kyung-Jin Lee is the mentor who said to me long ago that sometimes we need to have faith in others' faith in us. I have leaned on Jim's faith in me for over a decade now. *Open in Emergency* could not have happened without it.

6   Thank you to the editors for reminding me of the dance at the Society for Disability Studies conference as an example of bodily and affective disruption in a scholarly conference, which Simi Linton (2005) and Sami Schalk (2013) have both reflected on and theorized.

7   This letter to Elia appears as the editor's note in *Open in Emergency* (2016, 2019).

8   Here, I think of "classical" thinkers, including women-of-color feminists such as Audre Lorde, as well some of our most public and impactful contemporary theorizers of race, such as essayist Ta-Nehisi Coates, literary scholar and writer Viet Thanh Nguyen, geographer and prison scholar Ruth Wilson Gilmore, feminist theorist Sara Ahmed, poet and performance studies scholar Fred Moten, and literary scholar Christina Sharpe.

9   Email to editors at AALR, December 2016 (bold emphasis mine).

10   I include the response here to show readers what it looks like to do not only close reading of mental health shenanigans but also careful, thoughtful communication work (and relationship work) in and about our editorial practice.

11   The WHO (2014) defines mental health as "a state of well-being in which every individual realizes his or her own potential, can cope with the normal stresses of life, can work productively and fruitfully, and is able to make a contribution to her or his community."

References

American Psychological Association. 2012. "Suicide among Asian Americans." www.apa.org /pi/oema/resources/ethnicity-health/asian-american/suicide-fact-sheet.pdf.

Clare, Eli. 2017. *Brilliant Imperfection: Grappling with Cure.* Durham, NC: Duke University Press.

Dolmage, Jay T. 2015. "Universal Design: Places to Start." *Disability Studies Quarterly* 35, no. 2. dsq-sds.org/article/view/4632/3946.

Dolmage, Jay T. 2017. *Academic Ableism: Disability and Higher Education.* Ann Arbor: Michigan University Press.

Hamraie, Aimi. 2017. *Building Access: Universal Design and the Politics of Disability.* 3rd ed. Minneapolis: University of Minnesota Press.

Hedva, Johanna. 2019. "Sick Woman Theory." In Khúc 2019/20: 140–48.

Kafer, Alison. 2013. *Feminist Queer Crip.* Bloomington: Indiana University Press.

Khúc, Mimi, ed. 2016. "Open in Emergency: A Special Issue on Asian American Mental Health." Special issue, *Asian American Literary Review* 7, no. 2.

Khúc, Mimi, ed. 2019/20. "Open in Emergency: A Special Issue on Asian American Mental Health, Second Edition." Special issue, *Asian American Literary Review* 10, no. 2.

Kim, Jina B. 2014. "'People of the Apokalis': Spatial Disability and the Bhopal Disaster." *Disability Studies Quarterly* 34, no. 3. dsq-sds.org/article/view/3795/3271.

Linton, Simi. 2005. *My Body Politic: A Memoir.* Ann Arbor: University of Michigan Press.

Ninh, erin Khuê. 2011. *Ingratitude: The Debt-Bound Daughter in Asian American Literature.* New York: NYU Press.

Noh, Eliza. 2007. "Asian American Women and Suicide: Problems of Responsibility and Healing." *Women and Therapy* 30, no. 3/4: 87–107.

Park, Lisa. 1997. "A Letter to My Sister." In *Making More Waves: New Writing by Asian American Women,* edited by Elaine H. Kim, Lilia V. Villanueva, and Asian Women United of California, 65–71. Boston: Beacon Press.

Schalk, Sami. 2013. "Coming to Claim Crip: Disidentification with/in Disability Studies." *Disability Studies Quarterly* 33, no. 2. dsq-sds.org/article/view/3705/3240.

Shomura, Chad. 2019. "Chadcat's Corner of Heart-to-Hearts: A Public Feelings Project." In Khúc 2019/20: 11–18.

Thom, Kai Cheng. 2019. "The Myth of Mental Health." In Khúc 2019/20: 1–10.

World Health Organization. 2014. "Mental Health: A State of Well-being." www.who.int /features/factfiles/mental_health/en/.

Matt Hyunh and Leah Lakshmi Piepzna-Samarasinha, curated by Mimi Khúc

The Crip Tarot Card

The Crip is the twenty-sixth card in the major arcana. Not a magical cripple, not tragic or inspirational or I-could-never-be-you! Just an ordinary, extraordinary disabled person, with their ear defenders and heating pad, making art, making trouble, making rest. You are, as disabled Black queer poet Audre Lorde taught us, always defining yourself for yourself, so as not to be "crunched into other people's fantasies... and eaten alive." When this card comes to you, it points to disabled wisdom coming into your life. Are you newly disabled, or newly claiming a disabled identity? Or are you an old hand, but coming into a new disability experience? Are you experiencing disability as silent shame, vulnerable power, or beloved community and struggle? Meditate on how you want to use your one wild and precious crip life. The Crip asks you to consider how you are finding and claiming your power, sitting with isolation and struggle, and finding kin, including kinship with yourself. If you are not disabled (or aren't yet), ask yourself the same questions. How are you learning from, respecting, centering, and enjoying disabled art, politics, community, and magic? How are you dreaming disabled dreams of a world where every body-mind is loved and valued on our own terms? ❋ Leah Lakshmi Piepzna-Samarasinha

THE CRIP

Curator Statement: Mimi Khúc

The Crip is one of thirty cards in the Asian American Tarot, an original deck of tarot cards I curated as part of my hybrid book arts project on mental health, *Open in Emergency* (first published in 2016 and then in an expanded second edition in 2019/2020). Each card names an archetype that structures the psychic and material life of Asian Americans, and draws upon knowledge production in Asian American studies and Asian American communities to theorize that archetype's shape and reach. Each features original art and text, a collaboration between a visual artist and a scholar or literary writer. Each ends with guidance, a gentle directive to the reader for what to do now that they have drawn this card in a tarot reading. The Asian American Tarot is art-meets-scholarship-meets-wellness-practice-equals-magic-for-our-times.

The Crip is the twenty-sixth card in the major arcana, and it is here welcoming us all on our disability journeys.

The South Atlantic Quarterly 120:2, April 2021
DOI 10.1215/00382876-8916130 © 2021 Duke University Press

Artist Statement: Matt Huynh

The annotated version of *The Crip* below constitutes Matt Huynh's artist statement.

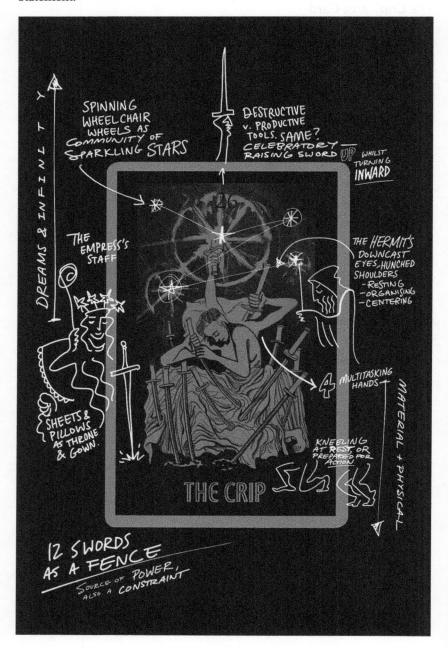

Artist Statement: Leah Lakshmi Piepzna-Samarasinha

I am a queer, disabled, and neurodivergent mixed Lankan/Irish/Roma writer who has been reading tarot for myself and as a community-based healing practice small business for over twenty years. When Mimi reached out to me about creating a card focused around disability for the second edition, I was very excited. Tarot is a disabled, queer, and neurodiverse/Mad way of healing. There is a strong tradition of tarot readers being sick, disabled, Mad, and ND (neurodivergent). As people who have lived experience and expertise with extreme states, living between the worlds and a close relationship with dreamlife, bedlife, and the possibility of death, we bring those strengths to our work. Cyree Jarelle Johnson (2018) of Temperance Queer Tarot, a writer, disability justice worker, and tarot reader I respect, writes about his experience as a Black trans tarot reader with lupus:

> As someone who does ancestral work, particularly with the dead, the fact that I am sick is a major reason I am able to do what I do. What well and non-disabled workers see as my weakness is actually my strength. . . . Living with the threat of death has given me a kind of intimacy with that great transformation that well people simply cannot access.

In creating the text for *The Crip*, I have been excited to create a card that speaks to disabled strengths, community, and lived experience in a way that goes beyond common ableist tropes. I wanted disabled readers to see themselves reflected with respect and complexity, for abled readers to have a window into an anti-ableist framing of disability, and for all readers to be able to see the vibrant richness of disabled experience.

Reference

Johnson, Cyree Jarelle (@temperancequeertarot). 2018. "Celebrate Sick and Disabled Magic." Instagram photo, July 1. www.instagram.com/p/Bktc_aZByyK/.

Jasbir K. Puar

Spatial Debilities:
Slow Life and Carceral
Capitalism in Palestine

Palestinian artist Khaled Jarrar's performance
piece *Blood for Sale* took place on New York City's
Wall Street in October 2018, during a week when
the US stock exchange/market took one of its
worst tumbles since the financial crisis of 2008.
In this piece, the prices of fifty vials of Jarrar's
blood were tied to the share prices of the fifteen
top-ranked US defense contractors. In the performance, Jarrar held a large trunk supported by a
shoulder sling, with the vials displayed behind a
glass window in the trunk, like shop wares.[1] For
the duration of one week, during the traditional
Wall Street market hours, Monday through Friday from 9:30 a.m. to 4:00 p.m., Jarrar announced
"Blood for Sale!" to curious and startled passers-by.

Not far from Zuccotti Park's Occupy Wall
Street, on native land and the burial grounds of
black slaves, Jarrar's enactment of the quantifica-
tion of disaster capitalism literalizes the question
of the worth of life, of life itself as a commodity,
through the worth of human blood. This brilliant
conceptualization of the value of Palestinian life
asks passers-by to evaluate whether a vial of Palestinian blood is worth the price of one share of
stock in Smith and Wesson, for example, first valued at $19.48 when he started his performance

The South Atlantic Quarterly 120:2, April 2021
DOI 10.1215/00382876-8916144   © 2021 Duke University Press

piece. Jarrar is focused on the abstraction of human life and the logics of market commodification in deeply material and immediate ways. To audience members who would rather donate money because they are reluctant to hand-carry a ten-millimeter vial of his blood, he said: "As Americans, you pay taxes for the war machine—your government is a war machine. . . . Believe me, there is some blood on your hands" (quoted in Weber 2018). This performance also resonates with blood quantum rules, initially a system that the federal government imposed on Native American tribes in an effort to limit their citizenship. While Jarrar wished to draw attention to the myriad forms of global violence carried out by the military-industrial complex, often focusing on the Middle East, especially Yemen, he related that there was pause when he brought up Israel: "You get some sympathy. But when it comes to Israel, a few of them changed their face and just left" (quoted in Weber 2018). Jarrar's performance brings to the fore the fact that we can entertain a liberal critique of the global violence of the military-industrial complex only by erasing the value of Palestinian blood, by forgetting how much global networks of militarization depend on the literal shedding of Palestinian blood. In other words, his performance makes the price of global violence visible *as* Palestinian people, bodies, and blood.

Jarrar's clever project has stayed with me because of the strong resonance with my own work on maiming in Palestine and for the way it captures the ambivalence surrounding the value of Palestinian life. As I argue in *The Right to Maim* (Puar 2017), the production of variegated and uneven metrics of bodily capacity and debility in Palestine is neither incidental nor the unfortunate effect of collateral damage but is intrinsic to the functioning of settler-colonial occupation. The latter part of this book looks at the deliberate production of injury—that is, the maiming of existence—in Palestine by Israeli forces. While this section of the book focuses predominantly on the 2014 war on Gaza, it also amalgamates significant yet preliminary data from the West Bank during the first and second intifadas.[2] There is so much data collected over decades for the purposes of political advocacy and humanitarian funding that is yet to be gathered and synthesized. That is to say, we have only begun to comprehend the deep history—the "historical accumulation" (Seikaly 2016)—of maiming in Palestine; these evolving archives are scattered, discontinuous, and sprawling.

The subterranean practice of maiming, often hidden by the sensational focus on civilian deaths, was on full display during the Great March of Return protests in Gaza, which began on March 30, 2018, during which the US mainstream media prominently focused, for the first time (as far as I can assess), on the undeniable spectacle of shooting to maim. Coverage from the *Washington Post* and the *Los Angeles Times*, as well as numerous progressive media such as Democracy Now and reports from Doctors without Borders, Human Rights Watch, and other human rights organizations, queried the thousands of below-the-knee injuries sustained from snipers targeting protestors, noting high rates of amputation due not only to the severity of injuries but also to the lack of minimal health care supplies and facilities and the denial of patient transport to medical facilities in the West Bank. The targeting of journalists and medics was also a focus of this reportage. Reaching its peak on May 15, 2018, with newspapers juxtaposing pictures of Ivanka Trump's visit to Jerusalem with scenes from Gaza of protestors being shot, this shift in media attention is worthy of comment in no small part because during the 2014 siege of Gaza the number of injuries was always reported as an addendum to civilian deaths, commonly referred to as "collateral damage."

The media focus on injured protestors may also be because, as Rashid Khalidi (2018) explains, in the history of Israeli rule of Palestine, the unabashed unleashing of military force against a civilian population, where all protestors are considered terrorists and therefore targets for injury and death, was unprecedented (for discussion, see Erakat 2019: 200–205). Nevertheless, we can trace then defense minister Yitzak Rabin's notorious "broken bones" or "break their bones" policy from the first intifada to its technologically updated corollary in precision sniper targeting. The libidinal economy of picking off bodies one by one, a massacre by other means, generates an affective renewal of settler subjectivity. During the first year alone, as the Great March continued every Friday, tens of thousands of protestors were injured, more than seven thousand of them in the lower limbs. Many of those injured await amputations and other surgeries; many need multiple surgeries extending over at least two years; without adequate antibiotics during these delays, super viruses proliferate (Abu-Sitta and Puar 2019). In other words, there is the moment of injury, but there is also the life trajectory of a maiming, the progression of which, as Palestinian poet and human rights activist Jehan Bsesio (Abu-Sitta 2019) pointedly notes, "outlasts media cycles."

Collectively, these recent reports, as well as earlier ones, contribute to an overall sense of how the Israeli military modulated their tactics. Disabling protestors as a means of hindering resistance while still claiming a humanitarian stance of sparing and preserving life is an enactment of what Lisa Bhungalia (2019) calls a "performance of moral violence" by the Israel Defense Forces, which claims to be the "most moral army in the world." This toggling between the sovereign "right to kill" and the biopolitical project of "let live" and "let die" is what I term "the right to maim" (Puar 2017). The right to maim, justified as moral because it doesn't kill, is a mode of producing value from disposable bodies while all but ensuring a slow death. Maiming is also a tactical refusal of producing a victim-subject, an abnegation of access to the version of the "human" manifested by human rights discourses. The harrowing question of what is deliberate and what is accidental haunts this connection between injury and death. If in 2014, for example, the spectacle of more than two thousand civilian deaths reigned supreme while over ten thousand injuries were seemingly unremarkable, during the Great March we see a clear shift from maiming as incidental to maiming as intentional—sniper targeting allows for no pretense of the accidental. As a further manifestation of Rob Nixon's (2013) theorization of slow violence, the right to maim foregrounds the economic and ideological productivity of maintaining a population in a state of perpetual injuring, what I have theorized as an underexamined "will not let die/will not make die" vector of biopolitics (Puar 2017). What this vector exposes is the liberal conceit at the heart of biopolitical thought, that "letting live" is always a gift, in contradistinction to the sovereign right to kill or "make die," underscoring that death is not necessarily the ultimate assault on life.

Jarrar's searing piece highlights, indeed mocks, the logics of the commodification of life that are driven not only by death—we know, of course, that the value of human life is commodified and unevenly valorized—but increasingly by the human will and capacity *not to die* and by the biopolitical state's capacity to weaponize that determination to survive. In *Gore Capitalism*, Sayek Valencia (2018: 21) argues that "death has become the most profitable business in existence," noting that "violence itself" (162) and the "destruction of the body becomes in itself the product or commodity" (20) within hyperconsumerist neoliberal capitalism. I would add to this argument that not only death but also the hinge between death and injury are part of a key calculus through which violence itself is a commodity and that these tortured and mutilated bodies are recycled for profit instead of being disposed of. It is therefore necessary to understand how biopolitical states weaponize the determination and capacity not to die in the face of the demand to die, another "most profitable business" (21). In the context of the extreme exploitation and ongoing biopolitical disaggregation of life chances, or the narrowing of the "make life" vector, we must ask not only what (your) life is worth and what (your) death is worth but also what (your) not-death is worth. This reformulation exposes at its core the liberal conceit of the supposed inherent value of life over death and the humanitarian and biopolitical alibis, fantasies, and excesses that are enacted in the name of such a conceit.

This query of what your not-death is worth can, in some sense, be tentatively mapped through fleshing out the relations between disaster capitalism and what prison abolitionist and scholar Jackie Wang (2018) calls "carceral capitalism." The first formulation foregrounds the infrastructural and corporeal debilitation and the profit-making circuits that value and profit from an otherwise disposable population: here, the disaster is meant to be survived. The case of literal maiming in Gaza becomes part of a humanitarian economy of disaster capitalism that relies on spectacular forms of violence as the performative reiteration of the settler-colonial state and the value of Israeli lives as protected property. This is not to diminish protestors' incredible corporeal fortitude in Gaza during the Great March of Return, only to ask how their risk is turned into value. Value realization is two pronged, as Nikhil Pal Singh (2014: 1097) explains, and neither mode depends on "whether they [in this case, the biopolitical state] derive pecuniary benefits from such a relation." Following Singh on the public violence of policing, we could also say that disaster capitalism is driven by the "exemplary spectacles" that "tutor publics" (1097), not only in which bodies are expendable but also in which bodies are worth protecting. One of the most effective elements of disaster capitalism in the case of Gaza is that it shifts global attention from the vibrancy and epic magnitude of a liberation movement to the medical needs of an afflicted population (Abu Salim 2016). This spectacle of humanitarian crisis normalizes—indeed, tutors publics in the witnessing of—not killing, or not only killing but also maiming, effectively validating maiming as the (new? current? formerly submerged?) apex of sovereign power. It also communicates that Gazan bodies are valuable only as injured bodies.

If disaster capitalism relies on exemplary spectacles, carceral capitalism creates value through "quotidian surveillance" (Singh 2014: 1097) that unevenly valorizes and devalorizes space. Wang (2018) posits economies of debt and indebtedness as producing forms of spatial enclosure that do not rely on the spectacular but are, rather, achieved through temporal openings and foreclosures. To be clear, this frame does not obscure the many forms of carceral enclosure articulated within disciplinary modes of power: the prison, the checkpoint, the security wall. Historically, enclosure is understood as the privatization of land. But Wang extends the concept of enclosure to encompass time. Wang demonstrates that, insofar as debt economies create populations beholden to life terms and trajectories that severely circumscribe how time is or can be lived, mobility is policed through the use of debt as an apparatus of punishment that solicits time as the form of spatial enclosure. Some examples include administrative fee structures, exorbitant fines for late payments and missed court dates, student loans, and any number of costs that accumulate and ground people at home or in certain areas for fear of being pulled over and subsequently arrested. What I understand from Wang's work is that the analytic of carceral capitalism does not privilege the spectacle-making capacities of disaster capitalism but focuses instead on what precedes disaster capitalism, what it leaves in its wake, and what it erases in order to accrue value within humanitarian terms. Wang elaborates the interplay between exploitation, which "must keep people alive in order to extract from them," and disposability, which "must confine and kill to maintain the current racial order" (80). We might otherwise mark this as the interplay between biopolitics and necropolitics.

The point here is that disaster capitalism is not forged in relation to the nondisaster but, rather, relies on the strictures of carceral capitalism, securing the unspectacular slow deaths, the disposability of those who will be left rather than recycled. What the disaster-carceral relation means for Palestine is that Gaza is the humanitarian rescue object par excellence while quotidian debilitation is unremarkable. Conditions continue to deteriorate in parts of the West Bank also, particularly in relatively spatially remote and confined refugee camps, some of which are the oldest in the world.[3] "Disaster," then, is a perverse recognition designated to some populations (and events) and withheld from others. I am interested in how disaster capitalism encircles a disposable population not only to extract and exploit from it but also to divert attention from the creation of other populations as disposable. That is to say, the mechanisms of disaster capitalism itself, in this case the "cycles of destruction" and reinvestiture in Gaza, the speed of which have accelerated in the last decade (Feldman 2016: 99; see also Roy 1999), can be used to obscure the conditions for the disposability of other populations, indeed, the very grounds of disposability in the wake of disaster. Gaza becomes the frontline for humanitarian intervention, which itself sustains Gazans as users and consumers rather than as laborers (the unemployment rate among men can be as high as 70 percent). A combined disaster-carceral analysis allows a rearticulation of what a disaster is and how we locate it (de-exceptionalizing Gaza, as one quick example, in relation to Kashmir). What lies outside the disaster that is producing equally if not more debilitating conditions than the disaster proper? It's not just that the construct of disaster binds our attention but that it works in concert with the slow death and abandonment of others. This is not to say that one situation is worse than the other but, rather, to note the overall structures of capitalism that establish, according to variables of crisis and systematization, such distinctions in the first place.

In what follows, I think through the disaster-carceral frame via two forms of value creation for disposable bodies: first, the production of differential disability mobilities; second, and relatedly, slow life as spatial enclosure.

Differential Mobilities

On December 15, 2017, Ibrahim Abu Thurayeh was shot in the head and killed by the Israeli Defense Forces in Gaza. Protesting US president Donald Trump's December 4, 2017, announcement that the United States would be moving its embassy from Tel Aviv to Jerusalem, twenty-nine-year-old Abu Thurayeh was a wheelchair user and a double amputee (Maza 2017). His legs were amputated in 2008 when he was shot by an Israeli helicopter while at a rally at the Gazan border when he replaced an Israeli flag with a Palestinian flag (Maza 2017). Images of Abu Thurayeh, a well-known freedom fighter in Gaza, unarmed on the front lines of protest while upright on two amputated thighs, went viral and generated a media spectacle.

Moral outrage accrues quickly to the injuring of disabled protestors, unwittingly producing them as benign entities unable to resist and agitate. In fact, I suggest it accrues more quickly to that spectacle than to the actual fact of protestors being targeted for injury in the first place. Underpinning these ableist renderings of outrage is the simple fact that able-bodied resistors face the disability to come, face becoming disabled, existing in a field of debilitation where the euphemism for an injury that is unable to heal is the term *permanent disability*. There often seems to be less interest in the production of the very disabled body, for whom moral outrage is reserved, or in the role of this production in maintaining settler-colonial occupation. This asymmetry evokes a simple question: How do we square the contradictions between disability rights platforms and the right to maim?

In summary, this uneven expression of moral outrage ironically obscures how the disabled body comes to be in the first place. The life history of Abu Thurayeh represents this very intersection of the targeting to disable (shooting eyes, arms, knees) and targeting the disabled, the injuring and killing of the disabled by Israel Defense Force soldiers that happens not infrequently.[4] What this intersection suggests is that disability is always a proximate state of becoming. The disability to come, the unceasing production of disability that haunts many sectors of the Palestinian population, derives from the experience of many decades of resisting the occupation that can likely eventuate in debilitation if not in death. Very different from the disability to come from aging and senescence, this always imminent "turning into," from the able body to the disabled body, produces a range of proximate, gradated capacities and debilities rather than a self/other model of ability and disability.

A corollary facet of this relational proximity to disability—what I call being "in debility's position" (Puar 2017, xiv)—is reflected in one of the prime carceral logics of the occupation, the production of what Celeste Langan (2001) calls "mobility disability." Her starting point for theorizing mobility disability is from Rousseau's ([1762] 1973: 58) *Social Contract*:

> Every free action is produced by two causes working together: one is mental, namely the volition that determines the act; the other is physical, namely the power that carries the act out. When I walk towards something, it is necessary that I should will to go there and that my feet should carry me there. If a paralytic wills to run and an active man doesn't, they will both stay where they are.

Rewording the terms *paralytic* and *active*, Langan (2001: 459) remarks on Rousseau's conviction of the similar stasis of the "cripple who wants to run and the able-bodied man who doesn't." She writes: "To think about mobility disability is to think about norms of speed and ranges of motion; perhaps also of desired ends. . . . To consider those constraints is to notice how the built environment—social practices and material infrastructures—can create mobility disabilities that diminish the difference between the 'cripple' and the ambulatory person who may well wish to move."

Bringing together two different sets of scholarly literatures on mobility in Palestine allows a sketching of the contours of these differences and how they might be diminished. While the centrality of mobility restriction to the occupation has been eloquently elaborated by many researchers, these studies referentially default to a presumed able body that has the potential of mobility and suffers its subsequent hindering primarily through infrastructural, architectural, and administrative apparatuses of surveillance, containment, and restriction. Unwittingly reinforcing mobility disability as an individual condition rather than a generalized social condition of movement modulation as a form of collective punishment, this otherwise illuminating scholarship does not examine the varied modalities through which many have the logic of containing mobility literalized on their bodies in the form of impairment (Kotef 2015). Inversely, emergent research and policy literatures on disability in Palestine have largely focused on homebound populations and promoting access to work, education, and integration (Eide 2006; Jarar 2009; Palestinian Central Bureau of Statistics and Ministry of Social Affairs 2011). Defaulting to an implicit assumption that these forms of access are available to other Palestinian populations, this work projects homebound persons against an able-bodied Palestinian population through disability human rights empowerment frames, bypassing the complex forms of enclosure and obstacles to mobility that many if not most Palestinian sectors of society have to navigate (Abu Nahleh 2009; Al Qaddi 2003). This fissure maintains the global universalism and relevance of such frames and rationalizes the acquiescence of international actors to Israeli rule. In other words, global disability human rights frames predominate in part by obscuring these connections between those demarcated as disabled and the overall sphere of debility within which the "ambulatory," to return to Langan's language, are unable to move.[5]

The diminished difference that Langan highlights is intrinsic to the carceral state as a continuum that grounds bodies through spatial confinement.[6] The production of mobility impairment across populations, across a disabled/nondisabled binary, is a form of collective punishment for all Palestinians.[7] What is the relationship of those who have what is typically referred to as "mobility disabilities" to the gradation of mobility impairment that affects Palestinian mobility generally, regardless of abled or disabled bodily categorization? Reflecting an evolving and convivial notion of disability, by framing differential mobilities as a form of collective punishment we can potentially envision and create new lines of solidarity that link entities through gradations of debilitation rather than sedimenting the self/other binarization that the categorization of disability relies on. It is also the basis on which framings of disability that maintain self-other identity positions are destabilized and the potentiating conduit through which deeper solidarities can be fostered that eclipse "ally" formations perpetuated by disability rights frames of recognition. Seriously thinking through this "diminished difference" is an important entry point into the process of decolonizing disability.

Langan's notion of mobility disabilities marks how debilitating infrastructures turn able bodies into a range of disabled bodies. This gradation is embedded within the logic of the occupation, hinging not on a division between Israelis, who can move, in relation to Palestinians, who cannot, but rather, on an intricate apparatus of differential yet proximate mobility capacities, such that each body has a slightly different status than the one next to it. This highlights the "careful distribution of differential privileges and punishments" (Li 2016: 193), for example, between those living in 48 (the term for the settler-colonial state of Israel), Gaza, East Jerusalem, the West Bank, and the diaspora/s. If, as Langan claims, "mobility disability is . . . about norms of speed and ranges of motion," then the polarization neither between the mobility of the Israeli and the immobility of the Palestinian nor between the able-bodied Palestinian and the homebound mobility-disabled Palestinian can sustain analytic pressure. If speed and pace measure the extent, the quality, the amount, the severity of disability mobility, then mobility needs to be thought of differentially. As a foregone capacity of able bodies, speed, "range(s) of motion," and their calibration, that is, the creation of different kinds and types of speeds and motion, are all forms of social control.

What is the materialization of this modulation of speed and motion? And to return to Langan briefly one last time, what are its "desired ends"? If the speed and range of motion of bodies are enabled and inhibited differentially, mobility is the personal property of the body, a possession of the self. This production of mobility through Enlightenment framings of possessive individualism is leveraged to create discord, distrust, and envy, as no one body moves in the same way as the body next to it. As Toufic Haddad (2016: 110) describes, the post-Oslo technology of "closure" was intended to fragment the West Bank, class relations, and individuals. Glimpses of what one body cannot do in relation to what another can are prolifically available. Freezing the movement of Palestinians is not the apex of a splintering occupation. Rather, it is the constellation of potential mobilities that condition the consciousness of mobility disability in Palestine. Whether or not there is explicit intent to create a panoply of mobility disabilities is not my concern here. Rather, I am interested in the cumulative effects of the experience of various forms of (im)mobility.

If differential mobility alters what disability is, especially in relation to global human rights regimes propagating disability as a protected and potentially empowered status (Ben-Moshe et al. 2007; Jaffee 2016), are different lines of solidarity created through the breaking down of the nondisabled/disabled binary, solidarity that foregrounds the collective punishment of immobilization through and beyond the identification of the body that is disabled? How are not only disability but also mobility redefined, and new forms created, in a context of extreme confinement where mobility is unevenly being held hostage? What kinds of work-arounds that stem from subaltern capacities to innovate are enacted to craft livable forms of movement, to subvert constraints on movement, to challenge altogether what movement is (see Rai 2019)?

In the context of Palestine, the external constraints that engender mobility disabilities include varied obstacles to and modulations of movement of all kinds: checkpoints (Tawil-Souri 2011); administrative bureaucratic apparatuses that stall and foreclose travel, mobility for work, development and entre-

preneurial ventures, and the capacity to move and change residences—
baroque processes to apply for permits to travel and build, absence of public
services such as postal delivery, lack of bill payment infrastructures (Ophir et
al. 2009; Tawil-Souri 2011, 2012; Berda 2017); the manipulated production
and destruction of landscape and transport infrastructure, such as highways, tunnels, and forms of vertical space—including yet another layer of verticality via bandwidth regulation and withholding and the airscapes populated
by drones—that partition circuits of movement (Weizman 2002, 2012); the
withholding of temporal modernity through the terms of an indefinite political detente; practices of repetitive incarceration that affect not only Palestinian
men but also kin relations; the literal production of mobility disabilities
through the targeting of knees, eyes, and other body parts that will likely render a body homebound; and finally, what I turn to now, the withholding of
temporal modernity through denial of resolution, suspension in the space of
the indefinite, and the production of mobility disabilities via the temporal reg-
isters of slow life.

Slow Life

"Space is a political plastic," observes Israeli architect and social theorist Eyal
Weizman (2017: 187); "the minute you understand space as a political plastic, there is no difference between construction and destruction. It is simply
the reorganization of space." This reorganization of space in Palestine happens with considerable speed on the scale of the quotidian, and this speed is
often inverse to the deep longevity of the form it is violating: informal checkpoints appear and disappear, disrupting and rerouting transit between home
and work; settlement building is authorized and initiated with rapidity;
house demolitions destroy the evidence of generations of family life in a day;
olive trees that have been on the land for decades are quickly plundered and
maligned—this list could go on. But one cannot escape the reality that life in
Palestine is, in contrast to these forms of destruction, slowed down, is a version of slow life.

The idea of slow death focuses on the relation to death but does not
adequately theorize the *slow* aspect of slow death. In fact, slow death itself is
literalized as the slowing down of life, in this case of Palestinian life. Temporalities of slowness are manifest to Palestinians in the West Bank, where it
can easily take hours to travel one or two dozen kilometers. Israel systematically slows down the movement of Palestinians, their commerce, and their
products with permanent as well as sporadic "flying" checkpoints (many

within the West Bank itself), roadblocks, the apartheid wall, electronic fencing, and segregated roads and highways. Palestine itself becomes simultaneously bigger—because it takes so long to get anywhere—and smaller, as transit becomes arduous beyond necessary paths in this world of Areas A, B, and C, where it is so difficult to travel between areas without permits and identifications. Movement is suffocated. Distance is stretched and manipulated to create an entire population with mobility impairments. And yet space is shrunken, as people are held in place, rarely able to move far. Unlike accelerationist theorizations of space-time compression and the annihilation of space by time, the increased spatial disparity is not remedied with temporal simultaneity.[8] Rather, this simultaneity is withheld. Time itself is held hostage.

This is the slow aspect of slow death: slow death can entail a really slow life, too, a life that demands constant calibration of different speeds and the relation of speed to space. The occupation works in part by titrating control over temporality: by foreclosing or suspending access to speed, the immediacy of forms of contact, and the space-time compression so coveted in modernity and crucial to the circulation of goods, ideas, and bodies. This asphixiatory control society shifts from a narrative of increasing speed to forms of algorithmic, parallel, distributed, and networked time. It works through suspensions between connectivity and modes of slow attenuation, in direct contrast to the always-connected ideal, whereby, as Seb Franklin (2015: 84) explains, "immobility, fixity, and disconnection from channels of communication appear aberrant or pathological and thus lead to expulsion from circuits of representation and exclusion." Palestinians in the West Bank live in the temporal instability of the indefinite, with suspension driving arbitrariness and uncertainty, thereby deprived not only of the future but also of the thick potentiality of the present that leads to open futures. The suspended state of the indefinite, of waiting and waiting (it) out, wreaks multigenerational psychological and physical havoc. The uncertainty of the indefinite is countered only by the certainty of a dictated future. Time thus is the meter of power; it is one form that physical enclosure takes on. The cordoning of time through space contributes to an overall "lack of jurisdiction over the function of one's own senses" (Schuller 2018: 74) endemic to the operation of colonial rule, as well as a sense of being "stranded in time" (Lagerquist 2008). If biopolitics functions in part through the "racialization of temporality," this process entails several modes of temporal differentiation: withholding futurity, making impossible anything but a slowed (down) life, and immobilizing the body "within the past of civilization itself" (Schuller 2018: 58), thereby putting under duress ascriptions of the past, the present, and the future.

Palestinian studies scholar Julie Peteet (2008) calls the extraction of nonlabor time "stealing time":

> Time has thus become another commodity, like land and water, which Israel expropriates from the population in the occupied Palestinian territories. In the wake of the 1967 occupation of the West Bank and Gaza, native time was appropriated for the extraction of labor. Since then, Israel has weaned itself from Palestinian labor by turning to the global labor market, but has continued to steal Palestinian time through myriad tactics of enforced waiting.

In this description, we are alerted to an oscillation from the laboring body as a source of value extraction that leads to the depletion of available nonlabor time, what has been theorized as living labor, to the extraction of time as a commodity that secures the value of the occupation for the Israeli state. In the first instance of living labor, one well familiar to us, the extraction of time attempts to produce a depleted and therefore compliant population so beholden to the logistics of the everyday that forms of connectivity, communing, and collective resistance are thwarted. The extraction of time functions as the transfer of "vital energy" or "the substance of activity that produces life" (Vora 2015: 3) from colonized to colonizer, from global South to global North (we can perhaps consider "Israel/Palestine" a North/South relation), an extraction that recapitulates a long colonial history of mining bodies for their potentiality.

However, the second mode of extraction, the extraction of time *as* a commodity, challenges theories of affective labor that circumscribe affect as an attribute of the laboring body and that understand affective labor to be immaterial, intellectual, emotional, communicative, and immeasurable. By contrast, Patricia Clough et al. (2007: 62) focus on affect as the transfer and circulation of potentialities not only between bodies but also between scales of matter, that is, at subindividual levels. They explain the abstraction of the laborers' affect to what they call "affect-itself": "Capital [is] setting out a domain for the investment in and an accumulation of affect by abstracting human affect to affect-itself: it is affect-itself that labors, not only the body of the laborer taken as an [self-enclosed] autopoietic organism." As a material form, as matter, affect-itself is abstracted from the actual performance of an individual body; in fact, it is located as emanating not from any one body but, rather, from collectivities of subindividual capacities. Affect-itself labors to reorganize intensities, corporeal energies, and the atmospherics of occupation. Affect is therefore not only something that is exchanged and transmitted between bodies but also an object of control as well as a mode of controlling. Affect-itself is not bound to the increasingly deployed tautology, commonly attributed to Spinoza, that affect is "the capacity to affect and be affected" (Massumi 1990). Biopolitics is the work of rupturing the presumed reciprocity of affect, manifesting what I have elsewhere called the "geopolitics of racial ontology" (Puar 2017: 55). Within the fantasized reciprocity of this formulation, the scene in which the affected body can also with equal force be affecting, is where the work of biopolitical sorting and population management thrives. What is crucial for thinking about affect-itself is that the denial, withholding, and asymmetrical redistribution of affect is a form of subjugation, hence laboring in the service of occupation. Between Clough et al.'s (2007) intervention regarding scales and the inhumanism of matter—an inhumanism that would also include land, ecosystems, and the biopolitics of life and nonlife (Povinelli 2016)—and the withholding of affective multidirectionality as a productive force of exploitation, the concept of affective labor is considerably complicated. Affective labor might more accurately be thought of as the laboring of affect, laboring in the service of creating and re-creating spatial and temporal orientations of corporeality.

How, therefore, is value extracted from slowness? Let's take as one example the role of checkpoints. Rema Hammami (2015: 4–5) writes,

> Checkpoints generally do not function to stop Palestinian mobility in toto . . .
> [or] to routinize Palestinian movement. . . . This network of permeability . . .
> operates . . . to make the everyday experience of mobility arbitrary, chaotic,
> and uncertain. . . . Rather than an effect, this constant state of uncertainty is
> the very logic of Israeli sovereign violence that checkpoints instantiate, as
> well as produce.

This "constant state of uncertainty" is the crucible of the carceral logics of differential mobilities and the circumscribing of time through space. Checkpoints ensure one is never sure of reaching work on time. Fear of not getting to work then adds to the labor of getting to work; the checkpoints affectively expand labor time as well as produce an intensification of time. The fear of not reaching work on time produces migration patterns that then clear the land for more illegal settlements. One is never not at work, but not in the way that theories of immaterial labor proclaim, via the blurring of boundaries between the office and beyond. Rather, this is about the expansion of material labor beyond the contours of the laboring body and its output. While the checkpoints inhibit bodies from doing and expand the time required for productive labor, the constant state of uncertainty is the work of affect, the reshaping of senses of time and space, of movement itself. As Franklin (2015: 26) argues, this expansion of material labor beyond the laboring body entails two things: the "discretization of the labor process" fractalizes differing bodily potentials, the parts of which are more available for "perpetual monetization" than the whole of the laboring body, and this perpetual monetization is a process of valorization not bracketed to "those hours nominally set aside . . . as labor time." Bodies in line at checkpoints contribute to the profit of the occupation not only because their nonlabor is completely tied up in the reproduction of their labor time but also because this division disappears through the fractalizing of the emotive, cognitive, physiological capacities of bodies toward the perceptual fields and sensorium of being occupied and the constant modulation of horizons of movement. It's not just that bodies are too tired to resist but that the experience of the "constant state of uncertainty" becomes the condition of being, much like Hammami's incisive point about uncertainty being not the effect but the logic of the checkpoints. It is not slowness itself that is held hostage by capitalism, for indeed, speed is capture as much as slowness is capture. Rather, the endless calibration of relations between speed and slowness are part of the weaponization of temporality.

In the context of Palestine, where the checkpoint-crossing body increasingly labors to simply labor and is also extracted from affectively, time is stolen from the laboring body, expanding the time of the laboring, and also extracting what I will call, following Clough et al. (2007), "time-itself." In making this analogy between affect-itself and time-itself, I note that, while Peteet's (2008) stealing time marks the hours of the day that are lost to laboring in order to labor, a modality of extraction that attempts to inscribe limits, time-itself works on the level of the sensorium, comporting corporeality, soliciting psychic scrambling of what movement is, what mobility is, what the relation of space to movement to time is.

Time-itself is simultaneously the "body" or the form of matter that is laboring and also an affective commodity produced not only by the occupied but also by the occupation itself and therefore part of the profit—not so much the pecuniary aspect but the valuation—of the occupation. Time-itself, then, is "generalized matter" that does not hew to the "bounded-ness of the human body" or the "body-as-organism" that is a "closed system" (Clough et al. 2007: 65, 62). Thus, labor power is located not only in the laboring body but also in multiple scales of matter, one of which is affect-itself, differentiated within the body as "perceptive states, drives, and desires" (Franklin 2015: 19) that inform not the individual but the dividual. In other words—and this is a supposition—perhaps the most valuable extraction from each individual Palestinian body is not labor nor even labor time but time-itself—indeed, the time of the dividual. The production of dividuals is a metric-generating mode that does not so much dissemble the body or assume that its parts form a composite as it isolates subindividual and paraindividual capacities. Dividualization is one of the more oblique forms—that is to say, one less driven by spectacular maiming—of the valuation of (Palestinian) life.

These disruptions in the surety of claims about immaterial labor, affective labor, the laboring body, and "living labor" are indeed a reminder, as the recent work of Neferti X. M. Tadiar (2012) so potently demonstrates, that "life itself," another concept under duress in Palestine (but hardly only in Palestine), is at best unevenly valorized and that the modality of value extraction is tactical, unstable, and shifting. Theories of immaterial labor direct us to how the distinction between work and nonwork time, that is, between home and the office, is increasingly blurred through technologies and social medias that solicit our presence continuously. But these theories presume such a divide between labor and nonlabor time exists in the first place, reflecting a geopolitical exceptionalism that does not comprehend the forms of collective punishment enacted in withholding connectivity, simultaneity, and temporal legibility and legitimacy. As Gayatri Chakravorty Spivak (1985) reminded us decades ago in her thunderous piece "Scattered Speculations on the Question of Value," the concept of immaterial labor is predicated on submerged and underacknowledged stratifications, ones that not only unsettle the assumed privilege of "having a work day" but also map the relations between the information technology worker and those populations consigned to sanding down the waste of discarded motherboards. Yes, in Palestine as in so many other places, one is never not at work—but not quite in the way that theories of immaterial labor propose.

A Mass of Entanglements

Slow life, or positioning the disenfranchised as "slow," is an old technology of colonial rule and an older still designation of animacy, such that, for example, bodies with cognitive disabilities are often relegated to the inhuman (Chen 2012; Pickens 2019). Slowness, however, is not always inevitably captured as sheer debilitation. While a variety of "slow" movements have cropped up in recent decades to counter and shelter from the sheer force of speed in modernity, we learn less from those who have the privilege of taking it easy and more from the innovations of subaltern populations. In Palestine, what mobility is and how it is valued are always shifting. In his 2012 film titled *Infiltrators*, Jarrar focuses on the porosity of the apartheid wall. Images show Palestinians scaling certain junctures of the cement structure at night, at risk of being apprehended, even shot. The most moving scenes are of relatives meeting and passing notes and photos through very small gaps and crevices sought out in the fraught architecture of the wall. The tenderness of these interactions, listening for clues that signal presence on the other side, the carefully folded paper gingerly inserted into a gap, in hopes that it reaches its recipient—these intimacies reflect the collectivization of slow life (see also Piepzna-Samarasinha 2018). The value of connectivity is beyond the totalization of the occupation, and the spectrum of mobility disabilities inspires radically different (different from global North human rights models) notions of access, accommodation, and even ableism. An access map, commonly crowd-sourced, takes on a different valence in Palestine, where border crossings, checkpoints, and banned highways create the most obstacles to mobility for most of the population. Mental diagrams are commonly created and continually revised by taxi and bus drivers registering in real time, via social media, personal communications, and news on the radio, openings and closures of roads, delays at checkpoints, and the sites of violent encounters with Israeli forces and settlers. Navigations of mobility are inseparable from political mobilizations, in this case public transport as a form of resistant mobilization (see Griffen 2015; Sadik 2011). In the 1960s, 1970s, and 1980s the Gazan short story, developed as craft and as export, was produced in the unlikely confines of the siege. Handwritten and "smuggled out of the strip" for typing and, ideally, publication, the Gazan short story reflects the innovation of form that emerges not from the European writerly emphasis on time and solitude but from the conviviality of blockade and dense proximity (Abu Saif 2014: ix–x).

Slowness in these and many other instances indexes neither the foreclosure of modernity nor the debilitation of or obstacles to connection. Attending to the collectivization of temporalities neither overdetermines the saturation of technologies of temporal control nor partakes in exhortations of resiliency and survivorship that might then subsume questions of decolonization and justice. Presuming a totalizing, inescapable reach of modalities of control societies does the work of control; it is not politically useful to hyperbolize how and what control can control nor to sanguinely elevate that which is perceived to escape control. Pivoting attention from collective punishment toward the potential solidarities across differential mobilities is one such important example. Slow life beyond and below capture can be fruitfully thought of as a carapace of movement, stillness, and encounter with the quotidian rhythms of bodily comportment, capacity, and debility that shape and reshape the living of time. That is, slow life might encompass how time is spent not only in relation to the administrative units of carceral capitalism but affectively as "a mass of entanglements" (Barad 2018) wherein we find potentialities for considering how time is relived and remade.

Notes

1   For video of this piece, see Open Source Gallery Facebook Page, www.facebook.com /watch/live/?v=2212514832369678&ref=watch_permalink.

2   The relationship of injury to death has been, during many periods of the occupation, an explicitly tactical one (Andoni and Tolan 2001; Barrow-Friedman 2016; Blumenthal 2014; Hass 2016; Helweg-Larsen et al. 2004; Reinhart 2002). I draw together this archive of maiming from the following human rights organizations: Al-Haq, Amnesty International, the Al-Mezan Center for Human Rights, Doctors without Borders, the Palestinian Red Crescent Society, the United Nations, the BADIL Resource Center for Palestinian Residency and Refugee Rights, the Gaza Community Mental Health Program, the UN Relief and Works Agency, the Palestine Human Rights Information Center, the West Bank Database Project, Harvard University's FXB Center for Health and Human Rights, and Physicians for Human Rights.

3   My observations are based on research in the West Bank during the summer of 2018. I visited the health, rehabilitation, and disability centers of nine refugee camps and spoke with health practitioners and workers in nongovernmental organizations.

4   Although there are various journalistic articles, medical assessments, and reports from nongovernmental organizations (Hardigan 2016), documentation of the targeting of disabled Palestinians remains to be collected.

5   For scholarship generated by medical practitioners examining the general overall deteriorating health conditions of Palestinians in the West Bank and Gaza, see Graff 1993, Qato 2004, and Qlalweh, Duraidi, and Bronnum-Hansen 2012. This work emphasizes collective population debilitation that presents serious challenges to any generic notion of able-bodiedness but likewise complicates disability as a category of either diagnosis or identity.

6   As another example of this diminished difference, public health experts in Palestine claim that percentages of children diagnosed with mental illness have been inflated for several decades. While a wide population of youth present with symptoms of post-traumatic stress disorder, these symptoms are embedded in a broader traumascape of the occupation rather than isolated events of trauma that lead to medicalization. The overdiagnosis of post-traumatic stress disorder and mental illnesses—and thus a pathologization of the social suffering of occupied people—therefore eclipses the political problem of the occupation. Addressing the effects of settler colonialism through a redistribution of the disabled/nondisabled binary, thereby opening up new populations for medical treatment, collapses the terrain of generalized debilitation experienced by an occupied population into the more legible, and thus from a humanitarian and rights-based perspective more "manageable," binarization of ability and disability (Rabaia, Saleh, and Giacaman 2014).

7   Bethlehem Arab Society for Rehabilitation 2010; Bethlehem Arab Society for Rehabilitation, interview by the author, January 10 2016, Bethlehem, Palestine.

8   Accelerationism claims that the demise of capitalism can be accelerated through its own acceleration, as a force or momentum that eventually outruns itself, hoodwinks its own logic, in essence a homeopathic or pharmakon poison-is-the-cure type of making it worse so that it gets better, a trading in of present justice for future utopia. Palestine is indeed one place where we can see capitalism accelerating, not necessarily through

speed but through the withholding of speed as a primary quality enabling capacitation within and alongside capitalism. As the purported opposite of speed, slowness not only is an anathema to capitalism but also exemplifies an aspect of capitalism at its most accelerated. Its withholding deepens the exploitative capacities of capitalism due to its stranglehold on temporality. Relatedly, in the imaginary of the accelerationists, the unevenness of lived acceleration seems unthought. The ramifications of Palestine as the location of sacrifice for the greater global good merely restates the necessity of extreme exploitation often located "elsewhere" as the laboratory for the constant mangling of speed, pace, and duration.

References

Abu Nahleh, Lamis. 2009. "Gender and Disabilities: Marginal Issues in Palestinian Development and Rights Initiatives." *This Week in Palestine*, September 18. palestine-family.net/gender-and-disabilities-in-palestine/.

Abu Saif, Atef. 2014. Introduction to *The Book of Gaza: A City in Short Fiction*. London: Comma Press.

Abu Salim, Jehad. 2016. "From Fence to Fence: Gaza's Story in Its Own Words." In *Gaza as Metaphor*, edited by Helga Tawil-Souri and Dina Matar, 83–93. London: Hurst and Company.

Abu-Sitta, Ghassan, and Jasbir Puar. 2019. "Israel Is Trying to Maim Gaza Palestinians into Silence." *Al-Jazeera*, March 31. www.aljazeera.com/indepth/opinion/israel-maim-gazans-silence-190326085728986.html.

Abu-Sitta, Ghassan, Jehan Bseiso, Jasbir K. Puar, Francesco Sebregondi, and Helga Tawil Souri. 2020. "Forum on Biospheres of War: A Discussion on the Rights of Future Generations." *Jadaliyya*, March 30. www.jadaliyya.com/Details/40752.

Al Qaddi, Muthanna. 2003. "Disabled Palestinians Struggling for Their Rights." *Palestine Report* 10, no. 23. www.palestinereport.ps/article.php?article=190.

Andoni, Lamis, and Sandy Tolan. 2001. "Shoot to Maim." *Village Voice*, February 20. www.villagevoice.com/2001/02/20/shoot-to-maim/.

Barad, Karen. 2018. "Undoing the Future." Lecture presented at Barnard University, March 19. bcrw.barnard.edu/videos/karen-barad-undoing-the-future/.

Barrows-Friedman, Nora. 2016. "Israeli Captain: 'I Will Make You All Disabled.'" *Electronic Intifada*, September 1. electronicintifada.net/content/israeli-captain-i-will-make-you-all-disabled/17821.

Ben-Moshe, Liat, and Sumi Colligan, eds. 2007. "The State of Disability in Israel/Palestine." *Disability Studies Quarterly* 27, no. 4. dsq-sds.org/article/view/41/41.

Berda, Yael. 2017. *Living Emergency: Israel's Permit Regime in the Occupied West Bank*. Stanford, CA: Stanford University Press.

Bethlehem Arab Society for Rehabilitation. 2010. *Annual Report 2010*. basr.org/eng/?s=annual+report.

Bhungalia, Lisa. 2019. "Response to Jasbir Puar's Lecture 'Slow Life.'" Presented at the American Association of Geography annual meeting, Washington, DC.

Blumenthal, Max. 2014. "Evidence Emerges of 'Shoot to Cripple' Policy in the Occupied West Bank." *Alternet*, August 8. alternet.org/2014/08/evidence-emerges-israeli-shoot-cripple-policy-occupied-west-bank/.

Chen, Mel. 2012. *Animacies: Biopolitics, Racial Mattering, and Queer Affect.* Durham, NC: Duke University Press.

Clough, Patricia, Greg Goldberg, Rachel Schiff, Aaron Weeks, and Craig Willse. 2007. "Notes Towards a Theory of Affect-Itself." *Ephemera* 7: 60–77.

Eide, Arne H. 2006. "Impact of Community-Based Rehabilitation Programmes: The Case of Palestine." *Scandinavian Journal of Disability Research* 8, no. 4: 199–210. doi.org /10.1080/15017410500466750

Erakat, Noura. 2019. *Justice for Some: Law and the Question of Palestine.* Stanford, CA: Stanford University Press.

Feldman, Ilana. 2016. "Gaza: Isolation." In *Gaza as Metaphor*, edited by Helga Tawil-Souri and Dina Matar. London: Hurst.

Franklin, Seb. 2015. *Control: Digitality as Cultural Logic.* Cambridge, MA: MIT Press.

Graff, James A. 1993. "Crippling a People: Palestinian Children and Israeli State Violence." *Alif: Journal of Comparative Poetics* 13: 46–63.

Griffen, Maryam S. 2015. "Freedom Rides in Palestine: Racial Segregation and Grassroots Politics on the Bus." *Race and Class* 56, no. 4: 73–84. doi.org/10.1177/0306396814567410.

Haddad, Toufic. 2016. *Palestine Ltd.: Neoliberalism and Nationalism in the Occupied Territory.* London: Taurus.

Hammami, Rema. 2015. "On (Not) Suffering at the Checkpoint: Palestinian Narrative Strategies of Surviving Israel's Carceral Geography." *borderlands* 14, no. 1: 1–17.

Hardigan, Richard. 2016. "Palestinians with Disabilities Are Not Immune from Israeli Violence." *Mondoweiss*, September 12. mondoweiss.net/2016/09/palestinians-disabilities -violence/.

Hass, Amira. 2016. "Is the IDF Conducting a Kneecapping Campaign in the West Bank?" *Haaretz*, August 27.

Helweg-Larsen, Karin, Ashraf Hasan Abdel-Jabbar Al-Qadi, Jalal Al-Jabriri, and Henrik Bronnum-Hansen. 2004. "Systematic Medical Data Collection of Intentional Injuries during Armed Conflicts: A Pilot Study Conducted in West Bank, Palestine." *Scandinavian Journal of Public Health* 32, no 1: 17–23.

Jaffee, Laura Jordan. 2016. "Disrupting Global Disability Frameworks: Settler-Colonialism and the Geopolitics of Disability in Palestine/Israel," *Disability and Society* 31, no. 1: 116–30.

Jarar, Allam. 2009. "Disability in Palestine: Realities and Perspectives." *This Week in Palestine*, no. 137: 28–30.

Jarrar, Khaled. 2012. *Infiltrators.* Streaming video. 52 min. amazon.com/Infiltrators-Khaled -Jarrar/dp/B01EF0KLFO/ref=sr_1_6?dchild=1&keywords=infiltrators&qid=16056 31459&s=movies-tv&sr=1-6.

Khalidi, Rashid. 2018. "Rashid Khalidi: The Israeli Security Establishment Is Terrified of a Nonviolent Palestinian Movement." *Democracy Now*, April 19. democracynow.org/2018 /4/19/rashid_khalidi_the_israeli_security_establishment.

Kotef, Hagar. 2015. *Movement and the Ordering of Freedom: On Liberal Governances of Mobility.* Durham, NC: Duke University Press.

Lagerquist, Peter. 2008. "In the Labyrinth of Solitude: Time, Violence, and the Eternal Frontier." *Middle East Research and Information Project* 248. merip.org/2008/09/in-the -labyrinth-of-solitude/.

Langan, Celeste. 2001. "Mobility Disability." *Public Culture* 33, no. 3: 459–84.

Li, Darryl. 2016. "Gaza at the Frontiers of Zionism." In *Gaza as Metaphor*, edited by Helga Tawil-Souri and Dina Matar, 187–94. London: Hurst.

Massumi, Brian. 1990. *Expressionism in Philosophy: Spinoza*. Translated by Martin Joughin. Brooklyn, NY: Zone.

Maza, Cristina. 2017. "Israel Troops Shot Dead a Wheelchair-Bound Palestinian Protesting Trump's Jerusalem Capital Move." *Newsweek*, December 15. newsweek.com/man -wheelchair-killed-palestine-protesting-trumps-jerusalem-announcement-750019.

Nixon, Rob. 2013. *Slow Violence and the Environmentalism of the Poor*. Cambridge, MA: Harvard University Press.

Ophir, Adi, Michal Givoni, and Sari Hanafi. 2009. *The Power of Inclusive Exclusion: Anatomy of Israeli Rule in the Occupied Palestinian Territories*. New York: Zone Books.

Palestinian Central Bureau of Statistics and Ministry of Social Affairs. 2011. *Disability Survey, 2011: Press Conference Report*. June. www.pcbs.gov.ps/Portals/_pcbs/PressRelease /disability_e2011.pdf.

Peteet, Julie. 2008. "Stealing Time." *Middle East Research and Information Project*, no. 248. merip.org/2008/09/stealing-time/.

Pickens, Therí Alyce. 2019. *Mad Blackness :: Black Madness*. Durham, NC: Duke University Press.

Piepzna-Samarasinha, Leah Lakshmi. 2018. *Care Work: Dreaming Disability Justice*. New York: Arsenal Pulp Press.

Povinelli, Beth. 2016. *Geontologies*. Durham, NC: Duke University Press.

Puar, Jasbir. 2017. *The Right to Maim: Debility, Capacity, Disability*. Durham, NC: Duke University Press.

Qato, Dima. 2004. "The Politics of Deteriorating Health: The Case of Palestine." *International Journal of Health Services* 34, no. 2: 341–64.

Qlalweh, Kahled, Mohammed Duraidi, and Henrik Bronnum-Hansen. 2012. "Health Expectancy in the Occupied Palestinian Territory: Estimates from the Gaza Strip and the West Bank: Based on Surveys from 2006 to 2010." *bmj Open* 2, no. 6: 1–6.

Rabaia, Yoke, Mahasin F. Saleh, and Rita Giacaman. 2014. "Sick or Sad? Supporting Palestinian Children Living in Conditions of Chronic Political Violence." *Children and Society* 28: 172–81.

Rai, Amit. 2019. *Jugaad Time: Ecologies of Everyday Hacking in India*. Durham, NC: Duke University Press.

Reinhart, Tanya. 2002. *Israel/Palestine: How to End the War of 1948*. New York: Seven Stories.

Rousseau, Jean-Jacques. (1762) 1973. *The Social Contract; and Discourses*. Translated by G. D. H. Cole. London: Everyman's Library.

Roy, Sara. 1999. "De-development Revisited: Palestinian Economy and Society since Oslo." *Journal of Palestine Studies* 28, no. 3: 64–82.

Sadik, Noreen. 2011. "Introducing the Palestinian Freedom Riders." *New Internationalist*, November 18. newint.org/features/web-exclusive/2011/11/18/palestinian-freedom-riders -israel.

Schuller, Kyla. 2018. *The Biopolitics of Feeling: Race, Sex, and Science in the Nineteenth Century*. Durham, NC: Duke University Press.

Seikaly, Sherene. 2016. "Gaza as Archive." In *Gaza as Metaphor*, edited by Helga Tawil-Souri and Dina Matar, 225–31. London: Hurst.

Singh, Nikhil Pal. 2014. "The Whiteness of Police." *American Quarterly* 66, no. 4: 1091–99.

Spivak, Gayatri Chakravorty. 1985. "Scattered Speculations on the Question of Value." *Diacritics* 15, no. 4: 73–93.

Tadiar, Neferti X. M. 2012. "Life-Times in Fate Playing," *South Atlantic Quarterly* 111, no. 4: 783–802.

Tawil-Souri, Helga. 2011. "Qalandia Checkpoint as Space and Nonplace." *Space and Culture* 14, no. 1: 4–26.

Tawil-Souri, Helga. 2012. "Uneven Borders, Coloured (Im)mobilities: ID Cards in Palestine/Israel." *Geopolitics* 17, no. 1: 153–76.

Valencia, Sayek. 2018. *Gore Capitalism*. Cambridge, MA: MIT Press.

Vora, Kalindi. 2015. *Life Support: Biocapital and the New History of Outsourced Labor*. Minneapolis: University of Minnesota Press.

Wang, Jackie. 2018. *Carceral Capitalism*. Cambridge, MA: MIT Press.

Weber, Jasmine. 2018. "Artist Critiques Capitalism and War, Sells Vials of His Blood on Wall Street." *Hyperallergic*, October 12. hyperallergic.com/465528/artist-critiques-capitalism-and-war-sells-vials-of-his-blood-on-wall-street/.

Weizman, Eyal. 2002. "The Politics of Verticality." *OpenDemocracy*, April 24. www.opendemocracy.net/en/article_801jsp/.

Weizman, Eyal. 2012. *The Least of All Possible Evils: Humanitarian Violence from Arendt to Gaza*. New York: Verso.

Weizman, Eyal. 2017. "Architecture of Modulation: Resistance as Differential Vision." In *Manifestos for World Thought*, edited by Lucian Stone and Jason Bahbak Mohaghegh, 179–90. London: Rowman and Littlefield.

Alison Kafer

After Crip, Crip Afters

*N*ote *to readers:* In an attempt to mark crip time through form, this essay proceeds across two sets of numbers: the list that comprises the body of the text and the list of endnotes that accompany it. Readers may choose to read the two parts concurrently, following each endnote as it appears, or read them consecutively, so that the endnotes function as a kind of afterword. Charting the poly-rhythmic movement of crip time, the essay alternates between text and empty space.[1]

1.

I remain deeply attached to *crip*—as a word, an orientation, an affiliation, a feeling. I like the way it dragged me into a group I didn't know existed, and wasn't sure I wanted to join, but needed, desperately.

    About twenty years ago, an older disabled dyke— her words—rolled up next to me, from across a crowded room, and said, "I can always spot another queer crip." And suddenly I was exactly that, another queer crip.[2]

2.

And yet, the fact that I love the feel of the word across my skin, the sound of it on your tongue, doesn't change the fact that the word has edges and edges bind.

The South Atlantic Quarterly 120:2, April 2021
DOI 10.1215/00382876-8916158　© 2021 Duke University Press

3.

A few weeks ago, I was giving a talk only to be interrupted almost immediately by an audience member wanting to know why I was using the word. That word. I suddenly found myself without a good answer.

Or, uncertain that it was my question to answer.

4.

In questioning what comes after crip, or what might constitute crip afters, I am wondering what it means that I am still after crip, still wanting it, still full of desire.[3] But wondering, too, if it's time to get over crip, to think and feel and imagine beyond its bounds.

Or does that very phrasing render crip static, immobile, more noun than verb? Am I denying crip (its) expansiveness, narrowing the scope of crip (in) time?[4]

5.

What does *crip* require? What does it ask of me, of you, of us? In these times, in these crip times, what does it mean to be attached to crip? And what might such attachments make possible?[5]

Attachment as affiliation, as relationality, as solidarity. Disability not through identity but relation.[6]

6.

As much as I may say that *crip* is an umbrella term that speaks to more than mobility impairments or physical disabilities, I continue to find myself thinking only about these kinds of conditions but not those, to imagine futures for certain bodyminds but not others, to allow norms of capacity, achievement, productivity, and independence to shape the limits of my politics.

What comes after this awareness?

7.

How long does it take to foreclose on possibilities, to refuse connection, to deny relation? How do my failures to imagine others as crip restrict the coalitions to come?

8.

I am starting to worry that, too often, what comes after crip is a claim to innocence. In refusing the ableist stance that people are to blame for their illnesses and impairments—eating too much, eating too little; failing to exercise, failing to stretch; holding on too tightly, letting go too easily; creating stress, imagining pain; in the wrong places at the wrong times, not trying to improve—are we too easily making claims to innocence?[7]

Are we dismantling the structure of blame, or simply leaving it intact for others?[8]

9.

And what if we *are* to blame for our illnesses or disabilities or pains or incapacities? Does that make us less worthy of care?

Or what if blame resides not in us, but in those we love? Does that relation exceed the boundaries of crip, or crip politics, or crip community?

10.

I read old writing where I remember running. Is that memory only about marking loss, or am I somehow believing that that loss matters more because I used to run? Am I marking loss, or undeservedness?

I am reminded of all the disability memoirs, the illness narratives, in which the protagonist informs the reader of their former vitality and able-bodiedness and capacity, as if the tragedy of their condition is made evident only in contrast to what came before (as if tragedies, by definition, befall only those who don't deserve them). Disability studies has long challenged these narratives for their focus on overcoming, on the good work that good patients do to rehabilitate into good citizens after their tragic injuries or illnesses or catastrophes. But perhaps we need to pay as much attention to the way the *before* is narrated in these stories as to the *after*. Aren't these stories all ways of insisting that one's disability be read a certain way, a more positive way, because of what came before, because of who one was before?

Or because of how one was injured?

11.

How do these kinds of stories rely on the straightness of linear time, the belief that becoming disabled is a single moment, tangible, identifiable, turning life into a solid, singular, static before-and-after? Can we tell crip tales, crip time tales, with multiple befores and afters, proliferating befores and afters, all making more crip presents possible?[9]

12.

Last year I fell seriously ill, a mystery infection raging in my stump. Doctors, nurses, physician assistants all reminded me that I need to take better care of my diabetes, that if I'm not careful they'll have to reamputate. But I don't have diabetes, I would respond, my amputations aren't from diabetes, my voice rising with each repetition of the statement. How much of my response was about wanting to make sure the doctors were seeing me, and how much was about making sure they were seeing my innocence?

So many foreclosures in those denials.

13.

I want to remember sitting in the waiting room, waiting in the examination room, examining those around me, and finding relation.[10] Instead, I recover a scared desperation, frantic to be seen.

Every one of us should be getting all the care we need, regardless of how we came to be here. The language of desert is rife with disavowals. I know this. That doesn't stop the voice in my head from wanting Dr.——— to see me first, longest, most. From thinking I deserve it.

14.

Not rupture. Flow.

Crip simultaneity, crip concurrence.

15.

Many disabled people refer to those without disabilities as TABs, or "temporarily able-bodied." The term is pedagogical: learn from its use. Intended to shake folks loose from their assumptions that bodies don't change, the use of *temporarily* reminds us all that the abilities we take for granted today may disappear tomorrow, perhaps temporarily, perhaps not.

Although occasionally spoken with an edge, even a snarl, the term is often perversely, queerly, welcoming: "We crips are here for you when you're ready."

16.

Several years ago I wrote an essay in which I argued that disability studies must pay more attention to the "causes of disablement or debilitation," in large part because "these causes are often traumatic sites of violence, both individual and structural, both singular and chronic" (Kafer 2016: 6). Some of the most exciting work in the field is pursuing exactly these questions, questions that require more complicated examinations of disability pride and crip culture and desire. How are people becoming disabled, debilitated, run down, worn out by violence both fast and slow: capitalist exploitation, environmental racism, war, state violence, policing, infrastructural neglect, gender violence, denial of health care? And under such conditions, conditions that do not fall equally, what can it possibly mean to desire disability?[11]

17.

One way the field has responded to such queries, to the call to reckon with the fact that many become disabled through violence, is to suggest that some ways of becoming disabled are wrong: "There's nothing wrong with being disabled but there might be something wrong with how people become disabled." Or, as I read recently, by naming some disabilities—namely, those caused by "unethical practices" such as environmental racism and infrastructural neglect—as "unjust disabilities."

18.

But do such moves then position other disabilities as "just"? And are we then moving those conditions, whatever they are, beyond the realm of politics? To what extent do all these questions and positionings and namings continue the ableist move of presuming that disability matters only as it happens, and whatever comes next—living in the aftermath—is irrelevant?[12]

Too often *those* sites—the aftermath—are also sites of "unethical practices," of violence both fast and slow.

19.

Or maybe there *are* wrong ways to become disabled, but we can't presume to know which are (or aren't) those ways, which disabilities are (or aren't) caused by injustice. Trauma, violence, oppression, dispossession all leave long trails, and what might appear on the surface to be "mere" heart attacks or depression or premature labor may all have their links to histories and generations of unethical practices.[13]

20.

How do we witness and resist the injustices that cause disability without falling back on notions of innocence, notions that then allow us to blame others for their disabilities or to cast those others as beyond the reach of politics? Can we name injustice without disavowing those in its wake, using them only to tell stories, stories that too often leave them behind?[14]

21.

How have we learned to feel differently about different disabilities, about different people with disabilities, based on such notions of innocence or blame?

I remember an older white woman in an airport, kind, open, and friendly, chatting warmly with me for quite some time. After she said something about my being injured in action, after I corrected her assumption that I was a vet, she literally turned her body away from me, angry that she had cultivated such good feelings for an undeserving cripple.

22.

I attended a disability studies talk on campus yesterday, given by a disabled person, in which the first question was the following: "Can you talk about the psychological effects of realizing that you were going to have to live the rest of your life like this?"

Which is worse, the "this" or the "rest of your life"?

23.

I am trying to understand *crip time*—like *crip kin*, like *crip affiliation*, like all the other terms moving through my brain—as potential tools for thinking otherwise, as tools for mobilizing against ableism, white supremacy, patriarchy.[15]

But such moves will require us to insist on crip time's multiple temporalities, *slowness* already being rapidly devoured by capitalism, whiteness, and the neoliberal university's attention to "self-care."

24.

I want to think more about tempo, about speed, about moving quickly.[16] I see you in my mind's eye, whipping through city streets in your wheelchair, speeding past so that you're gone before people's ableist, racist comments land in your ear.

25.

But I'm thinking, too, of slowness. Of how easily *crip time* has been reduced to, narrowed to, *more time*—more time as a way of mobilizing disabled people into productivity rather than transforming systems; more time as a way of increasing productivity rather than refusing such values altogether; offering extra time on tests rather than doing away with timed tests; allowing us to work on our own time as long as the same amount of work gets done.[17]

Maybe we should think less of what crip time is and more of what crip time does, thinking beyond specific speeds, toward as yet unimagined imaginaries. What are the temporalities that unfold beyond, away from, askance of productivity, capacity, self-sufficiency, independence, achievement?[18]

26.

More time. More time does nothing for those students sitting in underresourced and oversurveilled schools, nothing for those warehoused in institutions. Who wants more time in toxic environments?

Slow time. School days slowed by surveillance, punishment, administrative violence; school days slowed in all kinds of ways, none of them about supporting students or their families.[19]

27.

More time, slowing time, as punishment. Think, here, of the time of waiting: for treatment, for diagnosis, for recognition; for the ambulance to arrive, for the doctor to see you; for asylum, for documentation, for release. Only some folks—white folks, well-resourced folks, folks living outside of institutions—wait with a real expectation that the treatment they want is coming and coming soon.[20]

28.

For many the waiting is not for treatment but for (additional) injury, for (more) trauma, for (quicker or slower) death—waiting for the disability that is coming, unfolding, already under way. Isn't this, too, a kind of crip time? The time of waiting to become crippled, the time of slowly wearing down as one waits for even more violence to come?

"Temporarily able-bodied" not as defiant refusal of the myth of ability but as threat, as looming reminder, as the weight of everyday life.[21]

29.

For whom is "living with" seen as more tragic than "dying of"? For whom do we make "living with" punishment?[22]

How long does it take to disavow?

30.

Count, account for, all the ways disability is mobilized to justify the death and disablement of others: victims of distant crimes joining parole board hearings to insist that release never comes, politicians referencing wartime casualties as rationale for continued attack on civilians no longer innocent but mere collateral damage.

These calls for justice on behalf of the disabled have nothing to do with disability justice. There is no anti-ableist politics at work here. Quite the contrary: mobilize ableist fears of living like "this" for "the rest of your life" to justify doing harm to others. Then turn around, away, from the disability left in your wake. There is no after here.

31.

I am writing these lines, thinking these thoughts, feeling these pulls in a country in which innocence is posed against punishment. If injury befalls the innocent, then someone must be punished; if someone is being punished, they must not be innocent. What does it mean, then, to insist on the innocence of the disabled? To require blamelessness as a condition of care?

I am wondering, in other words, that if claims to innocence are what come after crip, then how closely does punishment follow?

And for whom?[23]

32.

Is it possible to treat the coexistence of *crips* as in cripples with *Crips* as in gang members with something other than distancing and disavowal? How does my thinking about crip community shift if I stop thinking of these histories as fully separate (disability activists reclaimed the word over here, while gang members used the term over there, two discrete groups working simultaneously in isolation) and instead recognize those histories as mutually informative? Might both terms gesture to the result of debilitation? To the identities, communities, cohorts, relations made possible (made impossible) during, after, and through debilitation?[24]

Or, how has insisting on separations between these terms been about preserving innocence for some by pushing violence on others, seeing Crips only as cripplers, never as crippled? Or, more, seeing crips only as crippled, never as cripplers?[25]

33.

How long does it take to disavow?

34.

I was initially pulled into thinking about crip afters because I was trying to think my way out of aftermath, to think beyond the *post* in post-traumatic stress disorder. Which traumas are erased in assuming that everyone has lived *pre*trauma life, that distress comes to find you only after? Or in the assumption that one can move up and away from trauma, leaving it behind in time and space, safely nestled in the *post*?

Where is the present in post-traumatic stress disorder?

35.

What is the crip time of remembering? Or the temporality of preparing to remember? How does one take steps now to get ready for the future moment when one will delve into the past? Recovery time is ongoing, the work is never done.[26]

36.

Aftermath as what happens once the crisis ends, after the epidemic passes. But each of these—crisis, epidemic, aftermath, temporalities all—mobilize (only) particular kinds of responses.

37.

What comes after trauma? Can crip? Or does crip as radicalized stance, as community affiliation, feel less available, less useful, less hopeful to those disabled through violence?

Closer: My own disabilities are the result of violence—how am I to balance crip with an awareness that I became disabled alongside others who didn't survive, or others for whom a disability identity has felt neither resistant nor empowering?

38.

Is my telling you this a claim to innocence?

39.

I am yearning for ways to theorize, name, witness disability as extraordinary, as anomaly, as catastrophe, while recognizing and remembering disability as endemic, as daily, as part and parcel of living under capitalist white supremacy. For ways to notice that all of these, some of these, none of these are true for different communities and peoples and populations.

I am searching for ways to name disability caused by trauma, trauma caused by disability, disability caused by disability and trauma by trauma, without flattening out different scales of violence or dispossession or alienation.

And I want all of these to coexist—not smoothly, not easily, not without friction or contention—with the possibility, the hope, of and for crip futures.

40.

I've been asked to speak about crip ritual, about the theoretical and political possibilities of imagining crip practice, crip markers, crip ceremony. Not too long after I became disabled I met another young crip; she, too, had become disabled in her early twenties. She marked the day each year with a party, a ritual marking her transition into a different world, a celebration of survival and shape-shifting.

I have yet to figure out a ritual that makes sense for all three of us, the me here now, the me from back then, the you who died.

41.

There are more than three in this scenario.

42.

What is the temporality of survivor guilt? Where does it fit in crip time? Is survivor guilt the only relation imaginable?[27]

What are the bounds around *survivor* in these questions?

43.

Remember: what came before violence is often other violence. And what comes before disability is often other disabilities. Release the assumption—one borne of ableism, white innocence, a denial of violence across generations—that the time before crip is one without disability.

Notes

I am grateful to Beth Freeman and Ellen Samuels for creating this space and supporting me in it; I could not have written this piece if not for them. Conversations with Jina Kim, Nirmala Erevelles, Lisa Armstrong, and all the participants in the Feminist and Queer Disability Studies seminar at Smith College informed this essay, and I am grateful for their insights. Thanks to my brilliant FDP colleagues in the Center for Women's and Gender Studies at the University of Texas for engaging with this work, especially Grayson Hunt, Lisa Moore, Christen Smith, Ashley Coleman Taylor, Pavithra Vasudevan, and Michelle Velasquez-Potts. For reading drafts and talking through ideas, deep gratitude to Susan Burch, Mel Chen, Elaine Craddock, Eunjung Kim, Travis Chi Wing Lau, Julie Avril Minich, Dana Newlove, Alexis Riley, and Hershini Young. This piece is dedicated to Stacey Milbern (1987–2020).

1   Although I have since come to recognize the various kinds of work this kind of writing can do (allowing multiple entryways into a text, subverting linear argumentation in favor of a more recursive reflection, positioning no one idea as more important or more central than another, and making space for reading in different time scales and rhythms), I began writing in this way because I found myself unable to write otherwise. Although this piece is not intended as a response to Ellen Samuels's (2017) moving essay "Six Ways of Looking at Crip Time"—I am not offering, in other words, "Forty-Three Ways of Looking at Crip Time"—my thinking time through numbers was undoubtedly influenced by her approach. I have also been informed by the "care scores" created by Park McArthur and Constantina Zavitsanos (2013) and Carolyn Lazard (2016). I am grateful to Travis Chi Wing Lau and Hershini Young for encouraging me to consider the possibilities of crip form; on mad form and method, consult Eales 2016 and Pickens 2019. Thanks to Georgina Kleege for advice on formatting for screen readers.

2   Stacey Milbern describes this kind of invitation as an act of "crip doulaing," or "naming disability as a space we can be born into . . . supported and welcomed by other disabled people" so that we are not "left alone to figure out how to be . . . in this ableist world" (Piepzna-Samarasinha 2018: 241, 240). As I hope this recollection suggests, *crip*, as a world-making term, as a word marking the potential for collective action and radical reimagining, precedes its use in the academy and in scholarly texts. For additional uses of the term rooted in disability activism and culture, consult the ongoing work of organizations such as Sins Invalid (founded by Patty Berne and Leroy Moore) and the Disability Visibility Project (founded by Alice Wong); books such as Eli Clare's *Exile and Pride: Disability, Queerness, and Liberation* (1999) and Corbett O'Toole's *Fading Scars: My Queer Disability History* (2019); blogs such as *Crip Commentary* by Laura Hershey and *Leaving Evidence* by Mia Mingus; and artistic productions such as Chun-Shan (Sandie) Yi's "Crip Couture" and Sky Cubacub's Rebirth Garments. I note these origins not to bifurcate theory and activism but, rather, to note their imbrications; these, too, are sites of crip theory.

3   Elizabeth Freeman (2011: 27) makes a similar move regarding queer theory: "I'm still after queer theory. This might mean: . . . evidencing my usual incapacity to let go once I attach, I'm still after it; I haven't stopped desiring queer theory." In noting this echo, I am both sharing Freeman's queer yearning (I, too, continue to desire queer theory, a desire entangled with my want for crip) and feeling behind.

In continuing to use the language of desire, I am also actively writing against curative imaginaries that presume there can and should be no futures for sick and disabled people; by pairing *after crip* with *crip afters*, I am invoking possibilities for *after crip* other than disappearance or disavowal.

4   The grammar of *crip* has long been central to its theorizing. As evidenced by the sub-heading "Verbs: Queering and Cripping" in her essay on queer crip performance, Carrie Sandahl (2003: 37) accentuates the verb form as central to both terms' work: *to queer* and *to crip* are to put into action a "wry critique of hegemonic norms." Robert McRuer (2018: 21) has recently focused more intently on crip grammar, breaking down the different connotations of *crip* as noun, adjective, and verb: "In the same ways that 'crip' as noun does not simplistically mark a form of existence that can be known in advance, 'crip' as adjective cannot be reduced to a mere descriptor" but rather "remakes the substance in question." Given this special issue's focus on crip time, it seems worth remembering, as Mel Chen (2012: 71, 58) does, that each of these parts of speech "posses[es] radically different temporalities," and attending to their different valences can help us understand how terms such as *queer* and *crip* often "[follow] quite predictable paths of exclusion."

5   McRuer (2018: 30) notes that the term *crip times* "carries both harshness and potentiality," tracing how "crip radicalization . . . is the direct result of an age of austerity." Not all crip times are to be desired.

6   I am thinking here of the way Eunjung Kim (2017) carefully describes her affiliation with disability movements through the language of relationality, proximity, and affect. After "repeatedly finding [her]self on the edges of acceptable norms of physical and mental health," she joined a group of women organizing through "'the receptivity of feelings' (*kamsusŏng*), a disability-centered sensibility about . . . oppressive social and material conditions" that "reflects the efforts to challenge identity-centered epistemology" (22, 23). Sami Schalk (2013: n.p.) traces her identification with crip in similar terms, explaining that "the ways in which [her] fat, black, queer, woman's body/mind/desire/behavior is constantly read and reacted to as non-normative" render her "similarly situated in regard to many vectors of power as people with disabilities." Sins Invalid (n.d.) also highlights attention to power in their mission statement, naming their "deeply felt connections to all communities impacted by the medicalization of their bodies, including trans, gender variant and intersex people, and others whose bodies do not conform to our culture(s)' notions of 'normal' or 'functional.'" Each of these approaches challenges patterns of marginalization that take place through medicalized categories of incapacity, deformity, and deviance, regardless of whether "disability" is present. Reading Kim, Schalk, and Sins Invalid together (and informed by Cohen 1997), we can understand disability in terms of proximity (or lack thereof) to power.

7   I focus here on the personal, individualized rubrics of blame all too familiar to many sick and disabled people, but it is worth remembering in this context that the racialization of illness and disease also occurs through logics of blame. These rhetorics are at work now, with COVID-19 being described by some as the "Chinese virus" and Asian and Asian American people being targeted for racist and xenophobic violence. As the work of scholars such as Nayan Shah (2001) reminds us, however, these patterns of blame have long histories.

8   What I am suggesting, in other words, is that logics of innocence, blame, and punishment are foundational to understandings of disability and illness, often even within dis-

ability studies. What I am hoping is that theories of crip time can be one site for undoing these assumptions, as each of these logics presumes and perpetuates linear time.

Emerging work in disability studies offers careful examinations of these dynamics. Julie Avril Minich (2020) reveals how logics of blame and responsibility are used to justify the denial of health care to Latinx communities, while Lezlie Frye (2016) details how the development of disability rights in the United States drew on rhetorics of deservedness and responsibility that perpetuated anti-Black racism and the disenfranchisement of poor people. These types of projects are essential to the kind of reimagining I am hoping for here.

9   Much of the writing on crip time and the temporalities of illness and disability makes this point, challenging the assumption that disability is an event with a distinct before and after, as well as the presumption that the time of the before elicits only nostalgia and the time of the after only loss and regret. In their work on trans temporalities, Hil Malatino (2019: 644) urges attention to the "interregnum," or "the crucial and transformative moments between past and future, between the regime of what was and the promise of what might be, . . . a kind of nowness that shuttles transversally between different imaginaries of pasts and futures" as "a space of looseness and possibility."

10   Some disability activists, artists, and theorists have recognized the waiting room as a potential site for crip solidarity, community, and humor. In *Notes for the Waiting Room*, Lazard (2016: 10) offers a "Score for Patient Interaction," a seven-step meditation encouraging us to attend to those waiting with us: "Imagine yourself breathing in each person's pain and anxiety with every inhale. Then, with every exhale, imagine yourself breathing healing energy out in their direction . . . for as long as it takes to breed equal compassion for your suffering and the suffering of others, or until you are called in for your appointment."

11   Nirmala Erevelles's (2011: 29) version of this question continues to inspire: "Within what social conditions might we welcome the disability to come, to desire it?" Chen (2014: 175–76) urges us "to weigh questions of value carefully, well beyond a sheer reversal of negativity that can accompany some neoliberalized, otherwise highly capacitated identities of disability." "Perhaps welcoming 'the disability to come,'" as Hershini Young (2012: 401) explains, "entails working toward a long-deferred liberation based on human variation, landscapes that are adaptive, and the recognition of the pleasure and pain of living."

12   My understanding of the need to address afters is deeply indebted to and informed by conversations with Eunjung Kim. One thread running throughout her work is a concern with what comes after the critique of debilitating violence. Too often "disability is frozen in the moment of its creation," Kim (2017: 19) explains, with little regard for what happens to disabled people as they live with disabilities or, even more radically, to "the possibility of life with disability without violence" (234). Erevelles (2019) tracks a related pattern, noting the hypervisibility of disease, disability, and sick and disabled people in accounts of racist and imperialist violence but the invisibility of them in accounts of resistance to that violence. Liat Ben-Moshe (2020), Jina Kim (2020), and Akemi Nishida (2020) are among those charting the possibility that these critiques can coexist; it is possible, as Clare (2017: 60) puts it, to "witness, name, and resist the injustices that reshape and damage all kinds of body-minds . . . while not equating disability with injustice."

13   Analyses of environmental racism and settler colonialism offer potent examples of how violence upon bodies and land reverberates across generations, moving at multiple temporalities to debilitate and disable. Consult, among others, Cook 2005; Vasudevan 2019, 2020; and Voyles 2015.

         Christen A. Smith (2016: 31) uses the concept of sequelae to describe "the gendered, reverberating, deadly effects of state terror that infect the affective communities of the dead." State violence "also kills slowly over time" (38), she explains, as evidenced by the heart attacks, chronic illnesses, and premature deaths experienced by Black women after losing relatives to police killings. Ruth Wilson Gilmore (2007: 247) makes plain this conjunction between death and racism, defining the latter in relation to the former: "Racism, specifically, is the state-sanctioned or extralegal production and exploitation of group-differentiated vulnerability to premature death."

         COVID-19 offers a stark manifestation of these multiple temporalities, as those with "preexisting" or "underlying" health conditions—conditions often produced and exacerbated by the entanglements of racism, sexism, classism, xenophobia, homophobia, and transphobia—are falling ill with more frequency and more morbidity than those without those conditions.

14   Eve Tuck (2009) and Nirmala Erevelles (2019) have, in different ways, reflected critically on both the effect and affect of what Tuck calls "damage-centered research" (409).

15   Briefly, theories of crip time address how illness, disease, and disability are conceptualized in terms of time, affect one's experiences of time, and render adherence to normative expectations of time impossible, for example, timeliness, productivity, longevity, and development, or what Elizabeth Freeman (2010) calls "chrononormativity." But theories of crip time also highlight how people are refusing and resisting those very expectations, thereby creating new affective relations and orientations to time, temporality, and pasts/presents/futures.

16   I am echoing the work of other theorists who question the assumption that delay and slowness are the defining characteristics of nonnormative time, noting that failure is not only about being behind. Kate Thomas (2011: 73) identifies "a tacit consent in queer theory and culture that queer time is predominantly about being late, or seeking lateness," wondering instead "about being early, or proleptic." Margaret Price (2015: 273) raises a similar concern about crip theory, suggesting that fully attending to bodyminds and compulsory abledness (rather than only bodies and compulsory able-bodiedness) will require a reckoning with rapidity: "If you've ever had a 'psychotic break' or been around someone having one, you know that action in such moments tends to unfold *fast*. Crip time is not necessarily time slowed down. Sometimes it is accelerated to a terrifying cadence." Thus, following Malatino (2019: 645), we need "an approach to temporality that understands it as multiply enfolded, rather than merely delayed."

17   As Kemi Adeyemi (2019: 553) notes, drawing on the work of Sarah Sharma, "If slowness provides a moment of breath from the pressures neoliberalism brings to bear on the physical and psychic landscapes through which we circulate, it is often only to gather the reserves to reenter the 'real world' as newly centered and thus more efficient worker-subjects." Lazard (2013: n.p.) offers a similar critique in terms of illness and disability, recovery and rehabilitation: "Biomedical treatment operates on a capitalist understanding of time . . . the idea is to get back to work as quickly as possible. We do not have time to get you better. We have time to make you functional." Each of these theorists gestures

toward what Chen (2014: 174) describes as "the revenge of the clock," wherein not only is any shift in temporal expectation merely temporary, revoked as soon as one "improves," but also *we* place these limits on crip time ourselves, assuming that its purpose is to allow us to "catch up" on our work, rather than to refuse the expectations of work altogether. For an example of crip refusal of productivity, consult Taylor 2004.

18 Samuels (2017) notes, however, that actually inhabiting such temporalities may not feel good; theorizing the transgressive possibilities of crip time and living in crip time may bring different affective responses.

19 Michelle Fine, Andrew Cory Green, and Sonia Sanchez (2018: 55, 51) asked high school students in "racially segregated schools of high poverty, institutional instability, high teacher turnover, substantial use of long-term subs, and heavy investment in police and school safety officers" to map "how time feels in [their] bod[ies] in school." Students describe school days interrupted by lockdowns, immigration raids, and police interventions; more time in such a setting seldom results in more time for learning. As they put it bluntly, "More time in a systematically disinterested and dehumanizing building is no one's idea of justice" (63–64). Subini Ancy Annamma (2017: 67) notes similar patterns in her work with incarcerated disabled girls of color, tracking the accumulation of minutes, hours, days, weeks of instructional time lost to "socializing practices" such as counting off, "where [the girls] said their number out loud to make sure all students were present. Though this seemed like it would be a brief process, it was surprising how long it often took—if girls were not keeping their hands at their sides, not properly deferential, or did anything else that varied from expectations, adults often made them recount."

20 Johanna Hedva (2016: n.p.) highlights "the presumptions upon which" this expectation "relies: that our vulnerability should be seen and honored, and that we should all receive care, quickly and in a way that 'respects the autonomy of the patient.' . . . These presumptions are what we all should have. But we must ask the question of who is allowed to have them. . . . And in whom does society enforce the opposite?" As numerous studies have detailed, Black people in the United States experience vastly inferior medical care compared to white people; they are less likely to receive timely or adequate pain medication, for example, and more likely to be diagnosed at later stages of a disease, often necessitating more drastic interventions. Ambulance response times are slower in poor neighborhoods, meaning longer waits for treatment, and many poor people live in rural areas without nearby (and therefore also temporally close) facilities. For more on ongoing histories of anti-Black racism within medical practice, consult, e.g., Bailey and Mobley 2019; Burch and Joyner 2007; Nelson 2011; Roberts 1999, 2011; and Washington 2006. Minich 2020 and Cook 2005 offer examples of the health inequities faced by Latina/o/x and indigenous populations, respectively.

In these situations, slowness and delay operate as modes of debilitation and death rather than opportunities for crip subversion. Anne Mulhall (2014: n.p.) therefore urges caution about defining the "fragmentation of time" or the "suspended time of the pause" as inherently a mode of radical resistance: for what purpose is time being fragmented or paused, and at whose request? She highlights the asylum process as an example of such violent uses, "where time is explicitly co-opted as an instrument of domination" and "deployments and experiences of waiting and the pause . . . assure the corrosion over time of the subjected person."

21   As Jasbir K. Puar (2017: 12) explains, the assumption that "'we will all be disabled one day, if we live long enough'—the disability to come—is already built on an entitled hope and expectation for a certain longevity." Many people simply do not live long enough to become disabled, let alone to have their debilitation recognized as disability. Aimi Hamraie (2015) argues that this difference is one reason disability studies needs to develop a critical analysis of age and aging.

22   In other words, as Jina Kim (2020: 266) puts it, we need to recognize the ways in which "disability, debility, and illness have emerged as primary arenas for racialized punishment." Emerging work from Michelle Velasquez-Potts (2020) on force-feeding in carceral locations offers a powerful example of "living with" as punishment. Describing the deployment of feeding tubes as instruments of torture, she argues that the US military "invests in the animacy of its target with the goal of endless captivity" (1). Her work resonates with Puar's (2017) work on maiming rather than killing and with Jennifer Terry's (2017) examination of how the disabling violence of war is justified by the attendant developments in medical technologies.

23   Informed by those working in abolitionist movements (e.g., Ben-Moshe 2020; Davis 2003; Gilmore 2007), I am trying to think through the "less visible and yet potentially more dangerous" (Meiners 2016: 12) ways that claims to innocence circulate within much of disability studies and disability activism, as claims to innocence "naturalize jails and unfreedom . . . for too many" (12). Queer theory is similarly concerned with tracing the cultural workings of innocence; as Kathryn Bond Stockton (2009: 5) puts it in her work on the queerness of childhood, "How does innocence . . . cause its own violence?" I am pushing here on the continued linkage of disability with incompetence, maldevelopment, delay, and vulnerability, linkages that often manifest in the infantilization of disabled people. I'm pushing, too, on the racialization of each of these categories, concerned with how innocence is measured through proximity to whiteness. How, then, has the category of disabled, because of its links with these particular dimensions of infantilization, been defined in the United States through ideas about innocence, ideas that then render invisible the disabilities of racialized others? Or, to view through one specific lens, how have Black people been figured as invulnerable to injury through white supremacist logics that bind blackness to criminality rather than innocence? Bailey and Mobley 2019; Erevelles 2011, 2014, 2019; Frye 2016; Mollow 2017; Pickens 2019; Schalk 2018; and Vasudevan 2020 offer historical and contemporary examples of, in Young's (2005: 388) words, the "invalidat[ion of] black injury."

24   In response to questions about *crip* that presumed disability studies had appropriated the term from the Crips gang (a common misperception by those unfamiliar with the field), I have often narrated its origins precisely this way: as a tale of parallel histories. Doing so allows me to underscore the ableism at work in *crippled*, to challenge the antagonism of theory and activism, and to highlight the work of disability activists, artists, and theorists in imagining the word differently. But that narration of mere coincidence elides the imbrications of these histories; as McRuer (2006) notes, experiences and representations of disability feature prominently in explanations for how the gang acquired its name. Erevelles (2014) adds the school-to-prison pipeline and larger patterns of racialized surveillance, removal, and confinement as reasons for a deeper engagement with the relationship between *crip* and *Crips*.

Leroy Moore (Hix 2011: n.p.) offers another thoughtful path here, one that centers the dual experiences of Black disabled people as creative reworkers of language and as targets of policing. For Moore, who calls himself a "Black Kripple," it is important to acknowledge the history of disabled people reclaiming the words *crip* and *crippled* as sites of resistance. Notably, he offers as examples not 1970s white disability rights activists but Black blues musicians who named themselves "Crippled," as well as contemporary hip-hop artists riffing on those same words. He also recognizes the dangers, especially for Black men, of being perceived as gang members, explaining that he spells *crip* with a *K*—*Krip*—because he doesn't "want any mix up with the gang the Crips" (Hix 2011: n.p.). But Moore simultaneously argues for a disability politics attuned to police violence, carceral logics, and economic dispossession; his distancing from the Crips gang is based not in a disavowal of urban geographies but in a commitment to them.

25   I am grateful to a comment from Hershini Young for the framing of *crip* in relation to *crippler.*

26   In her 2018 memoir *Heart Berries*, Terese Marie Mailhot explains that she needed to gather herself before attempting to remember buried trauma. This kind of anticipatory stance—preparing for the violence to come, preparing for the aftermath of historical and ongoing violence—is reminiscent of the work marginalized people must do to navigate the whiteness, patriarchy, heteronormativity, and ableism of normative spaces. It also calls to mind the work people with environmental illnesses are forced to do by the prevalence of chemicals in our environments. These, too, are experiences of crip time.

27   S. Lochlann Jain (2007: 90) raises questions about the discourse of "survivors," noting that it "offers a politics steeped in an identity formation" that encourages a kind of distancing of oneself from unknown others; hoping that one falls within the percentage of those who survive requires other people to occupy the percentage who do not (Jain 2013).

References

Adeyemi, Kemi. 2019. "The Practice of Slowness: Black Queer Women and the Right to the City." *GLQ* 25, no. 4: 545–67.

Annamma, Subini Ancy. 2017. *The Pedagogy of Pathologization*. New York: Routledge.

Bailey, Moya, and Izetta Autumn Mobley. 2019. "Work in the Intersections: A Black Feminist Disability Framework." *Gender and Society* 33, no. 1: 19–40.

Ben-Moshe, Liat. 2020. *Decarcerating Disability*. Minneapolis: University of Minnesota Press.

Burch, Susan, and Hannah Joyner. 2007. *Unspeakable: The Story of Junius Wilson*. Chapel Hill: University of North Carolina Press.

Chen, Mel Y. 2012. *Animacies: Biopolitics, Racial Mattering, and Queer Affect*. Durham, NC: Duke University Press.

Chen, Mel Y. 2014. "Brain Fog: The Race for Cripistemology." *Journal of Literary and Cultural Disability Studies* 8, no. 2: 171–84.

Clare, Eli. 2017. *Brilliant Imperfection: Grappling with Cure*. Durham, NC: Duke University Press.

Cohen, Cathy. 1997. "Punks, Bulldaggers, and Welfare Queens: The Radical Potential of Queer Politics?" *GLQ* 3, no. 4: 437–65.

Cook, Katsi. 2005. Interview by Joyce Follet [transcript of video recording], October 26 and 27. Voices of Feminism Oral History Project, Sophia Smith Collection, Smith College, Northampton, MA.

Davis, Angela Y. 2003. *Are Prisons Obsolete?* New York: Seven Stories Press.

Eales, Lindsay. 2016. "Loose Leaf." *Canadian Journal of Disability Studies* 5, no. 3: 58–76.

Erevelles, Nirmala. 2011. *Disability and Difference in Global Contexts: Enabling a Transformative Body Politic.* New York: Palgrave Macmillan.

Erevelles, Nirmala. 2014. "Crippin' Jim Crow: Disability, Dis-location, and the School-to-Prison Pipeline." In *Disability Incarcerated: Imprisonment and Disability in the United States and Canada,* edited by Liat Ben-Moshe, Chris Chapman, and Allison Carey, 81–99. New York: Palgrave Macmillan.

Erevelles, Nirmala. 2019. "'Scenes of Subjection' in Public Education: Thinking Intersectionally as If Disability Matters." *Educational Studies* 55, no. 6: 592–605.

Fine, Michelle, Andrew Cory Greene, and Sonia Sanchez. 2018. "'Wicked Problems,' 'Flying Monkeys,' and Prec(ar)ious Lives: A Matter of Time?" In *Just Research in Contentious Times: Widening the Methodological Imagination,* by Michelle Fine, 49–70. New York: Teachers College Press.

Freeman, Elizabeth. 2010. *Time Binds: Queer Temporalities, Queer Histories.* Durham, NC: Duke University Press.

Freeman, Elizabeth. 2011. "Still After." In *After Sex? On Writing since Queer Theory,* edited by Janet Halley and Andrew Parker, 27–33. Durham, NC: Duke University Press.

Frye, Lezlie. 2016. "Birthing Disability, Reproducing Race: Uneasy Intersections in Post-Civil Rights Politics of U.S. Citizenship." PhD diss., New York University.

Gilmore, Ruth Wilson. 2007. *Golden Gulag: Prisons, Surplus, Crisis, and Opposition in Globalizing California.* Los Angeles: University of California Press.

Hamraie, Aimi. 2015. "Cultivating Accountability toward the Intersections of Race, Aging, and Disability." *Age, Culture, Humanities* 2: 337–46.

Hedva, Johanna. 2016. "Sick Woman Theory." *Mask Magazine.* www.maskmagazine.com/not-again/struggle/sick-woman-theory.

Hix, Lisa. 2011. "Interview with Leroy Moore, Founder of Krip Hop Nation." KQED, February 14. www.kqed.org/arts/43903/interview_with_leroy_moore_founder_of_krip_hop_nation.

Jain, S. Lochlann. 2007. "Living in Prognosis: Toward an Elegiac Politics." *Representations* 98, no. 1: 77–92.

Jain, S. Lochlann. 2013. *Malignant: How Cancer Becomes Us.* Los Angeles: University of California Press.

Kafer, Alison. 2016. "Un/Safe Disclosures: Scenes of Disability and Trauma." *Journal of Literary and Cultural Disability Studies* 10, no. 1: 1–20.

Kim, Eunjung. 2017. *Curative Violence: Rehabilitating Disability, Gender, and Sexuality in Modern Korea.* Durham, NC: Duke University Press.

Kim, Jina B. 2020. "Disability in an Age of Fascism." *American Quarterly* 72, no. 1: 265–76.

Lazard, Carolyn. 2013. "How to Be a Person in the Age of Autoimmunity." *Cluster Mag.* static1.squarespace.com/static/55c40d69e4b0a45eb985d566/t/58cebc9dc534a59fbdbf98c2/1489943709737/HowtobeaPersonintheAgeofAutoimmunity+%281%29.pdf.

Lazard, Carolyn. 2016. "Score for Patient Interaction." In *Notes for the Waiting Room,* edited by Taraneh Fazeli. digigiid.ee/en/exhibitions-archive/disarming-language/canaries-2.

Mailhot, Terese Marie. 2018. *Heart Berries: A Memoir.* Berkeley: Counterpoint.

Malatino, Hil. 2019. "Future Fatigue: Trans Intimacies and Trans Presents (or How to Survive the Interregnum)." *TSQ* 6, no. 4: 635–58.

McArthur, Park, and Constantina Zavitsanos. 2013. "Other Forms of Conviviality." *Women and Performance* 23, no. 1: 126–32.

McRuer, Robert. 2006. *Crip Theory: Cultural Signs of Queerness and Disability.* New York: NYU Press.

McRuer, Robert. 2018. *Crip Times: Disability, Globalization, and Resistance.* New York: NYU Press.

Meiners, Erica R. 2016. *For the Children? Protecting Innocence in a Carceral State.* Minneapolis: University of Minnesota Press.

Minich, Julie Avril. 2020. "Radical Health: Justice, Care, and Latinx Expressive Culture." Unpublished Manuscript.

Mollow, Anna. 2017. "Unvictimizable: Toward a Fat Black Disability Studies." *African American Review* 50, no. 2: 105–21.

Mulhall, Anne. 2014. "Dead Time: Queer Temporalities and the Deportation Regime." *Social Text Online,* July 10. socialtextjournal.org/periscope_article/dead-time-queer-temporalities-and-the-deportation-regime/.

Nelson, Alondra. 2011. *Body and Soul: The Black Panther Party and the Fight against Medical Discrimination.* Minneapolis: University of Minnesota Press.

Nishida, Akemi. 2020. "Dare to Care: Affective Living of Disability, Race, and Gender." Unpublished Manuscript.

Pickens, Therí Alyce. 2019. *Black Madness :: Mad Blackness.* Durham, NC: Duke University Press.

Piepzna-Samarasinha, Leah Lakshmi. 2018. "Crip Lineages, Crip Futures: A Conversation with Stacey Milbern." In *Care Work: Dreaming Disability Justice,* by Leah Lakshmi Piepzna-Samarasinha, 240–56. Vancouver: Arsenal Pulp Press.

Price, Margaret. 2015. "The Bodymind Problem and the Possibilities of Pain." *Hypatia* 30, no. 1: 268–84.

Puar, Jasbir K. 2017. *The Right to Maim: Debility, Capacity, Disability.* Durham, NC: Duke University Press.

Roberts, Dorothy. 1999. *Killing the Black Body: Race, Reproduction, and the Meaning of Liberty.* New York: Vintage.

Roberts, Dorothy. 2011. *Fatal Invention: How Science, Politics, and Big Business Re-create Race in the Twenty-First Century.* New York: The New Press.

Samuels, Ellen. 2017. "Six Ways of Looking at Crip Time." *Disability Studies Quarterly* 37, no. 3. dsq-sds.org/article/view/5824/4684.

Sandahl, Carrie. 2003. "Queering the Crip or Cripping the Queer? Intersections of Queer and Crip Identities in Solo Autobiographical Performance." *GLQ* 9, no. 1–2: 25–56.

Schalk, Sami. 2013. "Coming to Claim Crip: Disidentification with/in Disability Studies." *Disability Studies Quarterly* 33, no. 2. dsq-sds.org/article/view/3705/3240.

Schalk, Sami. 2018. *Bodyminds Reimagined: (Dis)Ability, Race, and Gender in Black Women's Speculative Fiction.* Durham, NC: Duke University Press.

Shah, Nayan. 2001. *Contagious Divides: Epidemics and Race in San Francisco's Chinatown.* Berkeley: University of California Press.

Sins Invalid. n.d. "Our Mission." www.sinsinvalid.org/mission.html (accessed June 13, 2018).

Smith, Christen A. 2016. "Facing the Dragon: Black Mothering, Sequelae, and Gendered Necropolitics in the Americas." *Transforming Anthropology* 24, no. 1: 31–48.

Stockton, Kathryn Bond. 2009. *The Queer Child; or, Growing Sideways in the Twentieth Century.* Durham, NC: Duke University Press.

Taylor, Sunaura. 2004. "The Right Not to Work: Power and Disability." *Monthly Review* 55, no. 10. monthlyreview.org/2004/03/01/the-right-not-to-work-power-and-disability/.

Terry, Jennifer. 2017. *Attachments to War: Biomedical Logics and Violence in Twenty-First-Century America.* Durham, NC: Duke University Press.

Thomas, Kate. 2011. "Post-sex: On Being Too Slow, Too Stupid, Too Soon." In *After Sex? On Writing since Queer Theory,* edited by Janet Halley and Andrew Parker, 66–75. Durham, NC: Duke University Press.

Tuck, Eve. 2009. "Suspending Damage: A Letter to Communities." *Harvard Educational Review* 79, no. 3: 409–27.

Vasudevan, Pavithra. 2019. "An Intimate Inventory of Race and Waste." *Antipode,* January 15. doi.org/10.1111/anti.12501.

Vasudevan, Pavithra. 2020. "Entangled in Flesh: Bodily Archives of Industrial Ruination." Paper presented at the Center for Women's and Gender Studies, University of Texas, Austin, April 15.

Velasquez-Potts, Michelle. 2020. "Suspended Animation: Force-Feeding and the Visuality of Torture." Paper presented at the Center for Women's and Gender Studies, University of Texas, Austin, March 4.

Voyles, Traci Brynne. 2015. *Wastelanding: Legacies of Uranium Mining in Navajo Country.* Minneapolis: University of Minnesota Press.

Washington, Harriet. 2006. *Medical Apartheid: The Dark History of Medical Experimentation on Black Americans from Colonial Times to the Present.* New York: Doubleday.

Young, Hershini. 2005. "Inheriting the Criminalized Black Body: Race, Gender, and Slavery in *Eva's Man.*" *African American Review* 39, no. 3: 377–93.

Young, Hershini. 2012. "'Sound of Kuduro Knocking at My Door': Kuduro Dance and the Poetics of Debility." *African American Review* 45, no. 3: 391–402.

Protests in Lebanon

Karim Makdisi, Editor

These pieces were finalized in September 2020. Since then, the situation in Lebanon has continued to rapidly deteriorate. The early hope produced by the 2019 mass protests has eroded, as Lebanon's elite successfully retrenched, external intervention deepened, and the bulk of the Lebanese descended into poverty and insecurity. Still, new waves of protest—for better or for worse—are inevitable as the status quo is unsustainable.

—Karim Makdisi, February 2021

Karim Makdisi

Lebanon's October 2019 Uprising:
From Solidarity to Division and Descent
into the Known Unknown

This dossier examines the early promise and energy of Lebanon's mass protest movement of October 2019. After fifteen years of civil war (1975–90) and three decades of postwar neoliberal policies, people rose up against a kleptocratic ruling class of sectarian leaders and financiers that had captured, and bankrupted, the state. Protestors railed against structural corruption and demanded immediate reforms to end the overtly clientelist structure embedded in the very core of Lebanon's political and economic system.

During the protests' intoxicating early days and its carnival-like atmosphere, there was a lot of hope for revolutionary change. The essays here describe the conversion of previously walled-up public space as venues for popular dissent (Kosmatopoulos, this issue); grappling of educators with their new political roles on the street (Mouawad, this issue); emergence of new labor unions to foster worker solidarity and escape from the patronage straitjacket (Bou Khater, this issue); and even the imagination of alternative economies of mutual solidarity against the ravages of neoliberalism (Bauman, this issue).

My essay frames these protests and the hopes of the protestors. It examines why the sudden announcement of a series of regressive taxes that, in reality, had become the norm for three decades triggered such universal anger and mobilization. It also briefly charts the uprising's demise amid the unmasking of a nationwide banking Ponzi scheme, galloping inflation, palpable insecurity, national and protestor group division, and COVID-19 lockdowns. With the country in disarray, most people had been reduced to survival mode.

The South Atlantic Quarterly 120:2, April 2021
DOI 10.1215/00382876-8916176 © 2021 Duke University Press

By the time a massive blast, the largest nonnuclear explosion on record anywhere in the world, ripped through Beirut's port in August 2020, Lebanon's protests had become a footnote as French president, Emanuel "Papa" Macron personally took center stage and unveiled a plan to stabilize Lebanon through IMF-approved reforms. The irony of Macron's plan necessitating the return of not only the country's pre-uprising political status-quo but also possibly the very prime minister who was forced to resign in the wake of the protests one year earlier was lost on no one. If this fails, there may be even darker days.

The October 2019 WhatsApp Tax: The Straw That Broke the Camel's Back

The protests' proximate cause was a series of draconian indirect taxes targeting the middle- and lower-income population. In particular, the tax on WhatsApp calls, an essential social and work medium for most Lebanese across sectarian and regional divides, was essentially the straw that broke the camel's back. It was seen as an especially provocative and malevolent move by a parasitic ruling elite that had essentially bankrupted the country, gotten away with it, and now demanded the rest to foot the bill, as they had been doing for two decades already. All this so that these politicians may continue onwards with their corruption schemes.

With a steep downturn in economic prospects and a looming financial collapse, enough, it seemed, was enough. Cue dramatic scenes of mostly young women and men pouring into Beirut's city center, waving Lebanese flags in a deliberate, unifying renunciation of sectarian political party paraphernalia. In an impressively choreographed performance, dozens of small, inexpensive motorcycles so prevalent among Lebanon's working class emptied out of less affluent Beiruti neighborhoods to join the demonstrations. Many arrived from the Dahiya area, generally described by Western reporters and analysts as a "Hizbullah stronghold" or, even more mischievously, "Shia." Their arrival on the scene was symbolically a huge event, as it signified that the usually socially and politically disconnected areas and classes of Beirut were brought together by economic despair, not a predetermined political agenda.

All called in unison for the downfall of the government/regime that comprised the main sectarian political parties. The protests' primary objective was the wholesale removal of these *haramiye* (thieves), or "mafia," as they were generally described. An imagined and newly empowered citizen movement would hold these politicians fully accountable, force them to return *amwal al manhouba* (plundered money), and reclaim the state through a series of reforms that included, most urgently, the creation of a judiciary independent of sectarian and clientelist loyalties. Left-leaning protestors unleashed their considerable anger, and some violence, on the large commercial banks and the Central Bank. They demanded a new form of politics from below based on social justice, breaking up the bank cartel, and redistributing wealth; and they rejected proposed neoliberal reforms and structural adjustment plans as conditions for aid by European donors and the IMF respectively.

During the nightly teach-ins, rallies, and calls for solidarity across regional, sectarian and class lines, civil society groups distributed food and water for free, and the army largely stood down. People rediscovered the convening power of downtown Beirut that, in the post–civil war period, had been transformed from its traditional organic bustling center and melting pot for all Lebanese to a largely walled off, privatized, and sanitized playground for the affluent, a mere postcard of its past vitality. Loudly cursing and hanging effigies of politicians, spray-painting anti-sectarian and pro-revolution graffiti on governmental buildings, torching tires and garbage dumpsters, smashing ATMs and bank windows felt liberating and unifying.

Protests in Beirut were organized around three adjacent, though very distinct, spaces in the newly reclaimed downtown district. The first, comprising the bulk of the protestors, occupied the central area around the Martyr Square, the old *maydan* (open space) enclosed as an urban public space during the 1860s and renamed during the French Mandate to commemorate the public hanging of cross-confessional Lebanese nationalists by the Ottoman military commander Jamal Pasha during World War I. Protestors proclaimed that 2019 would mark the start of a new Republic, the moment a new wave of cross-confessional citizen groups recovered the country from the parasitic elite. Characterized by its carnival-like atmosphere and spontaneously built food stalls, the Martyr Square protests were largely peaceful, energized, family-oriented, and distinctly optimistic about the future.

The second space was close by, a smaller venue named Azarieh, with its teach-ins and often heated debates for those cautiously optimistic and curious to learn more about their country's problems and potential solutions. Speakers in the various booths and tents competed with one another to frame the road ahead for a civil (non-sectarian) state. The more prominent groups such as Beirut Madinati (Beirut is My City) and Mouwatinoun wa Mouwatinat fi Dawla (Citizens in a State) attracted hundreds of citizen-visitors.

The third location was for the more intense and hardcore leftist crowds, a thin corridor between Martyr Square and the heavily army-fortified Grand

Serail—the splendid former Ottoman Garrison and French High Commissioner Mandate base, converted after independence into the Lebanese prime minister's palace and government headquarters. The Serail is, in turn, adjacent on either side to the equally fortified Lebanese Parliament building and United Nations house. Under cover of darkness, crowds of young men engaged security forces in nightly cat-and-mouse battles. As rocks, bottles, and flares were thrown toward the Serail, riot police charged out behind the barbed wire, hitting and grabbing any stragglers.

Significantly, similar spontaneous protests occurred across Lebanon's peripheral regions and major coastal cities, most notably in Tripoli, Lebanon's second largest city and the North's capital (Doumat 2019). Tripoli and its seriously neglected predominately Sunni Muslim hinterland had over the years become hugely impoverished even as several billionaires, including two former prime ministers, jockeyed for political influence and election votes. Sectarian agitators had wormed their way into the political fabric of this area. Now, however, tents and peaceful nightly rallies were being held in Tripoli's main Al-Nour (the light) square, with an array of NGOs, a string of speakers, and nightly popular DJ-led concerts and glitzy lighting that belied the city's very conservative image.

Much attention, at least within liberal Beiruti circles and among foreign correspondents, was also given to small protests in southern Lebanon, including the important city of Nabatiyeh. Much as the protests in Beirut's Dahiye neighborhood, they were widely cast as the first overt dissent against the two dominant Shia parties: Amal (whose politically powerful, and infamously corrupt, leader and former warlord had captured the influential speaker of Parliament position for over two decades) and Hizbullah (Houssari 2019). In reality, while residents of southern Lebanon shared with all other Lebanese a deep sense of anger with the endemic corruption, overwhelming popular support for Hizbullah did not wane. Southern Lebanese don't perceive Hizbullah as corrupt. Rather, their huge reservoir of good will toward Hizbullah stems from the group's demonstrated record of resisting the Israelis and providing security, community support, and political empowerment to its constituents.

Those early days of unity across class, sect, gender, and generations were the sort of idealized moments of anti-sectarian national sentiment that Lebanese, particularly urban liberals, long imagined but deep down feared were more fantasy than reality. *Killu yaani killun* (all of them means all of them) was the main slogan in reference to protestors' nonpartisan, nonsectarian national call for the removal of all politicians regardless of their sectarian affiliations. Other chants were designed to connect to other protests in the Arab world, with *yalla erhal* (leave now) and *Ash-shaab yurid esqat al-nizam* (the people want the downfall of the regime/political system) echoing Syrian and Egyptian protestors respectively.

After quickly withdrawing the WhatsApp and other regressive taxes and promising a veritable laundry list of reforms, pledged on TV from the safety of his palace, an apparently contrite Prime Minister Saad Hariri resigned ten days after the start of the persistent protests that had swelled in scope and size. The street, many thought, or (more dangerously) assumed, had finally brought down not just the government but the very system itself. These feelings of solidarity, compassion, and euphoria filled the air. It was not to last. The political class was retrenching, foreign interference gathering pace, and the big bankers along with the governor of the Central Bank remained steadfast in their refusal to acknowledge responsibility.

Post–Civil War Sectarian Pact and Neoliberal Reconstruction: Setting up the Structural Rot and Normalizing Corruption

The protests' root causes originated in the internationally sponsored, post–civil war power-sharing agreement signed in 1989 in Ta'if, Saudi Arabia, after fifteen years of devastating war and hundreds of thousands of deaths and disappearances. Many of the sectarian leaders *still in power today* simply substituted their blood-soaked warlord fatigues for the kind of nondescript clothing that power-sharing agreements produce in order to satisfy international diplomats, mediators, and regional sponsors.

This national reconciliation pact framed Lebanon's new politics in overtly sectarian terms, even amending the Constitution and electoral laws and establishing a principle of *muhasassa* (sectarian distribution of civil servants). Guaranteed by the US, France, Syria, and Saudi Arabia, the pact promised an end to the bloodshed (with former warlords and criminals-cum-politicians now protected by an amnesty law) and internal stability (with the Syrian military and despised intelligence services ruling as overlords). As war militias were disarmed, Lebanon's resistance movement, now dominated by Hizbullah, grew in effectiveness, popularity, and professionalism during the 1990s against Israel's long and harsh occupation of southern Lebanon (1982–2000).

The postwar pact also framed Lebanon's huge reconstruction plans in clear neoliberal terms, with the overwhelming influx of Gulf money and a newly constitutionally empowered Sunni prime minister beholden to Saudi Arabia. Rafiq Hariri, the larger-than-life Lebanese prime minister who dominated Lebanon's politics and ran Beirut's massive reconstruction during the 1990s, remained a Saudi citizen, and loyal subject, throughout his time in office. Lebanon was to become some version of Dubai and, eventually, fold into the US-led 1990s negotiations to strike a peace deal with the Israelis to unlock even more money.

Politicians promised good governance, privatization, sustainable development, greening of institutions, integrated water management, public participation, civil society consultation, expert advice, and other neoliberal reforms required to unlock massive development aid from donors, international organizations, and international financial institutions. Instead, under the guise of internationally sanctioned state-building, Lebanon's intertwined financial and political elite ruthlessly plundered public assets, wealth, and resources, unlawfully privatizing and destroying Lebanon's famous coastline and mountain peaks and ramming through a deeply regressive taxation system. They used the vast wealth they accumulated to create iron-clad patronage networks and docile voters in their respective, well-delineated spheres of influence.

Supported by the World Bank and UN, Lebanon's politicians also systematically dismantled Lebanon's productive and rural economies via ruthless neoliberal policies, creating in its place a rent-seeking rentier economy reliant on financial services, large-scale tourism from Gulf countries, huge-scale real estate speculation, and money-laundering. Farmers became taxi drivers, artisanal workers became waiters and hotel staff, university graduates became bank employees, environmentalists became NGO project managers, engineers became building foremen, academics became experts and consultants, and citizens became consumers.

Against this, with huge sums of money flowing in and conspicuous consumption exploding, Lebanon quickly became, for the wealthy, a seriously fun place to be. It was high up on international cool lists with its appeal of fantastic food, hip bars and cafés, thriving gay scene, UNESCO heritage sites, and beautiful private beaches and mountain resorts supplemented by a dash of war chic and perennial risk potential for Hizbullah-Israeli spats along Lebanon's southern border.

To pay for all this, successive postwar governments and people alike borrowed unsustainably against Lebanon's future by letting the financiers work their magic. What the latter produced was an elaborate Ponzi scheme. The dominant, traditional private banks wooed Lebanon's vast reservoir of wealthy expats and Gulf investors with banking secrecy laws and super-high interest rates. In turn, the Central Bank borrowed from these private banks at even higher interests, reaching an incredible 30 percent in the mid-1990s, in order to fund the government's huge reconstruction projects that, in turn, maintained the sectarian leaders' patronage networks and lavish lifestyles. Lebanon became a fully dollarized economy, strengthening consumer purchasing power and creating dependence on imports—from food, fuel, and medicines to fine clothing and luxury items—for 80 percent of its products.

By the time protests began in 2019, and this huge Ponzi scheme was uncovered, it was too late. There was a run on the banks as throngs of people demanded their money. Banks first severely restricted depositors' monthly withdrawals of US dollars before stopping them altogether by spring 2020 as cash reserves ran out. For the first time in its history, Lebanon declared bankruptcy in order to use what was left to subsidize dwindling food, medicine, and fuel supplies for its people, half of whom were now below the poverty line. Lebanon's national currency lost up to 80 percent of its value as hyperinflation hit people hard.

Lebanon's neoliberal economic policies and corruption had produced a public debt 150 percent of GDP, among the highest in the world. It had also created some of the highest levels of inequality worldwide: the richest 1 percent received 25 percent of national income, and the richest 0.1 percent (under four thousand people) earned more than the bottom 50 percent (around two million) (Assouad 2019).

The Protest Movement in 2020: Division and Despair

The protests in Lebanon have been alternatively called *thawra* (revolution) by the idealists, who openly curse the traditional sectarian party leaders, with their large-scale patronage networks, and insist that restructuring the political and economic system is not only viable but non-negotiable; *harak* (movement) by the pragmatists, who argue that, in the absence of a genuine revolution, engagement with the traditional political parties is a necessary short-term strategy toward a civil state; and *mu'amara* (conspiracy) by those convinced that Western and Gulf embassies, using their Lebanese proxies, infiltrated the movement early on as part of a larger regional struggle against Iran and Hizbullah.

The ambivalence over these labels and their corresponding discourses—that can coexist or compete, usually depending on the regional or international dynamics—grew over time to the point that when COVID-19 locked the country down during spring 2020, the political divide rather than the popular demands to hold politicians and bankers accountable came to define the protests.

For months, COVID-19 fears and a palpable sense of foreboding left Lebanon, with its collapsing economy, galloping inflation, and bankrupt financial system, in a dystopian form of purgatory. The idealists retreated to the safety of social media, and the pragmatists bemoaned the lack of unified and coherent political demands by the two hundred plus protestor splinter groups. Those who focused on foreign infiltration asked where the funding was coming from for the expensive fireworks and concerts in Beirut and Tripoli. Why was the protest movement's iconic symbol in Martyr Square, a nine-meter wooden "fist of dignity," so reminiscent of Otpor's, the Serbian anti-Milosevic student movement that was allegedly funded by US-government-affiliated organizations?[1]

As this schism gathered pace, another, more serious one was opening up. Hizbullah, it appeared, was the big elephant in the room. It is the most powerful political group in Lebanon, the only real military force, with a large constituency largely drawn from lower- and working-class Shia in the South, Beirut suburbs, and in the Beqaa Valley. With massive national reconstruction centered around Beirut and the US-led "peace process" in full swing during the 1990s, Hizbullah's resistance to Israel's brutal occupation of southern Lebanon became more effective until it forced Israel's withdrawal in 2000. However, the US "war on terror" and 2003 invasion of Iraq fundamentally altered the entire dynamic of regional politics. Hizbullah's main protector, Syria, was now under huge pressure to withdraw from Lebanon. Rafiq Hariri's 2005 assassination in a massive car bomb in downtown Beirut ushered in a new period of internal sectarian strife, another catastrophic Israeli invasion, and various international interventions in Lebanon. To protect its interests, Hizbullah became part and parcel of the Lebanese state and joined successive national unity governments along with its allies and adversaries.

Following the 2016 election of Donald Trump in the US, relations among the Lebanese parties became increasingly strained as the US pursued a "maximum pressure" policy and harsh sanctions regime against Iran and its regional allies. The catastrophic war in Syria (including Hizbullah's participation), and the coming to power in Saudi Arabia of the virulently anti-Iran and Hizbullah Crown Prince Mohamad bin Sultan, exacerbated this tension and renewed the sense that the Saudi-Western-Israeli targeting of Iran and Hizbullah would reach its end game before the end of Trump's first term. In this geopolitical game, the protestors' voice became irrelevant.

The Beirut Port Blast Buries the Protest Movement and Draws in "Papa" Macron

On August 4, 2020, 2,750 tons of ammonia nitrate, stored illegally and without any safety measures for six years in the unremarkable warehouse number 12 in Beirut's port, ripped through the city, killing and wounded hundreds and displacing three hundred thousand residents from nearby neighborhoods. It was the single biggest nonnuclear explosion ever recorded globally, heard across the Mediterranean to Cyprus, and rendered Beirut's population collectively traumatized in a way that even its most conflict-hardened residents had not felt before. The politicians, bureaucrats, and financiers inevitably played the merry-go-round blame game, covering up a stunning act of state negligence in which all the traditional political parties were implicated. Appropriately cynical Lebanese know that judicial and army investigations will be botched and will not lead to clear answers and accountability: they never do.

A sense of solidarity returned briefly to the streets as an array of civil society and religious groups took the initiative in the immediate rescue and relief operations in the absence of a coherent official response. For people congregated in the area or glued to their TVs, if the port blast had symbolized the essence of the Lebanese state's necropolitics—the imagery of the "living dead" seemed apt—then a dramatic three-day rescue operation around a destroyed building led by volunteer TOPOS Chile rescue team—with its motto "no one is dead until we find them"—epitomized hope and redemption. By the time the Chilean team leader Francisco Lermanda finally confirmed "we can say there's no sign of life inside of the building," people could have been forgiven for thinking he was talking about the Lebanese state.

The Beirut port blast and its aftermath encapsulated Lebanon's political turmoil in compressed time, transforming Lebanon's political landscape, as people moved quickly from shock to hope to despair to renewed division. French President Emmanuel "Papa" Macron flew to Beirut to inspect the damage and announced a French-led diplomatic intervention that he would personally lead to revive the moribund political system and push through IMF structural adjustment plans. Lebanon's traditional elite and politicians are locked in negotiations, not to save Lebanon or its people, but rather their influence and privileges.

Macron's plan was the carrot to Trump's stick that included ratcheting up of his "maximum pressure" policy against Iran and Hizbullah and strong-arming the Arab world into normalizing relations with the Israelis. It was lost on no one that Beirut's port, Lebanon's lifeline to the outside and would-be base for the potentially huge recently discovered offshore gas reserves, was mysteriously destroyed at precisely the time Haifa's port is making a bid to be the preeminent one in the Eastern Mediterranean to connect the region with Europe. A month after the blast, and a day after the UAE signed an official treaty with Israel to normalize ties, Dubai's state-owned DP World signed a deal to partner with an Israeli group in developing Haifa's port. Just after that, Lebanon suddenly announced that it had agreed to hold talks, albeit indirectly through UN and US mediators, with Israel to delineate the maritime boundaries.[2]

On the eve of the protests' first anniversary, we were not merely back to square one but in a situation worse than where we started. There is now real poverty, the kind never seen before in modern Lebanon. Children are hungry and parents unable to provide basic food. Unemployment is at record levels, young women and men are emigrating at unprecedented rates, and people's bank deposits and savings have disappeared even as they have to deal with rampant inflation and currency devaluation. The country is bankrupt, and its Central Bank reserves are so critically low that—barring some external intervention—core medicine, food, and fuel subsidies will soon be lifted to catastrophic effect.

One year on, Macron's neoliberal plan is the only game in town, and protesters need to urgently remobilize for the struggles ahead. If this fails, Lebanon faces a descent into the known unknown.

Notes

1   The young man who constructed the fist insisted his creation was totally "spontaneous" and categorically dismissed any politically motivated motives and comparisons to the Serbian fist (Henoud 2019).

2   These talks have, predictably, stalled as Lebanon continues to resist an unjust US-imposed solution that favors Israel. Future progress will surely depend on the outcome of the struggle over the regional order.

References

Assouad, Lydia. 2019. "The Ravages of Inequality." *Diwan*, Carnegie Middle East Center, November 19. carnegie-mec.org/diwan/80133?lang=en.

Domat, Chole. 2019. "Impoverished and Ignored, Tripoli Rises to Become Heart of Lebanon's Protests." *Middle East Eye*, November 7. middleeasteye.net/news/protesters-fight-corruption-lebanons-northern-city-tripoli.

Henoud, Carla. 2019. "Tarek Chehab's Fist of Dignity." *L'Orient Le Jour*, November 9. lorientlejour.com/article/1194481/tarek-chehabs-fist-of-dignity.html.

Houssari, Najla. 2019. "Nabatieh Rises against Hezbollah and Amal." *Arab News*, October 26. arabnews.com/node/1574416/middle-east.

Nikolas Kosmatopoulos

Unhatching the Egg in Lebanon's 2019 Protests:
Activism, Purity, and the Real-Estatization
of Civil Society

Lebanon's October 2019 uprising succeeded in bringing down a government, but failed to forge a new political alliance among the country's civil society. One of the uprising's most ambitious aims, advanced by participants and commentators alike, was the ushering in of a new social contract beyond sectarian divisions. To this end, protestors used national paraphernalia, waved large Lebanese flags, and displayed patriotic folklore, in deliberate contrast to party or sectarian affiliation symbols deemed divisive. For them, nothing less than the wholesale rejection of the political class in toto would do: the main slogan "kilun ya3nni kilun" means "all means all," in reference to all the leaders who had dominated Lebanon's polity and economy since the end of the fifteen-year civil war (1975–1990). Some protestors went as far as to diagnose in the protests the real end of the civil war, whose effects and divisions have been haunting state and society over the past three decades. Indeed, the civil war cast a long shadow on the uprising.

In this brief auto-ethnographic essay I revisit the story of the Beirut City Center Dome, also known as the "Egg." A 1960s brutalist-modernist cinema abandoned to snipers during Lebanon's civil war, it was transformed into an inaccessible and "amnesiac" (Nagle 2017) postwar landmark and finally, briefly, became a stage for a direct action politics in the early days of the October 2019 mass protests. During the first week of the demonstrations, the Egg hosted a short-lived experiment in politicizing war ruins and making them relevant to contemporary politics. The experiment to turn the Egg into "Eggupation"—the symbolic metamorphosis into a platform for

The South Atlantic Quarterly 120:2, April 2021
DOI 10.1215/00382876-8916190   © 2021 Duke University Press

direct action—caused quite a few passionate reactions among many individuals and groups presumably in favor of popular politics: excitement, curiosity, and mobilization but also outright rejection. Perhaps then, revisiting the story of the Eggupation might reveal deeper insights about the intricacies of postwar politics in Lebanon's civil society. Mostly, I am interested in testing the argument that a postwar model of expert-driven peace, which involves compartmentalizing the political society and its demands while devolving power into real estate investors—prime ministers (Baumann 2016; Makdisi 1997), crucially depends on the constant reproduction of technomoral hierarchies between experts and their subjects (Kosmatopoulos 2014). In the context of mass mobilization, as in the October uprising, I consider "real estate" to be a fitting metaphor to describe the process through which potentially emancipatory projects, such as the Eggupation, fail to materialize within a toxic climate that tends to equate political critique with purity competitions and boundary work.

I show thus how the Eggupation, a brief but highly symbolic presence in the urban topography of dissent in Beirut downtown, became entangled in the real estate jurisdictions of civil society experts and various gatekeepers. Tellingly, just after effectively shutting down the Egg, many of these critics went on to establish similar initiatives in public politics, as in events with speakers in tents and stands, often reproducing on the ground the fragmented geography of the postwar civil society (Sinno 2020). Hence, unlike other uprisings in the region, such as those in Egypt, Greece, Turkey, or Iraq, for which the taking over of iconic urban spaces and their metamorphosis into political edifices was a fundamental strategy for the popular movement, the real-estatization of civil society, namely, the fragmentation between expert-controlled domains in Lebanon, persisted. Next to the Egg, and beyond it, the compartmentalization of popular politics continued unabated, utterly unable to morph into a collectively formed platform for effective political change.

Hatching the Egg: An Activist Experiment in the Urban Topography of Popular Dissent

The idea to politicize the Egg was born when the October uprising began to settle into a permanent occupation of Beirut's downtown and other cities in Lebanon. The uprising's initial instigators, a mobile mass of young motorcyclists animating, as inflating rivers of popular anger, an otherwise soulless bourgeois downtown, seemed to have totally withdrawn or settled in the downtown protests. These lively representatives of the popular classes that roamed streets and blocked intersections, beeping and yelling, had yielded their place to an ever growing, and class-wise more diverse, crowd that had begun to spread in the squares around the country.

This protest followed an established pattern in successive popular demonstrations since the exodus of the Syrian military rule in 2005. Before the 2019 uprising, the so-called YouStink protests in 2015 were the latest manifestations (Khneisser 2019).[1] In October, walking among the protestors, one could already discern masses of people oscillating between two main geographically distinct poles. On one hand, the crowds facing the seat of the government in the Ottoman Serai, now protected by barbed wire, were obviously poorer, angrier, willing to engage in acts of violent dissent. The other pole constituted a steadily growing crowd in the Martyrs Square that seemed content with occupying space, along with more or less established parties and civil society initiatives, and celebrating the national uprising.

This observation revived in my mind similar protest geographies in which I had participated before in the United States and in Greece. These often revolved around the occupation of symbolic squares in the nation's administrative or economic capital. My self-schooling in these matters had been advanced through my involvement in the Aganaktismenoi Movement in Athens, Greece, between May and August 2011, as well as the Occupy Wall Street movement in New York in September 2011 (Graeber 2011). I also followed as closely as I could news and analyses of the urban uprisings in Egypt and Spain, both of which followed a similar aim, namely, occupying the central square, the symbolic heart of the state. Clearly, each uprising revealed a different urban map of popular dissent. But they all had one, and now I could also observe a similar map being formed in Beirut. As manifested in all these uprisings, being able to hold space is crucial for not only self-defense and popular self-confidence but also the advancement of political visions. Political visions can be advanced through the practice to speak out, exchange with others, articulate demands, form alliances, discuss strategy, and plan next steps collectively.

In Greece, for example, the protest movement fiercely defended the urban space it occupied, while ensuring its popular repurposing. Within the early weeks, a series of other occupation projects occurred: They removed the cement from a parking lot to create a people-run public park in the neighborhood of Exarcheia, which still allows the memory of the uprising to flourish. They turned a derelict hotel, the City Plaza Hotel, a few blocks away into a self-governed space for refugees and migrants from Syria, Afghanistan, and elsewhere. They transformed an abandoned theater in the

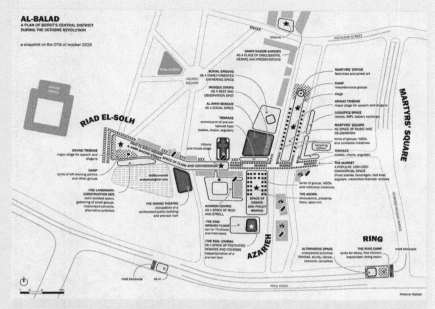

Figure 1. Al-Balad, a plan of Beirut's Central District during the 2019 Lebanese Uprising. Created by Antoine Atallah.

tourist neighborhood of Psyrri, earmarked for gentrification, into a popular stage for political events, music concerts, theater plays, dance ensembles, and fundraising parties.

With these memories in mind, I looked at the Beirut protests through a similar lens. I could hardly overlook the haunting presence of the so-called Egg, the derelict cinema. While partaking in the protests, seeking to understand them as an anthropologist-activist, I would take detours and visit the Egg, often alone. I could easily reenact in my mind a popular assembly in its oval belly, with people filing up the abandoned stairs. The stark contradiction between a long-gone modernist glory and the current abandonment reflected a creative tension between a silenced past and an unclaimed present. Echoes and shadows in the belly made up a mélange of melancholy and meaningfulness. Walking past the Egg's belly, one would find shaky stairs leading to the top of the building. The feeling of anguish when on it felt like a suitable metaphor for the risks attached to any effort to deploy its haunting presence for a contemporary politics.

Then, in the street outside of the Egg, I ran into a sociologist colleague, and we briefly exchanged on the current events. We shared similar insights about the unfolding protest movement but also a deep appreciation for direct

Figure 2. People looking to the street from inside the Egg. Photograph by the author.

action as well as few experiences in similar projects. He had taken active part in the 2011 uprising in Egypt, but also participated in projects in Europe, reflecting an intense engagement with direct action and urban spatiality. We discussed the prospect of using the Egg to host debates and teach-ins. Among them, we envisioned a discussion about possible lessons from protest movements in Egypt, Greece, and elsewhere in the region. Linking urban spatiality to solidarity could be meaningful to the current uprising in Lebanon, particularly at the current phase of territorialization and rapid politicization.

The next day, the Egg project was discussed in an American University of Beirut (AUB) faculty-led discussion at the landmark United Nations Economic and Social Commission for West Asia garden in downtown. In this meeting, two main action plans emerged. I would summarize them under unionization and direct action, respectively. Aware of our privileged status as university professors in a private upscale university, some of us had doubts about the feasibility to unionize along horizontal lines, but nonetheless did not perceive this plan as contradictory or even antagonistic to direct action initiatives, such as space occupation. Both were addressing different needs of the current movement. So, we moved on with the plan, while joined by others, among them an Armenian colleague in the Fine Arts Department.

We decided that the first step, as a way of testing the waters, was to organize a teach-in at the Egg. Classes in schools and universities had been mostly suspended, but the planned session in my Political Anthropology course was conveniently titled "Capitalism and Crisis." Without much hesitation, I suggested holding this session in the Egg, and emailed my students the change of location with a message that began with the following words: *Dear all in revolt, During these historic times of hope and struggle for a better tomorrow, "the protests will be our classroom and the classroom will be the street," until further notice.* As it happens, one of my students "leaked" the message on Twitter, where it was picked up by a local journalist with a broad following.

The next day's "teach-in" was packed with all kinds of people. Apart from my students, others had obviously seen the announcement on Twitter and joined. The teach-in turned quickly into an open discussion about direct action, radical pedagogy, and experiences from uprisings in other countries. Responding to inquiries, we then brought up a suggestion for an event about uprisings in Egypt, Greece, and Armenia. Others suggested many other interesting ideas. One person half-jokingly suggested to call it Eggupation, which we all found provocative and creative. The Egg was hatched.

Unhatching the Egg: Purity and Danger in the Uncivil Society

The instant popularity of the endeavor caught us by surprise. Local and international media had already been reporting about it since the first teach-in. We declined to talk to them, however. Conscious of our controversial status as foreigners and university professors in an elite US-chartered institution, we did not want our professional identity to get in the way of the initiative, nor did we want to harvest personal gains from this attention. Yet, the experiment that we had just thrown ourselves into would not allow for such luxuries of choice. Soon after, the news about the Eggupation spread. The excitement about its possibilities, but also the incitement against its potentialities, took us by storm. Every move—events, announcements, and responses to social media inquiries—was mired in open antagonism, mirroring a controversy that was growing, and turning dangerous.

Initially, a brief text outlining aims, tools, and plans was posted on the Eggupation Facebook page, which had more than two thousand members in two days. Busy with planning, most of us didn't pay much attention to the text, but our critics did.[2] In particular, the invitation to solicit and filter proposals for sit-ins, direct action, and discussions seemed to have hit a nerve, especially among young professionals and gatekeepers of cultural and academic milieus. "The revolution will not be curated," wrote an angry critic, dismayed by what she saw as efforts to filter popular wisdom. A few others falsely accused us of blocking access to the building, despite the fact that the Eggupation organized altogether three two-hour-long events in the entirety of its short life. Others lamented that by organizing events we effectively (attempted to) empty the streets from people [sic]. A few weeks later, a friend, at first supportive of the initiative, told me that the choice of the Egg—elevated above the street level—manifested the elitism in the experiment.

Then, the idea to invite Charbel Nahas, a controversial public figure, previous minister of labor and leader of a progressive oppositional party in Lebanon, was met with strong criticism among both other university colleagues and Eggupation activists. Most were concerned about safeguarding some sort of purity border. Thus, some questioned whether a former minister could be part of the protest movement, reiterating the slogan "kilun yaɜnni kilun," meaning all means all. For these purists, serving in a previous government made one automatically part of "kilun." Yet, this attack neglected widely known facts about this rather unique minister's ousting from the government in 2012 because of his relentless defense of workers' rights and against corruption of telecoms.

Other critics voiced concerns about the repercussions of "politicizing" the initiative by hosting a known party leader. The heated discussions that ensued revolved around the impossible desire of keeping a popular political platform pure from certain forms of politics perceived as "dirty." On the other hand, those invested in more "messy" kinds of politics were eager to open the initiative to controversial figures that could be challenged through open and free dialogue. Nonetheless, boundary work and purity competitions continued unabated. Another impossible boundary that emerged was that between academics and politics, highlighted through the hybrid identity of the invitee. Although the initial invitation was meant for a public intellectual and university teacher, there was no way that this identity would remain purified from his other features, the party leadership being primary among them.

Finally, the event was held, and it was a resounding success. More than four hundred people attended, asked questions, and raised all kinds of issues about party and street politics, popular strategies, and the challenges for the movement down the road. In the aftermath of the event, an interesting dynamic emerged in the Eggupation group. The boundary warriors sought to issue a public statement condemning the guest speaker for not respecting the border between academics and "politics." Since he spoke about current politics also as a party leader, members wanted to openly chastise him for this. Debating purity borders, the group exchanged arguments about what constitutes a "party event" when, for example, no party cadres control the discussion. Anyone could have taken the floor to challenge the speaker in an open platform. The internal uproar continued, so the group reconvened in a nearby bar. Despite the immense success of the event, the main agenda item was the public statement against the alleged boundary transgressor. Out of both courtesy to the guest and genuine disrespect to purity contests in politics, the statement was never issued.

In the next days, the Eggupation support base was growing but critics became louder. Our Facebook page had turned into an ugly theater of angry and visceral comments. When the Facebook comments became vile, we decided to shut them down, for which we received even more criticism. When the attacks turned threatening—some were calling for a physical confrontation, while one of us was receiving death threats over WhatsApp—we decided to shut down the initiative altogether.

Shocked by the vileness surrounding us, we circulated the following— obviously defensive—statement:

> Eggupation announces the conclusion of its teach-in cycles until further notice. Events took place inside, outside and transcended the Egg. Eggupation—a figure of speech—hosted three of these events in the Egg, and had no hand (but much joy) in any other events happening in the building (hence we disabled posts to avoid misconceptions). The Egg belongs to the people and has no doors. See you in the streets! In solidarity.

The Egg was unhatched.

Concluding Thoughts

At the outset, I suggested that the story of the Egg might reveal deeper insights about the politics of civil society in contemporary Lebanon. My first point is that the Egg, a war ruin, failed to create a "common space for political debates, proposals for direct action, teach-ins, suggestions for political transformation," as per the founding text.

Instead, purity competitions rendered its politicization obsolete. Another war ruin could serve as animated background for the retelling of the history of downtown (an AUB colleague organized history tours in the "grand teatro"). Yet, any effort to turn a war ruin into a lively site for the messy contemporary politics provoked fierce reactions. In my observation, the boundary warriors were mostly members of the educated urban middle class, who took on the role of gatekeeping the entrance to the past. In my eyes, a real estate mentality had effectively shut down the possibility of re-articulating the denied memory of an ever-present haunting war as a hopeful politics of today.

To be fair, real estate mentalities existed in the Athenian protests too. Indeed, its topography divided the so-called upper and lower squares. The upper square—vulgar, nationalist, moralist—coalesced around the populist slogan "thieves, thieves" directed against the totality of Parliament members—opposition and government alike, another reiteration of "kilun yaʒnni kilun." The upper square crowd understood politics as a division between friends and foes of the nation. The lower square, occupying the main Syntagma Square, was organized around a regular popular assembly and the working groups that it designated. Eventually, the assembly became the cradle and carrier of an affirmative political will, a kind of popular parliament that promoted a series of demands, public policy proposals, and collective platforms.

Returning to Lebanon, the second point I want to make is about the necessary closure of the war memory that a compartmentalized civil society could not achieve. My own research on the global peace and development industry manifests that depoliticizing expert politics of peace—which I call Master Peace—divided civil society into small cottage industries based on the primacy of technomorality. As a result, the necessary closure of the war through an emancipatory politics was rendered impossible. As the Eggupation story might indicate, this legacy can also help to analyze the failure to achieve a unified political vision in the aftermath of the October uprising.

Notes

1   The "youstink" movement began as a protest to the government's failure to solve a severe waste crisis caused by the shutting down of the regional waste dump in Naameh (south of Beirut). The closure led Sukleen, a private waste company, to suspend collection, causing piles of rubbish to fill the streets, rivers, valleys. For a critical approach on the 2015 protests through the lens of "technomorals" see Khneisser 2019.

2   This is the full text:

> In view of the general strike and the continued revolution, we are a group of academics, artists, teachers, students and intellectual workers who are organizing a common space to hold political debates, proposals for direct action, teach-ins, share new and existing programs and suggestions for political transformation, as well as to hear and learn from each other. We will be calling on to hear from people from a broad spectrum of political and social organizations who have concrete proposals and/or analyses of current events. The space is the Egg, the

time is the afternoon (3:30 p.m.). As one of us has stated, "The Egg is the place from which the new social order is hatched." More modestly, perhaps it can be one of those places from which to imagine a new beginning. The Egg is on the streets, yet provides a space for concentrated thinking and debate. Our motivation is critical pedagogy as a political practice, one that aims at a critique of the existing social order and thinks of the means of its transformation. For this, we believe we need analyses of the concrete situation, as well as hear affirmative proposals. We don't believe that during political action thinking and theory need to pause and give way to the regime of the urgency of action. Theory is practice and practice is theory. The goal is to learn from the streets and to transform the streets into a classroom while formulating a common vision for a new politics.

Please submit a VERY SHORT (one paragraph and preferred time) proposals to for teach-ins, direct actions, workshops, open presentations and so on.

PLEASE SEND THE PROPOSALS TO EggThawra@gmail.com.

While we are open to all kinds of interventions and agendas, the organizing committee will have to filter the proposals according to the broad goals we have defined for ourselves:

- Critical pedagogy which entails public and free of charge education geared towards a program of a critique of the current relations of production in the specific context of Lebanon
- Helping to forge a strong socialist alliance
- Sharing our experiences from various revolutions and social movements
- Organizing situational events that intervene in the public protests
- Creating a space to lay out and discuss various political and economic programs for transition
- Developing modes of institutionalization of our efforts that will also last beyond the street revolts

References

Baumann, Hannes. 2016. *Citizen Hariri: Lebanon's Neoliberal Reconstruction*. Oxford, UK: Oxford University Press.

Graeber, David. 2011. "Occupy Wall Street Rediscovers the Radical Imagination." *Guardian*, September 25. theguardian.com/commentisfree/cifamerica/2011/sep/25/occupy -wall-street-protest.

Khneisser, Mona. 2019. "The Marketing of Protest and Antinomies of Collective Organization in Lebanon." *Critical Sociology* 45, nos. 7–8: 1111–32.

Kosmatopoulos, Nikolas. 2014. "The Birth of the Workshop: Technomorals, Peace Expertise, and the Care of the Self in the Middle East." *Public Culture* 26, no. 3 (74): 529–58.

Makdisi, Saree. 1997. "Laying Claim to Beirut: Urban Narrative and Spatial Identity in the Age of Solidere." *Critical Inquiry* 23, no. 3: 661–705.

Nagle, John. 2017. "Ghosts, Memory, and the Right to the Divided City: Resisting Amnesia in Beirut City Centre." *Antipode* 49, no. 1: 149–68.

Sinno, Wael. 2020. "How People Reclaimed Public Spaces in Beirut during the 2019 Lebanese Uprising." *Journal of Public Space* 5, no. 1: 193–218.

Hannes Baumann

Dumping Humpty-Dumpty:
Blockages and Opportunities for Lebanon's
Economy after the October 2019 Protests

On October 17, 2019, Lebanon's capital, Beirut, erupted in protests. The government had proposed a range of taxes, including on voice calls via messaging services such as WhatsApp—an essential service in Lebanon, where mobile telephony is hugely overpriced. The protests spread throughout the country and demonstrators denounced not only the new taxes but also the corruption of the country's political class, which had presided over a failing economy and failing public services—from electricity to water, from health to education.

The protests followed a summer of disasters. Firefighters were unable to suppress raging forest blazes because their helicopters had not been serviced in years. Most ominously, the value of the currency was deteriorating. Between 1997 and 2019 the US dollar and the Lebanese lira were used interchangeably in everyday transactions, and Lebanese could choose whether they wanted to maintain their bank deposits in either currency. By September 2019, banks were restricting access to dollars and some traders refused to accept Lebanese lira. The currency slide led to rising panic among Lebanese who were facing the prospect of high inflation and plummeting living standards when the majority were already at the precipice of poverty.

The disasters continued. Governments were unable to halt the slide of the currency. By August 2020, the Lebanese currency had lost about 80 percent of its value since October 2019. COVID-19 struck, and while a lockdown prevented a catastrophic spread of infections, it further depressed economic activity. Then, on August 4, an enormous explosion at Beirut port delivered

The South Atlantic Quarterly 120:2, April 2021
DOI 10.1215/00382876-8916204 © 2021 Duke University Press

the coup de grâce to a city in crisis. At the time of writing, 180 have been confirmed dead and over 6,000 have been injured.

Lebanese demonstrators are protesting their corrupt political class, which is responsible for the failing economy and public services. A crucial piece of the puzzle of Lebanese corruption is the way the regional and global political economy enable Lebanese corruption. I will focus on the collapse of the currency because it was at the heart of Lebanon's political economy after the end of the civil war in 1990. For years, a coalition of forces inside and outside of Lebanon kept the system ticking until it disintegrated just before the October protests. It is neither possible nor desirable to put Humpty-Dumpty back together again. What new constellations of internal and external forces are trying to reshape Lebanese capitalism? In other words: What are protestors up against?

The Transnational Coalition behind the Currency Peg

Maintaining the dollar peg equaled a near-impossible balancing act in a country that imports most of its needs, exports relatively little, runs persistent government deficits, and has accrued one of the highest debt levels in the world. What is surprising about Lebanon's currency crisis in 2019 is not that it happened, but that the country's unsustainable economic model avoided currency collapse for over twenty years. The key to maintaining the peg was to offer attractive interest rates that would entice capital from abroad, which would, in turn, finance the current account and government budget deficits: in a period of historically low interest rates around the globe, Lebanon's commercial banks would commonly offer around 10 percent interest even on ordinary deposits (Cornish 2019).

These capital inflows came mostly in the shape of deposits from the large and wealthy Lebanese diaspora and from Gulf citizens. Lebanese banks—owned by a small coterie of politically connected individuals—were earning handsome profits by mediating these inflows and channeling them primarily into government debt and central bank debt instruments. Commercial bank profits in the three years from 2014 to 2016 reached US$5.5 billion after tax (Association of Banks in Lebanon 2017: 135). The different components of the coalition—central bank, commercial banks, diaspora, politicians—were not discrete entities but overlapped. Politicians held major stakes in the banks (Chaaban 2019). Prior to taking his post in 1993, central bank governor Riad Salameh had worked at Merrill Lynch, where he managed the account of Rafiq Hariri. Hariri was a Lebanese-born Saudi contractor who became prime minister in 1992 and was the driving force of Lebanon's reconstruction after the end of the civil war in 1990 (Baumann 2016). Another key figure was Fuad Siniura, Hariri's school friend and manager of one of his banks who served as finance minister during Hariri's repeated stints as prime minister in the 1990s and early 2000s. Hariri epitomized the blurred lines between Lebanese diaspora capital, often accumulated in the Gulf countries, domestic capital, and the state. His assassination in 2005 caused a political earthquake. His son Saad took on his political mantle and much of his business empire.

The financial benefits of the debt-fueled and precarious scheme to maintain the peg were distributed highly unevenly. The bulk of the profits flowed to a small group of commercial banks and depositors—with both banking ownership and deposit structure concentrated in a small number of hands. Lebanon's middle and lower classes earned little from this scheme, although they did benefit from the ability to afford imports, which were made relatively cheaper by the peg. By 2014, income was so unequal that the top 10 percent of income earners were receiving 57.1 percent of the income, while the bottom 50 percent were left with a mere 10.6 percent (Assouad 2017).

In times of crisis, confidence in the peg was severely tested, and there were several points in the 2000s when investors looked like they might abandon Lebanon. At those points Gulf governments would provide well-publicized capital injections to bolster confidence. During Israel's 2006 war with Lebanon, Saudi Arabia and Kuwait deposited US$1.5 billion with the central bank. One report suggested that foreign donors were thus providing an "implicit guarantee" for Lebanon (Schimmelpfennig and Gardner 2008). The reasons for Gulf support were both political and economic. First, it was designed to bolster Saudi Arabia's Lebanese ally Rafiq Hariri and later his son Saad. Second, Lebanon's finance, real estate, and tourism sectors were a profitable outlet for Gulf investment. They became even more attractive investment options after the 2008 global financial crisis choked off lucrative opportunities elsewhere.

The Unravelling of the Currency Peg

Over the last ten years, the coalition that had kept the currency peg in place was slowly unravelling. The push and pull factors that had channeled capital into Lebanese bank accounts were disappearing. The Syrian war after 2011 threatened to destabilize Lebanon. One effect was the influx of refugees. Another was the collapse of Gulf tourism, which had been an important driving force of Lebanon's hospitality and real estate sectors. An oil price slump in 2014 reduced the amount of cash the Lebanese diaspora in the Gulf and Gulf investors were able to deposit in Lebanon. Meanwhile, public infrastructure was deteriorating further and coming under strain through having to serve over one million Syrian refugees fleeing war. During the 2015 "garbage crisis," mountains of uncollected waste in the streets of Beirut sparked a wave of protests, which were a precursor to what was to happen in October 2019.

Gulf financial support eventually grew more uncertain. Initially, Saudi Arabia strongly supported Saad Hariri after his father's assassination in 2005. Over time, however, Riyadh came to abandon their local ally. King Salman's son, Crown Prince Muhammad bin Salman, who has emerged as Saudi Arabia's new strongman, has fractious relations with Hariri, whose inherited construction empire effectively collapsed after being cut off from royal contracts in 2015 (Dalton and Parasie 2017). In 2017, bin Salman strong-armed Hariri into resigning from the post of prime minister by holding him in confinement in the Saudi capital (Barnard and Abi-Habib 2017). Although Hariri was eventually able to return to Beirut and resume his post as prime minister, relations with Riyadh had broken down and his pleas for aid for Lebanon's financial system fell on deaf ears.

With capital inflows slowing down and Gulf support waning, the central bank was forced into desperate measures. It designed complex deals with Lebanese commercial banks, which involved paying exorbitant interest rates to keep US dollars flowing into Lebanon. Central bank governor Riad Salameh referred to them as "financial engineering," but critics dubbed it a Ponzi scheme (Cornish 2020). By the summer of 2019, the central bank could no longer stem capital outflows. US dollars were becoming scarce. Soon after the protests started, commercial banks started imposing limits on the amount of US dollars depositors could withdraw, sparking intense popular anger at the commercial banks. As the Lebanese government failed to respond to the October 2019 protests with meaningful political or economic change, the currency plunge continued unabated.

The protests forced Prime Minister Saad Hariri to step down at the end of October 2019. The new prime minister, academic Hassan Diab, carried no political heft and proved unable to stand up to the commercial banks, who were trying to minimize their losses. The Diab government's failure to present a united front to the International Monetary Fund (IMF) led to a breakdown of negotiations for a rescue package. This came after successive governments since the early 2000s had first negotiated neoliberal reform packages with foreign donors and then failed to carry out the promised privatization policies and fiscal retrenchment—from a series of conferences dubbed Paris I–III in the 2000s to the CEDRE conference of 2018. After the port explosion, Diab's government became untenable and he resigned.

What Political Constellation Are Protestors Facing after the Beirut Port Explosion?

The days after the Beirut port explosion saw an immediate cleanup marked by civic initiatives and an absence of the state, as well as a return to protests and a brutal crackdown by security forces. The economic situation became ever more critical. Buildings in the immediate vicinity of the port had collapsed, but there was also extensive property damage for miles around. Initial estimates suggested that three hundred thousand people had been made homeless and put the cost of reconstruction at US$15 billion. While such a headline figure can convey the scale of the economic challenge, it fails to convey the political challenge the Lebanese protestors now face to rebuild more equitably and sustainably.

At the time of writing, protestors are facing an array of domestic and international actors and the specter of geopolitics. Two days after the blast happened, French president Emmanuel Macron flew into Beirut to walk among the ruins near the port. He promised that no French aid would go to Lebanon's corrupt elites, and he organized a donor conference that pledged nearly US$300 million in emergency funds. French goals are not entirely congruent with those of the protestors: the president is concerned about Lebanese "stability" and potential refugee flows to Europe as well as the strategic balance in the Eastern Mediterranean, where Beirut is a crucial port. Lebanese politicians are likely to reinvent themselves as reformists to gain entry into a new "national unity government" envisioned by Macron.

Hizballah is the most powerful political force in Lebanon and has put its weight behind the political class. Its main concern is not social and economic reform but its struggle against Israel (Daher 2016). It sees the existing system as the best way to stave off any challenges to its status as an armed resistance movement. Iran is set to continue its support for their local ally. The flipside of the coin is that the United States is likely to use their influence over IMF decision-making to push for the exclusion of Hizballah from the political process and its disarmament (Wimmen 2020). This comes on top of sanctions on Hizballah officials imposed in 2019 and recent US sanctions on the Syrian regime—dubbed the "Caesar Act." They target those with military and financial ties to the Assad regime in Lebanon, putting not only Hizballah into the crosshairs but also the many Lebanese who keep the extensive, economically crucial, and often illicit trade between the two countries going. Sanctions on Lebanese banks or trading houses could have a further crippling effect on Lebanon's economy.

Given the dire situation of Lebanon's finances, the country has had to approach the IMF for emergency aid. The IMF has signaled its willingness to help, but such a bail-out comes with strings attached. The deep "structural reforms" the IMF generally demands would hurt the interests of the former warlords who have colonized state agencies. Some protestors in Lebanon see the IMF as a necessary ally in breaking the economic stranglehold of the sectarian elite (Salloukh and Newman 2020). The political class may therefore try to block an IMF agreement. The only thing worse than an IMF agreement with punishing neoliberal reforms may be no IMF agreement at all. Things could get a lot worse if no further outside support is forthcoming and if Lebanon's elites are left in charge. It is difficult to overstate the cynicism of Lebanon's political class, who had left almost three thousand tons of a highly explosive substance lying around in the center of the capital despite widespread knowledge of its destructive potential. Many former warlords had spent the civil war (1975–1990) profiting from rackets for food or fuel within the cantons they controlled. They may revert to such means of economic and political control should Lebanon descend further down the road of economic collapse.

While an IMF agreement may be a necessary evil for Lebanon, it is likely to involve the usual mix of privatization and austerity. The IMF has recently softened its tone, but its neoliberal instincts are still intact and fly into the face of protestors' demands. After all, what brought protestors onto the streets on October 17 had been opposition to the very kind of measures the IMF is likely to ask for: austerity in combination with tax rises and reduced spending on the public sector. Lebanon's public sector is indeed riddled with clientelism (Salloukh 2019). A reformed public sector could be at the forefront of providing desperately needed public services in education, health, electricity, waste collection, and much more, but this would require extra money. Balancing the books cannot be the only guiding principle.

A November 2019 position paper by Lebanese economists fills in many of the gaps within IMF-style reform proposals (Arab Reform Initiative 2019). Public finances cannot be put on an even keel through expenditure cuts alone. The state needs to recover stolen assets and, crucially, tax the wealthy, who pay very little in taxes. Currently, much of government revenue comes from regressive taxes such as value added tax or the proposed "WhatsApp tax" that had brought protestors out on the streets in October. The economists caution that privatization under current circumstances would represent a fire sale that brings in relatively little cash, while benefiting the well-connected oligarchs who dominate the economy. They call instead for an expanded social safety net and propose mechanisms for transparency and monitoring of public agencies to reduce corruption. Finally, they want to bring unions, professional associations, and employers around the table to provide input into policy making, which up to now has been opaque and driven by politicians' interests.

The greatest cause for hope lies not with the IMF, foreign donors, or foreign capital but the initiative of Lebanese citizens as well as refugees and migrant workers in the country. Alternative economies of mutual solidarity have been emerging in the wake of the 2015 trash crisis, the 2019 protests, and COVID-19. The aftermath of the explosion saw a huge civic effort to clear up the affected areas, with teams of volunteers from around Lebanon traveling to the capital to help. This stands in contrast to top-down "reconstruction" after the civil war, when properties in the city center were handed over to a single private developing company that turned it into a luxury enclave for tourists and wealthy Lebanese (Fawaz 2020). A new alternative economy must make space for these grassroots initiatives that do not profit Lebanon's "one percent" but increase solidarity among citizens as well as the Syrians, Palestinians, and migrant workers who live in the country.

References

Arab Reform Initiative. 2019. "For an Emergency Economic Rescue Plan for Lebanon." *arabreform* *.net*, November 10. arab-reform.net/publication/for-an-emergency-economic-rescue -plan-for-lebanon/.
Association of Banks in Lebanon. 2017. *Annual Report 2017*. Beirut: ABL.
Assouad, Lydia. 2017. *Rethinking the Lebanese Economic Miracle: The Extreme Concentration of Income and Wealth in Lebanon 2005–2014*. WID.world Working Paper, Paris.
Barnard, Anne, and Maria Abi-Habib. 2017. "Why Saad Hariri Had That Strange Sojourn in Saudi Arabia." *New York Times*, December 24. nytimes.com/2017/12/24/world/middle east/saudi-arabia-saad-hariri-mohammed-bin-salman-lebanon.html.
Baumann, Hannes. 2016. *Citizen Hariri: Lebanon's Neoliberal Reconstruction*. London: Hurst.
Chaaban, Jad. 2019. "I've Got the Power: Mapping Connections between Lebanon's Banking Sector and the Ruling Class." In *Crony Capitalism in the Middle East: Business and Politics from Liberalization to the Arab Spring*, edited by Ishac Diwan, Adeel Malik, and Izak Atiyas, 330–43. Oxford: Oxford University Press.
Cornish, Chloe. 2019. "End of the Party: Why Lebanon's Debt Crisis Has Left it Vulnerable." *Financial Times*. December 31. ft.com/content/078b2e4a-266a-11ea-9305-4234e74b0ef3.

Cornish, Chloe. 2020. "Lebanon Central Bank Chief in Spotlight over $6bn Boost to Assets." *Financial Times*, July 21. ft.com/content/d2d63b9b-9669-4ec0-93e9-ed97cbeb9261.

Daher, Joseph. 2016. *Hezbollah: The Political Economy of Lebanon's Party of God*. London: Pluto.

Dalton, Matthew, and Nicolas Parasie. 2017. "With Saudi Ties Fraying, Lebanese Premier's Construction Empire Crumbles." *Wall Street Journal*, November 24. wsj.com/articles /with-saudi-ties-fraying-lebanese-premiers-construction-empire-crumbles-1511519402.

Fawaz, Mona. 2020. "To Pre-empt Disaster Capitalism, Beirut Urgently Needs a People-Centred Recovery." *New Arab*, August 15. english.alaraby.co.uk/english/comment/2020/8/15 /to-pre-empt-disaster-capitalism-beirut-needs-a-people-centred-recovery.

Salloukh, Bassel. 2019. "Taif and the Lebanese State: The Political Economy of a Very Sectarian Public Sector." *Nationalism and Ethnic Politics* 25, no. 1: 43–60.

Salloukh, Bassel, and Julia Newman. 2020. "Will a New Lebanon Arise from the Ashes of Beirut?" *Qantara*, August 11. https://en.qantara.de/node/41186.

Schimmelpfennig, Axel, and Edward Gardner. 2008. *Lebanon—Weathering the Perfect Storms*. Washington, DC: IMF.

Wimmen, Heiko. 2020. "Why the US Should Allow Lebanon's IMF Loan Application." *Responsible Statecraft* (blog), June 11. responsiblestatecraft.org/2020/06/11/why-the-us-should -allow-lebanons-imf-loan-application/.

Lea Bou Khater

Lebanon's October 2019 Revolution:
Inquiry into Recomposing Labor's Power

In a world dominated by neoliberalism, there is renewed attention to labor organizing and radical forms of action outside the institutional framework. In Lebanon, the October 2019 Revolution brought to the forefront the capacity of labor to recompose its power in the face of the long-standing capitalist effort to decompose it. In this essay, I first examine the outbreak of social unrest in 2019 that accompanied the failure of neoliberal policies. Second, I explain the absence and silence of the labor movement amid the 2019 revolution by state interference and at the service of a longstanding laissez-faire economy. I finally conclude by examining recent attempts of professionals to organize from within the October Revolution and the challenges they currently grapple with.

The effects of social and economic injustice in Lebanon intensified and culminated in social unrest in October 2019. Thousands of Lebanese citizens took the streets on October 17, 2019, after the cabinet approved a new tax (US$0.20 per day fee) on internet-based phone calls over services like WhatsApp. While the largest protest took place in Beirut, protesters also gathered for the first time in other main cities like Tripoli, Saida, Tyre, and Baalbeck. As a result, Prime Minister Saad Hariri resigned, and in January 2020, a new technocratic government was formed. Against the backdrop of an enduring decline in foreign reserves, popular dissent was accompanied with a bank closure for fourteen days triggering a currency crisis and uncontrolled bank rush, followed by an unofficial capital control and a hidden haircut on deposits. In March 2020, for the first time the state decided to default

The South Atlantic Quarterly 120:2, April 2021
DOI 10.1215/00382876-8916218　© 2021 Duke University Press

on a US$1.2 billion Eurobond debt, while the Lebanese pound plummeted to a record low, losing around 80 percent of its value and causing basic staples prices to soar. More than half of the population was projected to fall into poverty by the end of 2020 (World Bank 2019).

In fact, Lebanon had been pushed to breaking point by the failure of neoliberal policies that have exacerbated inequality, and poverty. Since the end of the French mandate in 1943, the ruling elite molded state institutions in a way that benefited their financial interests, which implied a weak state and a free market economy (Gates 1998: 50). The state's laissez-faire relationship with the private sector has increasingly deteriorated throughout the history of Lebanon, leading to durable inequalities and the dismantled commitments of the welfare state in guaranteeing social and economic justice. Ever since the end of the Lebanese Civil War (1975–1990), Lebanon has adopted antigrowth financial and monetary policies that hinged on a regressive public revenue structure that discouraged productive investment, a reliance on remittances, a balance of payment deficit, and a high public debt. Currently public debt stands at 150 percent of GDP, and the cost of financing the debt services leaves only 60 percent of the budget for all other government expenditures (IMF 2019). Drawing upon the main macroeconomic policies that prevailed after 1990, and political instability that included the recurrent Israeli attacks (1993, 1996, 2006) against south Lebanon, the assassination of former Prime Minister Hariri in 2005, and the outbreak of the Syrian refugee crisis in 2011, Lebanon failed to achieve economic and social progress. The GDP growth dropped from a high of 10.1 percent in 2009 to 0.9 percent in 2011 and to less than 1 percent on average during 2011–2019.

In 2019, on the eve of the October Revolution, 44 percent of residents lacked any form of social protection. The informal economy comprised around 40 percent of the workforce as it witnessed an accelerated growth of precarious, informal, and temporary workers that infiltrated all economic sectors from unskilled to professional labor (Central Administration of Statistics 2020). Ten percent of the Lebanese adult population had captured 45 percent of the wealth between 2005 and 2014 (Assouad 2017). More recently, data from a leaked 2020 document by the Banking Control Commission of Lebanon showed that 1 percent of depositors held 52 percent of deposits in 2018. In a survey conducted during the first ten days of the October Revolution,[1] more than 87 percent of responses indicated that economic reasons were behind the participation of interviewed protestors (Bou Khater and Majed 2020: 17).

The Lebanese Labor Movement in Chains

Neoliberal economic policies have also gutted a labor movement that had previously succeeded in improving working and living conditions, especially throughout the 1960s and early 1970s. Fierce trade liberalization and reliance on foreign capital and remittances deformed the economy and labor market. Soaring debt service precipitated monetary and fiscal policies that crowded out the productive sector, leading to a "jobless economy" (World Bank 2012). The activity rate—the share of the population over fifteen years old who are working or actively looking for a job—has remained stagnant and low (around 50 percent in 2019 compared to 47 percent in 2004). The vast majority of enterprises were micro-size (employing fewer than five workers), which has a negative impact on labor organizing given the limited capacity for association of workers in small enterprises. Migrant workers, who make up almost 20 percent of the total workforce, are excluded from labor organizing (Central Administration of Statistics 2020).

In addition to restrictive labor market features, the labor movement is subdued by legal restrictions. The 1946 Lebanese Labour Code significantly limits freedom of association: according to Article 86, no trade unions may be established without prior authorization from the Ministry of Labour; according to Article 50, the only union members protected from dismissal are those elected as union board members. In line with these restrictions, Lebanon never ratified the International Labour Organization Convention No. 87 of 1948 on Freedom of Association and Protection of the Right to Organize, which eliminates any requirement that union formation be preauthorized.

Co-optation of the General Confederation of Workers

The labor movement is also marred by an obsolete organizational structure that lacks democratic and proportional representation. The labor movement in Lebanon is represented by the General Confederation of Workers in Lebanon (GCWL), an umbrella organization comprising fifty-nine federations of trade unions (2015). According to the GCWL 1970 charter—which remains unchanged until today—each federation is represented by four members in the GCWL Representative Council, irrespective of its membership size (i.e., a federation comprising five thousand members and a federation of five hundred members are equally represented by four members each). Moreover, these four members are appointed by the federation executive council rather than being directly elected by the members of the federation itself. Finally, these nonelected representatives elect at their turn the GCWL Executive Council and its president. The sectarian allocation of major seats in governmental institutions was also mirrored in the allocation of seats at the GCWL. In fact, the leadership of the confederation has always been Christian since its creation in 1968 without any legal provisions citing that, with an amendment only at the level of the vice president, which became a position reserved for Muslims. This amendment took into account the new balance of power installed after the Ta'if Agreement, which ended the civil war in 1990. The sectarian restriction of the presidency of the GCWL was an indication of the absorption of the labor movement in the sectarian political system and being subject to its repercussions.

This undemocratic structure visibly leaves room for political manipulation and intervention. Indeed, the state and the ruling elite strove to starve trade unions and block their opposition to socioeconomic policies. They also made repeated sets of demands by withholding the GCWL's budget allocation, intervening in executive council elections, and disproportionately authorizing federations of specific political affiliations in order to influence or even control the decision-making process within the confederation.

The central tool used by the ruling elite through the Ministry of Labour was the excessive authorization of federations. The creation of additional trade union federations, which is a process described as "hatching," allowed the government to achieve a progovernment majority within the GCWL executive council. The above-mentioned lack of proportional representation facilitated this task. The number of federations in the GCWL increased from twenty-two in 1993 to thirty-six in 2001 to fifty-nine in 2015.

As expected, the co-optation of the labor movement from the 1990s has hindered opposition to aggressive neoliberal policies and to its nefarious social repercussions. By the late 1990s, the GCWL had become an extension of the ruling elite's interests, and its positions continue to be severed from the conditions and demands of the workforce it claims to represent. By way of illustration: In 2011, the GCWL opted not to support an unprecedented hike in the monthly minimum wage for private sector employees, from US$333 to US$580 (proposed by the minister of labor at the time as part of a progressive reform package). Instead, the GCWL sided with business associations to support the prime minister's proposal of capping it at US$450.

Incorporation of Public Sector Leagues

Political interference in labor organizing is not limited to the GCWL and the private sector. The Union Coordination Committee (UCC), a coalition of the public primary and secondary school teachers' leagues, the Association of the Private Schools Teachers, and the League of Public Sector Employees were also co-opted in 2017, largely as a reaction to their past success. Aided by its democratic and centralized structure, and propelled by an enormous contingent of civil servants (around 130,000), the UCC led a successful campaign between 2012 and 2017 to demand a new salary scale for public sector employees that takes into account the 121 percent inflation between 1996 and 2012. Success came despite the fact that, like private sector workers, public sector employees face legal obstacles to organizing. Civil servants are forbidden from directly engaging in political affairs, joining a political party, or participating in strikes. According to Article 65 of Law Decree No. 112, a civil servant's participation in a strike is akin to a resignation. As a reaction to the mobilization that culminated in a new salary scale, candidates affiliated to ten political parties allied to successfully oust UCC representatives in the next elections.

Labor Organizing in the October 2019 Revolution

In this context, it is understandable that neither the GCWL nor the UCC called for any strikes or demonstrations in the aftermath of the October 2019 Revolution. In fact, the GCWL waited nineteen days after the onset of the protests to issue a brief and taciturn statement calling for the prompt formation of a new government (General Confederation of Workers in Lebanon 2019).

It is in this labor landscape that a group of professionals have begun organizing under the umbrella of a newly formed Lebanese Association of Professionals (LAP). According to interviewed members, the LAP was inspired by the Sudanese Professional Association (SPA). The SPA played a seminal role in the Sudanese uprising in 2018 by organizing and scheduling protests, which first focused on wage increases for public sector workers and the authorization of trade unions but soon demanded the "removal of the ruling National Congress Party, the structural transformation of governance in Sudan, and a transition to democracy" (Medani 2019).

In Lebanon, various groups of professionals have used the impetus of the October protests to coordinate alternative labor movements. They quickly joined forces and together they formed the LAP on October 28, 2019, and issued an introductory paper stating their participation in the October uprising in protest against the political and economic system in place, refusing all ensuing social, economic, financial, and monetary policies, and calling for a democratic transition to a secular state based on social justice. The LAP is now composed of several associations of university professors, engineers, physicians, artists, journalists and media workers, and workers in non-governmental organizations. Associations are still in a nascent form and each comprises only around two hundred members.

The founding of the LAP stems from the accumulation of mobilizations and experiences in the previous years. Several founding members of the LAP were activists in previous popular protests and mobilizations since 2005, the year that saw the largest nationwide protests, dubbed the Cedar Revolution, which took place in demand of the withdrawal of the Syrian troops from Lebanon following the assassination of Prime Minister Rafiq Hariri. Some members of the Independent Professors Association were already dedicated activists within the national/public Lebanese University way before the 2019 revolution. "Our activism and our demands are not new. But the momentum of the October Revolution has put our demands on the forefront and brought us all together under the LAP," said Wafa Noun, a university professor and activist (pers. comm., March 25, 2020).

Several members told me how the 2015 mobilization was an important turning point in terms of the need for labor organizing and overcoming the fear of traditional frameworks of representation. A series of protests took place in July 2015 against the inability of the government to elaborate a national waste management strategy leading to the worst trash crisis in the history of Lebanon. The movement grew beyond addressing waste management and voiced political demands pertaining mainly to transparency and accountability and the organization of parliamentary elections. Most importantly the movement was able to gather around it people of different political affiliations, from diverse regions, who came together to protest against the diminishing presence of the state. However, this nascent cross-regional and cross-sectarian solidarity was soon tamed by the ruling elite, which united in its manipulation and enticement of sectarian identities through several rallies and events in a way to supersede and divert popular demands away from pressing political and socioeconomic reforms. The movement weakened and faded away. At this juncture, interviewed activists experienced the limited capabilities of unstructured and leaderless movements, such as the 2015 movement in challenging the ruling elite. They have brought to the fore the importance and the need for organizing that would guarantee sustainability over time and coordination and geographic spread throughout the country in the face of the ruling elite's attempts at decomposing contentious movements.

As a nascent association, the LAP faces organizational challenges that still require lengthy discussions and probably the envisioning of new approaches to organizing that supersede the traditional structures of trade unions or professional orders and the required official preauthorization. A serious challenge is the structure of the LAP, which remains under discussion and whereby currently the decision-making process is ambiguous and does not guarantee the representativeness of the different associations. These obstacles have already questioned the viability of the LAP as an umbrella body that coordinates among different members and sets the political tone of the movement regarding the October Revolution and all positions to be taken vis-à-vis the new government in place and its decisions. The umbrella organization might need more time to acquire a representative structure and raise questions pertaining to its internal regulations, decision-making process, and outreach.

Meanwhile member associations of the LAP have started to operate in a standalone way for the organizing of professionals and the protection of labor rights and working conditions marred with informality and lack of social and legal protection. Member associations also face organizational challenges. For instance, some organizers raised the issue of inclusion and exclusion criteria of members in terms of type of occupation (employers, self-employed, and employees) or even nationality (are international workers and employees included?) and the impact of such decision on representation and decision-making processes. Even if the LAP is today facing structural and organizational challenges, it has a least demonstrated the capacity to imagine and experiment with new forms of social organizations.

Several months following the October Revolution, the economic and financial crises and the outbreak of COVID-19 have led to underemployment, salary cuts, and mass layoffs in violation of the Code of Labour that stipulates predismissal negotiations between employers and the Ministry of Labour. The impact of the crises on unskilled labor has also fueled the urgency of labor action. In fact, migrant workers, the most vulnerable category of workers legally, socially, economically, and linguistically, and whose association is legally constrained, organized several protests against salary cuts and layoffs. In May 2020, four hundred migrant cleaning workers of Bangladeshi and Indian nationality organized week-long strikes and protests asking for one day off per week, to be paid in the first five days of the month, and to stop all physical and verbal abuse against them. Sudanese workers have also organized a series of protest against layoffs and in demand of wage adjustment. Migrant domestic workers, whose union, founded in 2017, was in fact unauthorized by the Ministry of Labour in violation of the International Labour Organization Convention No. 87 of 1948 on Freedom of Association and Protection of the Right to Organize, are also facing harsh working conditions and foreign currency shortage and have organized community assistance and a series of protests.

These attempts of new types of organizing and strategies to recompose labor power aim to allow labor to deploy power against the existing ruling elite and recomposition of capital. The ruling elite may attempt the co-optation of new labor organizations as it previously did to the GCWL and the UCC. But the October Revolution, the deepening economic crisis, the financial crash, and the ensuing pauperization of the majority of the population have weakened the authority and legitimacy of the ruling elite and traditional patron-client sectarian relations. Like the Arab uprisings, one of the major achievements of the October Revolution so far is the paradigm shift it generated. After decades of simply succumbing to sectarian leadership, citizens have seized the public sphere to oppose the political system and voice their demands, and it seems that there is no return to the status quo ante. This context allows a better environment and prospects for the new labor mobilization dynamics and in turn a successful struggle for change.

Note

1   Structured interviewing conducted with a sample of 1,183 protesters targeted at various protest sites across Lebanon from October 19 to October 31.

References

Assouad, Lydia. 2017. "Rethinking the Lebanese Economic Miracle: The Extreme Concentration of Income and Wealth in Lebanon 2005–2014." World Inequality Database Working Paper Series No 2017/13.

Bou Khater, Lea. 2018. "Understanding State Incorporation of the Workers' Movement in Early Post-War Lebanon and its Backlash on Civil Society." *Civil Society Review*, no. 3: 48–71.

Bou Khater, Lea, and Rima Majed. 2020. *Lebanon's 2019 October Revolution: Who Mobilized and Why?* The Asfari Institute for Civil Society and Citizenship. www.activearabvoices.org/uploads/8/0/8/4/80849840/leb-oct-rev_-_v.1.3-digital.pdf.

Central Administration of Statistics. 2020. *Labour Force and Household Living Conditions Survey 2018–2019 Lebanon*. cas.gov.lb/images/Publications/Labour%20Force%20and%20Household%20Living%20Conditions%20Survey%202018-2019.pdf.

Gates, Carolyn. 1998. *Merchant Republic of Lebanon: Rise of an Open Economy*. London: Center for Lebanese Studies in association with I. B. Tauris Publishers.

General Confederation of Workers in Lebanon. 2019. "Statement of the Executive Bureau on 5 November 2019." cgtl-lb.org/NewsDetails.aspx?NewsID=13370.

IMF (International Monetary Fund). 2019. "Lebanon: Staff Concluding Statement of the 2019 Article IV Mission." July 2. imf.org/en/News/Articles/2019/07/02/mcs070219-lebanon -staff-concluding-statement-of-the-2019-article-iv-mission.

Medani, Khalid M. 2019. "The New Mobilization Dynamics of Sudan's Popular Uprising: The Virtue of Learning from the Past." *Jadaliyya*, February 23. jadaliyya.com/Details/38376 /Quick-Thoughts-The-Sudanese-Protests-with-Khalid-Medani.

World Bank. 2019. "Lebanon Is in the Midst of Economic, Financial, and Social Hardship, Situation Could Get worse." Press release, November 6. worldbank.org/en/news/press -release/2019/11/06/world-bank-lebanon-is-in-the-midst-of-economic-financial-and -social-hardship-situation-could-get-worse.

World Bank. 2012. *Republic of Lebanon—Good Jobs Needed: The Role of Macro, Investment, Education, Labor and Social Protection Policies*. Washington, DC: World Bank. https://open knowledge.worldbank.org/handle/10986/13217.

Jamil Mouawad

Teaching Lebanon's Politics in Times of the Uprising

Triggered by a government decision to tax WhatsApp calls, Lebanon witnessed in October 2019 (and onwards) waves of mass protests that have spawned an uprising unprecedented in the country's recent history. The "October 17 uprising" was not just an outcry against a dire economic situation, Lebanon's ruling class, and their unapologetic corruption. In fact, these protests—as is the case with any other aspiring revolutionary moment—also pushed people to reimagine their reality and act upon it. But the utopia of revolutionary moments conflates a number of distinct challenges, one of which is the way to go about one's professional life (in this case teaching) and how to balance the desire to protest on the streets with the importance of carrying on with teaching and classes.

When classes were suspended because of the protests and I could no longer meet the students on campus, I had to contend with losing the opportunity to teach the Politics in Lebanon class that might help us better explain the underlining factors of these protests.

I argue that in a revolutionary moment an engaged academic should not only preach to the converted but must also account for those that are or feel disempowered or estranged, whether because they feel indifferent to "politics in action" or alienated for political reasons, or because they simply oppose the protests. I had to clearly think and reflect on how to return to the "class"—as an ultimate space for critical thinking—even when teaching in the classroom was no longer a possibility. The shift from the classroom to the street prompted two questions: (1) Should we as faculty work to direct

The South Atlantic Quarterly 120:2, April 2021
DOI 10.1215/00382876-8916232 © 2021 Duke University Press

behavior in this very specific moment and perhaps fall into the trap of "rhetorical movement" that relies on persuasive talks (Howard 1966) and aims to change the opinion of students? (2) How can we avoid alienating those who are undecided, not necessarily convinced, or, perhaps more importantly, oppose these protests?

At times, when courses were suspended because of the protests, many professors decided to give talks or teach-ins in the main square (Martyr's Square) where protests were taking place. I learned that leaving the classroom behind and opting for teach-ins was not necessarily the best option. Conversely, I advocate for the classroom, even when confined inside the walls—and events unfolding on the street—as a space for openness and creativity. A classroom gathers everyone in one space and renders the space relatively neutral, yet political. Neutral, because it is open for students who happen to have different political leanings, unlike the square where teach-ins take place. Political, for it is there where they have the opportunity to safely voice their concerns or objection to the demands, slogans, and repertoires of mobilizations. The task was not easy, especially when the generation we teach is directly affected by the polarization that has prevailed in the country since 2005, a date when Syrian troops withdrew from Lebanon after the assassination of former prime minister Hariri.

Teaching Politics in Lebanon before October 17

When I ask students in each introductory session to give three words they directly associate with politics in Lebanon, *sectarianism* and *conflict* appear to be the most cited. This reflects the conventional and mainstream understanding of politics in Lebanon as a society comprising a jigsaw puzzle of communities.

Rarely do students ask questions related to class stratification or wealth inequalities, let alone everyday life. Likewise, the sectarian variable and framework shies away from these questions as well. According to this mainstream understanding of politics, Lebanon does not have social classes but, rather, sects (Traboulsi 2014), even though Lebanon is ranked among the countries with the most pronounced inequalities, where the top 1 and 10 percent of the adult population receive 25 and 55 percent of national income on average, respectively (Assouad 2017).

This question gains particular importance in recent history, specifically for students belonging to the post-2005 generation, marked by the assassination of former prime minister Rafic Hariri (2005), a prominent figure in reconstruction process after the civil war, with a neoliberal approach to state affairs and management. This led to the inauguration of an acute and long-lasting rivalry between March 8 and March 14 supporters: March 8, a group led by Hezbollah—a party committed to resist Israel—and March 14, a pro-Western group led by the Future movement with an anti-(regime) Syrian stance. Underneath this polarization lies the echo of regional tension between Saudi Arabia and Iran, which is translated internally into an imagined Sunni-Shia sectarian conflict. Student contributions clearly reflect this understanding of politics, namely, an over-politicized generation shaped by this binary that reifies the divisions in society and renders politics outside this two-group framework almost impossible.

This often causes tension in class as students expect teachers or their peers to be either pro–March 8 or pro–March 14. Accordingly, for some, any sense of independence from these two groups is indeed an "apolitical stance," a position that does not necessarily relate to the conflict or main challenges Lebanon is facing. I find myself repeatedly explaining to students that this course is designed to teach "politics in Lebanon," how the system functions, how it affects our everyday life and future, and that it is not a course about "Lebanese politics," which is framed by the interests of the ruling class and how they define politics.

At the start of each semester, I draw a long time line on the board and ask students to fill it out with dates they find relevant to understanding Lebanese history. Most of the events listed are related to "conflicts" (wars, assassinations, etc.) or reaching "consensus" among representatives of political parties and groups (national pact 1943, Doha Accord 2008, etc.). Politics accordingly is about the political system and ruling class and rarely about everyday life or the average citizens (social movements, right-based questions, etc.). It is only after 2015, the year of mass mobilizations (the You Stink! movement) against the trash crisis that hit Lebanon after piles of waste filled the street, that social movements start to appear as key dates. This signals a turning point in recent history where citizens took to the streets to accuse the ruling class for failing to provide public services and for corruption. Later in 2020, they again took to the streets to protest the additional sins of financial collapse and the Beirut blast, the result of an analysis that diverged from the rather tired praxis framework where ruling elites are only pawns in the hands of regional powers (Saudi Arabia-Iran).

2019–20: An Abnormal Academic Year

The academic year 2019–20 will most likely be remembered as a most challenging year for universities, colleges, and schools in Lebanon. At the heart of the challenge was the interruption of education as protestors flooded the streets in October 2019, only one month after the semester started.

Facing the somewhat confusing situation during the first days of the mass protests, and with the absence of unions for professors or a clear decision from the administration on whether or not to suspend classes, uncertainty prevailed: Do we teach? Do we not? If so, when and where? Meanwhile, some professors started to look for alternative teaching methods, including public talks, teach-ins, meeting in cafés, or online classrooms. More radical professors supporting the protestors advocated for the complete suspension of classes: "We won't go back to normality, because normality was the problem," inspired by a Chilean slogan,[1] attested to the place of the Lebanese protests as part of a global movement against capitalism and neoliberalism. Previously invisible tensions cropped up, as professors were forced to choose between their obligations toward students, especially those who did not want to miss their academic year, and showing solidarity with peer professors who decided not to teach.

The interruption of classes was not only the result of pro-protest professors who left campus because, as they said, "the streets are a classroom and the classroom is on the streets." In fact, universities emptied of protesting students also pressured the presidents of leading private Lebanese universities to publicly support the demonstrations and call for the suspension of courses "until further notice." The American University of Beirut (AUB) and Saint-Joseph University (USJ) issued a joint statement on October 25 and condemned "all attempts to suppress the protests" while at the same time clearly stating that they "cannot but share in the commitment of faculty, students, staff, and alumni who are already participating in the struggle for the rights of all Lebanese without exception."[2]

Leading private universities, credited with historically educating the middle classes and congratulating themselves for fashioning the Levantine and Lebanese elites of the early twentieth century, had clearly sided with a group of students and professors, thus further alienating those students and professors in their respective universities who had chosen to remain silent because they were either politically opposed to the protests or simply because they preferred to finish the academic year uninterrupted and join the protests.

Against the backdrop of a prominent conviction, "life cannot go back to normal," many questions were raised in parallel about the practical need to go back to normal. In private universities where tuitions cost up to US$20,000 or 30,000 per year, with looming financial collapse and the Lebanese lira gradually losing its value, many students, especially those who were graduating that year and hoping to go about their life, wondered whether to continue their studies abroad or enter professional life. Finding a job outside Lebanon amid financial collapse would have been for some the only way to ensure a prosperous future.

Of course, responding to these unusual circumstances, professors resorted to different strategies, including but not limited to online teaching and public lectures related to the desired political changes. The decision reverted to binary reasoning for some: either you demonstrate or you teach, either you demonstrate or you attend classes. However, questions were also raised about the extent to which one can or should divert the class into the service of the demonstrations by showing unconditional support to protestors. To what extent should we neglect those who are not taking part of the protests, but might also have the need to express themselves in class and not on the streets?

PSPA 256: Politics in Lebanon

I recall the email I sent to students after being astounded by the number of messages I received asking me about their course. In retrospect, I realize that those who wanted to resume classes were not necessarily part of a "counter-revolutionary voice." In fact, this is something that I did not consider at the time: some students were against the protestors because they opposed the political parties they are aligned with. Moreover, protestors were raising what has become a famous slogan: "all of them means all of them," in reference to everyone who has taken a public office in postwar Lebanon, including all traditional parties combined outside the polarized vision of March 8 or March 14. Despite its fleeting character, the October 17 uprising presented the opportunity to forge the possibility of politics outside the binary of March 8 or March 14.

After a considerable amount of thought, I started to outline a strategy that was guided by three principles: (1) my convictions and full participation in the protests, (2) the extreme relevance of the course to the context, and (3) the need to foster dialogue between students, those who felt empowered by the revolution because they were convinced, along with those who felt alienated and disempowered because, in this instance, they were international students or because they supported the political parties in power. Guided by these considerations, I sent the following email to the students emphasizing the need to both gather as a class and be on the street:

Our PSPA 256 course (Politics in Lebanon) has never been more relevant, in these historic times. The street will be the classroom. Instead of cutting ourselves off from the outside in order to analyze "the outside" we will take a walk through the city of Beirut and I will explain the postwar political order that has given rise to ongoing protests. This tour is based on our previous discussions. We will meet at AUB medical gate and walk to Beirut Martyr's Square. . . .

A Tour

While a number of professors gave talks or teach-ins in the square where protests were taking place, I decided instead to give a tour. Why a tour? For two main reasons: First, it is an active, engaging process that allows students to see the different buildings and monuments that shaped postwar Lebanon. I wanted to walk them through the process that had led to these social protests (from colonialism, to war times, to real estate speculation, reconstruction, and finally the square). Second, the square in itself, I thought, was too polarizing, despite being a place for rejuvenating ideas and imaginaries. I was convinced that in such a charged moment, making "pro-regime" students face the protests and their demands, which called in part for the toppling of a regime—or a politician—they support, might have led to unproductive antagonisms.

The walk started at the AUB medical gate. I gathered the students outside the gate and introduced the idea of the walk and its objectives. I remember when a professor angrily protested what I was doing and said I was making AUB take a position (pro-protests) "that we will all pay for at a later stage." Although I did not have the chance to reply to him, the purpose of the walk was precisely not to take sides and not to fall into the binary of with or against the uprising. Our first stop was a pile of stinking garbage. Despite the unpleasant odor, I explained to them how, after the war, a neoliberal order landed smoothly in Lebanon. The ruling class outsourced state functions to private companies they themselves owned, which led them to accumulate resources and capture state institutions. The Lebanese in return get very bad services, and the ruling class exonerates itself from any responsibility. The second stop was next to two buildings belonging to the same family: a newly built highrise (more than twenty floors) next to a two-story mansion from the nineteenth century. The contrast between the two stops spoke volumes about Lebanon's economy, prosperity, and collapse. Lebanon's economy is based on laisser-faire laissez-passer, and in recent years, it was driven by market and real estate speculation, which led to a "bubble" that further accelerated the collapse. The third stop was an old building from the colonial era (Lebanon was under the French mandate 1920–43) that still attests to the terrors of the 1975–90 civil war and was never reconstructed, most likely because it does not fall under the mandate of Solidere, a private company that has acquired legal or managerial control over reconstruction of the center of Beirut (known as Downtown Beirut). The fourth stop was the Holiday Inn hotel, a landmark in Beirut's tourist scenes in the 1970s, during Beirut's "golden age" of economic prosperity, when it was hailed for being *La Suisse du Moyen-Orient*. The fifth stop was Downtown Beirut, just across the street from the destroyed hotel, where one encounters the reconstructed part of Beirut that represents part of Lebanon's postwar predicament: private accumulation, land expropriation, lack of public spaces, and championing of private interest to the detriment of the public good. Finally, we reached the square, where I told students to walk around on their own and analyze how the space interacts with the demands.

Going Back to Class . . . Teaching in the Classroom

When the power of the protestors gradually started to reach a halt, universities under the obligation to finish the academic year and the semester called for students and professors to go back to campuses. Going back to the classroom was an opportunity to see the uprising from another angle: the vantage point of those who were opposed to the protests, or those who had developed cynicism toward its "failure," "shortcomings," or even repertoires of contentions (lack of leadership, no unified demands across different groups, etc.). When we came back to class, the discussion was open as to whether the repertoires of contention, specifically road blocking, were justified. I also realized that going back to the classroom was accompanied not by a feeling of reunion but rather of fatigue and alienation. I felt that students—rightly so—had more and more concerns about the collapse, their future, and, most importantly, prospects for real change.

On the other hand, I felt that those who did not participate in the protests expressed themselves the most. In this sense, I came to understand the uprising as a political space that might also alienate, and I now advocate for the classroom as a space that should coexist with the streets, the one complementing the other. The uprising is/should be an opportunity to empower, not alienate.

Almost One Year After: A Blast and Forced Migration to Private Spaces

Almost one year after the October 17 uprising, which is still far from over for some, dramatic events keep unfolding in Lebanon: the COVID-19 pandemic, the Beirut blast that destroyed one-third of the city, and the free fall of the economy. Despair is gradually taking over. Here again, the course is somehow extremely relevant, yet exceptionally challenging.

I sent the following in an email to the students:

> These are exceptional times for everyone. Meeting you from behind the screen brings only sadness, sorrow and loneliness. These are not normal feelings to kick off the course. We should all acknowledge that. We don't live in normal times. We should all acknowledge that.
>
> What makes me even more sad is how relevant this course is to understanding contemporary Lebanese politics—at a time when, as never before, people need to gather and collectively reflect on our—Lebanon's—predicament. This alienation, imposed on us because of COVID-19, came only months after the public spaces were made open for everyone to express himself/herself. This forced withdrawal from the public to our private spaces is, indeed, alienating, to say the least.
>
> However, we should also be grateful for the virtual spaces we still have that allow us to discuss politics in Lebanon. This class—as never before—should be an opportunity for all of us, not only to learn about politics in Lebanon, but also to express ourselves, share our ideas (from our everyday life . . .), vent whatever frustrations we have, or voice whatever hope we have left . . . as we—and as never before—need to collectively think about the times we live in, about today's Lebanon.

Notes

1   No volveremos a la normalidad porque la normalidad era el problema.
2   USJ and AUB joint memo 20193, October 25, 2019. usj.edu.lb/news.php?id=8296.

References

Assouad, Lydia. 2017. "Rethinking the Lebanese Economic Miracle: The Extreme Concentration of Income and Wealth in Lebanon, 2005–2014". WID.world Working Paper No. 13, Paris. wid.world/document/rethinking-lebanese-economic-miracle-extreme-concentration-income-wealth-lebanon-2005-2014–wid-world-working-paper-201713/.

Howard, Martin. 1966. "The Rhetoric of Academic Protest." *Communication Studies* 17, no. 4: 244–50.

Traboulsi, Fawwaz. 2014. *Social Classes and Political Power in Lebanon*. Beirut: Heinrich Boell Foundation. lb.boell.org/en/2014/05/04/social-classes-and-political-power-lebanon.

Notes on Contributors

Moya Bailey is an assistant professor of Africana studies and women's, gender, and sexuality studies at Northeastern University. She is a scholar of critical race, feminist, and disability studies. Her book *#HashtagActivism: Networks of Race and Gender Justice* (2020) was coauthored with Sarah J. Jackson and Brooke Foucault Welles. She currently curates the #transformDH Tumblr initiative in digital humanities. She is also the digital alchemist for the Octavia E. Butler Legacy Network.

Hannes Baumann is a senior lecturer at the University of Liverpool. He is the author of *Citizen Hariri: Lebanon's Neoliberal Reconstruction* (2016).

Lea Bou Khater is a lecturer of development studies at the Lebanese American University. Her research interests are state-labor relations, social and protest movements, and social protection.

Amanda Cachia (www.amandacachia.com) is an independent curator and critic from Sydney, Australia. She received her PhD in art history, theory and criticism from the University of California San Diego in 2017. Her research focuses on modern and contemporary art; curatorial studies and activism; exhibition design and access; decolonizing the museum; and the politics of disability in visual culture. Cachia has curated approximately forty exhibitions, many of which contain social justice themes and content, including *Performing Crip Time: Bodies in Deliberate Motion* (2014).

María Elena Cepeda is a professor and cochair of Latina/o studies at Williams College, where she specializes in Latina/o/x popular culture and media. She is the author of *Musical ImagiNation: US-Colombian Identity and the "Latin Music Boom"* (2010) and coeditor of *The Routledge Companion to Latina/o Media* (2017).

Eli Clare is white, disabled, and genderqueer and lives near Lake Champlain in occupied Abenaki territory (currently known as Vermont) where he writes and proudly claims a penchant for rabble-rousing. He has written two books of creative nonfiction, *Brilliant Imperfection: Grappling with Cure* (2017) and *Exile and Pride: Disability, Queerness, and Liberation* (1999) (both published by Duke University Press) and a collection of poetry, *The Marrow's Telling: Words in Motion* (2007).

Finn Enke is a professor of history, gender and women's studies, and LGBTQ+ studies at University of Wisconsin, Madison. Finn is author of *Finding the Movement: Sexuality, Contested Space and Feminist Activism* (2007) and editor of *Transfeminist Perspectives Within and Beyond Transgender and Gender Studies*

(2012). Their books in progress include a graphic memoir, currently titled "With Finn and Wing: Growing Up Amphibious in a Nuclear Age," and an essay and comics collection, currently titled "Trans on Campus: Pedagogies of the Impossible."

Elizabeth Freeman is a professor of English at the University of California, Davis, and the author of *The Wedding Complex: Forms of Belonging in Modern American Culture* (2002), *Time Binds: Queer Temporalities, Queer Histories* (2010), and *Beside You in Time: Sense Methods and Queer Sociabilities in the American Nineteenth Century* (2019).

Matt Huynh is a Sydney-born, New York-based visual artist and storyteller. His illustrated essays, comics, and animations interrogate the vast impression of war, with a particular focus on amplifying diasporic voices, telling refugee narratives, and the experiences of asylum seekers and migrant communities. Huynh's paintings, comics, and murals have been exhibited by the MoMA, the Smithsonian, and New York Historical Society.

Alison Kafer is Embrey Associate Professor of Women's and Gender Studies and an associate professor of English at the University of Texas in Austin. She is the author of *Feminist, Queer, Crip* (2013).

Mimi Khúc is a writer, scholar, and teacher of things unwell. She is the managing editor of The Asian American Literary Review, a DC-based arts nonprofit, and the 2019–21 Scholar/Artist/Activist in Residence in Disability Studies at Georgetown University.

Jina B. Kim is an assistant professor of English and the study of women and gender at Smith College. She writes and teaches on the topics of critical disability studies, feminist- and queer-of-color critique, and contemporary ethnic American literature. She is currently at work on a manuscript that examines the literary-cultural afterlife of 1996 US welfare reform through the framework of crip-of-color critique.

Christine Sun Kim was born in California in 1980 and is now based in Berlin. Kim has built an acclaimed practice around sound, its visual representations and its circulation as social currency. Kim uses performance, video, drawing, writing, and technology to reflect on her experiences as part of the Deaf community and to comment on the social and political operations of sound. A keen observer of language, Kim employs American Sign Language, music notation, televisual captioning, and other systems of visual communication in a wide-ranging practice that address the intricacies of social exchange and the power of representation with illuminating wit and candor.

Nikolas Kosmatopoulos teaches International Affairs and Anthropology at the American University of Beirut. He is navigator of the Floating Laboratory of Action and Theory at Sea and founding member of the Decolonize Hellas collective. He researches violence and peace, maritime capital and solidarity activism, cosmopolitanism and cosmopolitics. In 2020–21 he is a Member at the Institute for Advanced Study in Princeton University.

Karim Makdisi is an associate professor of international politics and director of the Program in Public Policy and International Affairs at the American University of Beirut. He is coeditor, with Vijay Prashad, of *The Land of the Blue Helmets: United Nations in the Arab World* (2017).

Jamil Mouawad is a lecturer in politics at the American University of Beirut.

Leah Lakshmi Piepzna-Samarasinha is a queer, disabled, nonbinary femme poet, memoirist, and disability and transformative justice movement worker of Burgher/Tamil Sri Lankan and Irish/Roma ascent. She is the Lambda Award–winning author or coeditor of nine books, including (coedited with Ejeris Dixon) *Beyond Survival: Strategies and Stories from the Transformative Justice Movement* (2020), *Tonguebreaker* (2019), *Bridge of Flowers* (2019), *Care Work: Dreaming Disability Justice* (2018), *Dirty River* (2015), and *Bodymap* (2015). Since 2009, she has been a lead artist with the disability justice performance collective Sins Invalid.

Margaret Price is an associate professor of English and director of the Disability Studies Program at the Ohio State University. She has published one book, *Mad at School: Rhetorics of Mental Disability and Academic Life* (2011), as well as numerous articles, essays, stories, and poems. She is now at work on a forthcoming book titled *Crip Spacetime: A Reorientation to Disability Studies*.

Jasbir K. Puar is a professor of women's and gender studies at Rutgers University. She is the author of the award-winning books *The Right to Maim: Debility, Capacity, Disability* (2017) and *Terrorist Assemblages: Homonationalism in Queer Times* (2007), which has been translated into Spanish and French and reissued in 2017 in an expanded version for its tenth anniversary. In 2019 she was awarded the Kessler Award from the Center for Gay and Lesbian Studies, given yearly to scholars and activists whose work has significantly impacted scholarship and organizing.

Jake Pyne is an assistant professor in the York University School of Social Work, in Toronto. His research focuses on trans studies, critical disability studies, critical autism studies, fat studies and queer of color critique. He is currently at work on a book project about autistic and trans life titled "Building a Person."

Ellen Samuels is an associate professor of English at the University of Wisconsin–Madison and the author of *Fantasies of Identification: Disability, Gender, Race* (2014).

Sami Schalk is an associate professor of gender and women's studies at the University of Wisconsin–Madison. Her research focuses on disability, race, and gender in contemporary American literature and culture. She is the author of *Bodyminds Reimagined* (2018) and a forthcoming book on disability politics in Black activism.

Michael D. Snediker is an associate professor of English at the University of Houston and the author of *Contingent Figure: Chronic Pain and Queer Embodiment* as well as *Queer Optimism: Lyric Personhood and Other Felicitous Persuasions*. His most recent book of poems, *The New York Editions*, was published in 2017.

DOI 10.1215/00382876-8916247

Keep up to date on new scholarship

Issue alerts are a great way to stay current on all the cutting-edge scholarship from your favorite Duke University Press journals. This free service delivers tables of contents directly to your inbox, informing you of the latest groundbreaking work as soon as it is published.

To sign up for issue alerts:

1. Visit **dukeu.press/register** and register for an account. You do not need to provide a customer number.

2. After registering, visit **dukeu.press/alerts**.

3. Go to "Latest Issue Alerts" and click on "Add Alerts."

4. Select as many publications as you would like from the pop-up window and click "Add Alerts."

read.dukeupress.edu/journals

Printed and bound by CPI Group (UK) Ltd, Croydon, CR0 4YY

13/04/2025

14656471-0007